GOING OUT ON A LIMB

How Signals Led Me Beyond My Limits & Into Truth

Bernadette Logue

The sequel to the best seller:
Pinch Me—How Following The Signals Changed My Life

Brought to you by:

www.pinchmeliving.com

First Edition published in 2013 by Pinch Me Publishing

Cover image by iStockphoto.com

Cover design by Teddi Black

Editing by Caroline Webster

Also by the Author:

Pinch Me

Unleash Your Life

The content of this book is a personal story, with references to truths that are based solely upon the author's own personal beliefs and experiences. This book is intended to provide inspiration and information to assist you in creating a life you love. If you should decide to apply any of the information provided in this book, the author and publisher assume no responsibility for your actions or the consequences of your actions.

Although this is a nonfiction account, most names used throughout this book are fictitious for the purpose of privacy for the individuals.

978-0-473-23351-8 (Paperback)

978-0-473-23352-5 (eBook)

A copy of this publication is available from the National Library of New Zealand.

Contents

Dedication

For Aaron, my family and my baby dog:
all the love and support a soul
could ask for.

*"I would love to live like a river flows,
carried by the surprise of its own unfolding."*

- John O'Donohue

Preface

Carried by the surprise of your own unfolding ...

A process that is exciting and filled with intrigue. A process that is at times quite frightening. As you unfold it is like meeting a stranger that you somehow feel you have known forever. Sometimes the stranger feels like your long lost friend, sometimes an enemy you wish you'd never met. For in the unfolding you are led to discover parts of yourself that are blocks, behind which lie parts of yourself that are gifts.

Getting to the gifts takes traversing through blocks; at least it did for me. I am grateful that I realised this and didn't mistake those blocks to be all there was. For in hitting those blocks, those seeming enemies to joy, I realised that they held the key to how and where the river was flowing, or not flowing as the case may be!

The blocks in your life that keep you stuck are the access points to all your gifts within. The blocks are gifts in and of themselves. I wish I had been taught this in school.

My hope is that all people will experience their own unfolding. My vision for my life is to serve others and thereby contribute to the collective unfolding. Perhaps my words in some small way might help.

When I wrote *Pinch Me* and returned from Thailand back to New Zealand, it seemed signals had shown me the way home to my true self. This was not entirely the case as I was to soon discover. They had most definitely pointed the way home to my true self, but I had not taken the full journey to that home, yet. I had only scratched the surface. This book is the sequel to *Pinch Me* and picks up where that one left off.

In writing this second story, I got partway through and stopped. I almost didn't finish writing it. I considered filing the manuscript away somewhere dark. It felt at times that it belonged in the dark, because it contains things from the dark—the dark places within me. Those dark places are the enemies I met on my journey, my blocks. I am not proud of my experiences in those dark places, and at the same time I am not ashamed. I accept that I'm human and I'm doing the best with what I know, and that in fact I am writing my own unfolding, at times not knowing where it will lead me.

I completed this book and decided to publish it for one reason alone—to encourage and support others to flow with their own unfolding. To flow with the unfolding of yourself and discover how deep and dark the crevices of self are, in order to flow onward to the light, takes either courage or complete ignorance. At times I think I had a combination of both. But I realised at the end of the journey that others may never unfold, or may stop midway through the process, if they felt something was "wrong" when they met the parts of self that looked like enemies, the dark places. I want others to know what it looks like to traverse across the great unknown, through the dark into the light. I want others to know it is possible and to know how the theory plays out in practise. Well, at least how it played out for me.

It doesn't please me to think that you will soon read of my falling over many times. In fact it pained me to have to write the dark sections of this book. Every time I reached one, I wanted to skip over several chapters and pretend it never happened. I considered working out a way to leave it out of the book, but then realised that the unfolding was hollow without it. There is no book without it. So in all its glory, here it is.

I judged myself endlessly during my journey, wishing I were stronger, more present, and more capable of coping fearlessly. It took me some time to come to love my blocks for the gifts they were unveiling to me. In loving self, miraculous things occur.

I wish for you to love yourself. I wish for you to pick yourself up without judgment if you fall, knowing that we all fall and only some tell the tale as it really is. If this truthful tale helps you, please share it with others. If it does not, perhaps you know someone like me, and by reading this you may understand their unfolding a little better by hearing what it's like to be in the middle of it.

When you read this book, please hold in your mind a picture of a person taking a journey, being carried by the surprise of their own unfolding. That person is not me, it is you, reflected in the events of the world around you. For when we read, we read not of the other person's experience, rather we read to seek ourselves in the mirror of their words.

May the words that follow be a mirror to you of what you

know yourself to be capable of deep within, and give you strength to unfold as the majestic, divinely reflected soul that you are.

Love and blessings to you,

B

Chapter 1

C'est la vie Security

Perched on the edge of my bed, I stared at my phone. My mouth felt dry and my heart thudded. This moment felt reminiscent of another defining moment in my life some eighteen months earlier.

There are moments in life when you glimpse a sense of greater possibility for yourself. These moments are like little windows opening up. They are opportunities to step into the opening, to step out onto the edge. These moments are characterised by an inner knowing that you've outgrown the space you've been living in.

I stared beyond the glass window at the blanketing shades of green covering the valley, and then glanced back at the clock. It was 3:59 p.m.

He was waiting for me. I could not back out or change my mind. I had asked to speak to him on this day. I needed to tell him the thing that had to be said. That thing was that I had made a mistake. The commitment I had made to him only weeks earlier was a commitment made from fear. I thought I had gone past living in fear, but it seemed I had not.

Knowing When to Make the Call

The clocked ticked over. 4:00 p.m. I scrolled for his number in my phone, my mind all the while screaming, "What are you doing?" and my heart definitively announcing, "It's time."

Stephen went silent as soon as I told him.

"I made a mistake, I'm so sorry. I thought I could do this. I thought I could be what I need to be for you and the company, and do it well, and do what I need to do for myself, for my new life, for where my heart leads me. But I can't. I've realised I have to follow my heart and I have to commit myself fully to my new path in life. I have to take this leap of faith. I'm sorry to have changed my mind so soon. I thought I could do this but I can't. I have to resign."

The silence didn't last long, because Stephen somehow must have known that this was coming. I think, in retrospect, he could read me a like a book. I was probably more transparent than I realised. Perhaps he believed in me so much that he knew once my heart was entwined in this new life adventure that I wouldn't stop and I would leap into it to make it a success. The conversation was short, and he was accepting and supportive as always, turning his attention to what actions would be required to fill my space when I left.

Just like that it was done. I was leaving. At 3:59 p.m. I was the National Manager of a company, with a secure income and a stable future that I was certain of. For a long time, it had defined me. It gave me a place and a position in society, an acceptable and comforting position. I knew what it looked like, what it felt like, how it sounded, what it meant and how to do it. That, in fact, was part of the problem.

There was no growth or expansion for me left in that space. My soul longed to evolve. All souls long to evolve. We don't hunger for change. Change alone is not what we are called for. We hunger to expand the expression of who we are. Some people say that a change is as good as a holiday; if that is the case then evolution is as good as winning the lottery.

At 4:01 p.m. I was pending unemployment (ahem ... I mean *self*-employment!).

It had only been a few weeks since I returned home from my glorious three-month sabbatical in Thailand. Stephen had moulded and flexed to fit around my desire to go off and find myself like any corporate middle-aged woman turned newfound hippy does. He had been patient. I had returned full of zest for life, with an array of new, self-selected and shiny titles to help me frame my path forward as Author, Coach and Healer B. I was creating a life that would be everything I wanted; I knew I could achieve it by continuing to follow the signals, the very signals that had served me well for eighteen months. And I felt sure that if I just did both my day job and followed my new passion path it would all be fine. I could spread myself thin enough, no problem. I was the master of thin spreading. I could be National Manager B, and help run the company, and lead the staff, and grow the business even though it didn't feel like my joy (after all it was my income), and I could also be Author, Coach and Healer B in my spare time.

Leverage to Leap the Fence

This "being all things to all people" approach was really about me being a shit scared scaredy cat straddling the fence of indecision. I had three scared little paws on the old life side of the fence and I had one brave paw on the new life side of the fence. The scared paws had their claws out, dug firmly into safety, which is also commonly called a paycheck. The brave paw was on the other side of the fence feeling around to see what was there.

What exactly happened to me that allowed me to retract my scaredy cat claws from the paycheck that had made me feel so supported and secure? What allowed me to leap and land with all four paws on the yonder side of the fence when all that lay ahead was uncertainty?

The answer, of course, is signals. Well, signals and heart-led decisions. Both leveraged me forward.

I knew without a doubt that following signals was the way to experience inner peace and joy, to connect to my soul-level self, and so I could not ignore the new signals.

It started when I was out walking with my friend Emily at home on Waiheke Island. She said, "So, now that you're back from Thailand maybe you should just quit the job?"

That was followed by another enquiring gem from one of my dear sisters, "Have you thought about quitting?"

Emily and my sister both had faith in my ability to live fully in my new expression, in writing, coaching and healing. I reasoned to myself that the sensible thing was to stay put: *These conversations aren't signals, they're just conversations. Sure it's an obvious question to ask, but that doesn't mean I need to pay attention to it.*

My reasoning seemed solid. After all, the money was good and it was important to have secure income. Money makes the world go around after all (or so I thought), and I had no certainty of income if I resigned. I could grow my new venture, for sure, but that would take time and who knew how long. No, it was sensible to stay put.

The signals quickly put rest to that concern, with these lyrics haunting me on and off for weeks in my waking hours ...

"It's not about the money, money, money ... forget about the price tag." [1]

Then came the incessant nagging feeling that had taken up residence within me. If feelings could talk, this feeling was saying, "It's time. Leave." I thought if I moved, walked faster, thought of something else and occupied myself with other things then I wouldn't feel it anymore. But I was wrong.

Before my *Pinch Me* journey, I had never given any weight to horoscopes. Like everything else spiritually based that I had ignored for the first thirty-plus years of my life, they seemed at best entertainment and at worst a crock. I soon realised I must have been reading the wrong horoscopes. Meredith, my spirituality course teacher, recommended a particular astrology website which I looked at from time to time and found to be remarkably and spookily relatable. At this unsettling time I checked in to see what clarity the planetary placements might offer. It said it was time to take a chance on something I had known for sometime was right for me.

While at my job in the city one day, I realised I had the haunting song "Creep" going over and over in my head. Not a song I like, and one that I would recognise only by tune, with no idea what the lyrics were ...

"What the hell am I doing here? I don't belong here." [2]

It could not have been more obvious to me.

Oh god, I know what this means, I thought. *I could resign; I'm brave enough to do it. I just need to ascertain if that is brave and dumb, or brave and smart. There's a big difference.*

So somewhat unwillingly I had settled on my bed, legs dangling over the edge, shuffling back and forth to get comfy. Shaking out the tension in my shoulders, wondering if it was a very good idea to ask the forthcoming questions, knowing that the answers would open a can of worms I wasn't sure I wanted to open. But curiosity always gets the better of me, and I knew the signals would only get louder, and my feelings would only get stronger, if I ignored them.

I sat in meditation, preparing to communicate with the Energy Source, which I commonly now refer to simply as source or universal energy (personally, to me these terms also mean God, Creator and Divinity). I asked questions and received responses the way I had grown accustomed to—with a symbol in my minds eye of a tick or a cross, with a tweak of my head to the left or right indicating yes or no, and/or with clairaudience.

I asked, "*Are these signals guiding me to leave my job?*"
"*Yes.*"
I asked, "*Do I need to leave my job in order to progress towards my goals and dreams?*"
"*Yes.*"
I asked, "*Is it in my best interests to resign from my employment?*"
"*Yes.*"
I asked, "*Should I just leave my job?*"
"*Yes.*"
I asked, "*In order to achieve my dreams and to live the life I have envisioned before me, do I need to fully commit my time to it?*"
"*Yes.*"
I asked, "*Are you sure?*"
"*Yes.*"
I asked, "*Am I really connecting to source and pure guidance at present?*"
"*Yes.*"
I asked, "*Is there any way I could be making this up right now and the signals are not pointing me to leave my job?*"
"*No.*"
I asked, "*Couldn't I just leave my job a little bit, you know, like further reducing my hours?*"
"*No.*"
I asked, "*Couldn't I just do a bit of both?*"
"*No.*"
Exasperatedly I exclaimed in my head, "*So you want me to just quit?*"
"*Yes.*"
I sighed. "*But that's really challenging and we won't have any reliable immediate income, and we have to be realistic here. Aaron is committed to his new ventures and we can't both be chasing our dreams at the same time.*"
"*Be brave.*"
"*That's easy for you to say from up there. I'm so scared I*

think I'm paralysed!"

And then it appeared as a fleeting image in my minds eye: the months on a calendar. October, November, December, January, February, March. There was nothing after March.

I asked, *"Resign now but leave in March?"*

"Yes. Set in motion. Leave later."

March marked exactly six years since I had started at the company. It dawned on me that there might have been some correlation between this and a song that had been popping up on and off for the last few weeks.

This song played in my mind when I woke, it arrived in my daydreams as I wandered along the street, and it played on the radio when I entered shops. Someone even asked me, "Hey, this is a great song, what's it called?" The day I went to open a new bank account for my writing, coaching and healing company, I walked into the bank and the song was playing on the radio.

" ... with your high heels on ... something about the chase, six whole years ... lipstick all over your face ... something about just knowing when it's right." [3]

In my mind I always thought of my corporate consulting days as beating the streets with my lipstick masterfully applied and high heels click clacking on the pavement as I walked (or often ran) everywhere on a mission. I guess that was my six-year chase for the most traditional form of success.

The song was a signal referencing my career at a time when I was being signalled in all sorts of ways to make a move in that area of my life.

The song lyrics "It's not about the money, money, money" [4] were to continue to be a prominent message reaching out to me for the coming six months as I retrospectively um'd and ah'd about the logical sense of walking away from a career that had taken me thirteen years to build and a career that I considered to be a goldmine. A goldmine for materiality that is, not a goldmine for joy.

While being faced with signals to leave my job was confronting, it was not that I was merely leaving *a* job. It may look like that to you. Emotionally, I was leaving the biggest, best (ranked on title and paycheck) and most promising job I had ever had. And, just like with the last career crossroad I had found myself at back in Wellington, on the surface there was nothing at all "wrong" with the situation I was in. Believe me, I had left many jobs before. But I had always left to climb one rung higher on the "I'm important, successful, high achieving, blah blah blah" ladder, not to mention always remaining safely on the same familiar ladder that I knew.

The decision to leave my job was really to leave the only type of work I had ever known, the only way I knew how to support myself, and to leave with nothing more than passion and faith in my heart that the direction I was going in was the right one for me. Indeed, to me this signified leaving all security I had amidst many questions that didn't yet have answers.

This notion of spending "thirteen years building myself up"—what does that mean anyway? I have no idea, it sounds ridiculous in retrospect, but whatever it meant it felt like something I had to do in order to be okay and to avoid pain and failure. I had been accumulating in order to be independent and secure, but that's just good common sense. Isn't it?

Quitting felt like putting everything at risk and risking taking steps backward. Backward from what? From going forward of course! For life had conditioned me to believe that we move in a linear fashion, away from the past that lies behind, towards the future that lies ahead, on an upward slant at all times, all the while measuring ourselves on an invisible scale of life progression.

In fact, the truth was I would have risked more if I had stayed put and ignored my calling. I would have risked not realising all the infinite possibilities for myself. I would have traded off possibility, by accepting the known quantities in my life as being enough. Of course it was all more than enough at the base level of Maslow's hierarchy of needs, providing all the essential elements for living and sustaining, yet that was not the type of enough I needed. The enough I needed, at a deep level, would turn out to be incomparable to the enough I was used to on a surface level.

It makes no difference how much money you do or do not have, how far up the false ladder you are or are not, your position can look and feel as precarious as the next person based solely upon your perspective of what is possible and your relationship with money.

Life has a way of giving us the exact challenges we need to face in order to evolve and expand. During my *Pinch Me* journey I had been introduced to numerology and I subsequently utilised information pertaining to my life path number (derived from my date of birth) to help me understand my life challenges. My life path number is 8. One of the noted challenges for 8's is their relationship with money. To now be facing internal turmoil about leaving my career, because of fear around money, was painful, amusing, frustrating, enlightening, confusing and helpful all at once. If nothing else I would be giving myself an opportunity for some very real personal development by resigning with no certainty ahead.

In my notebooks I wrote the following entry, as I reflected upon the idea of following these "quitting" signals. So strong was my emotional reaction to this fear that my eyes welled up as I lent over the page, writing. On neatly ruled, tear-stained lines it read:

I cannot do it anymore. I called Aaron to tell him it's time I left. I called Charlotte to tell her I'm afraid. I guess this is "do or die"—do it or die inside. I feel so challenged by this move. But I know I have to listen to these signals. There are too many to ignore, and I know them to be true because they resonate. I can feel it is time. It's time for me to walk the talk. I've been losing perspective on one very important thing— that it's all possible, or not possible, depending on your perspective. I don't need to look at what I have had in the past and somehow work out how to replace it with a new venture. Replacing is not the point. Recreating is the job at hand, to establish something new from scratch and to let it rise up as a creation of its own, irrespective of what has come before. To let this flow, I have to let go. I cannot receive into my hand what I desire if I am so tightly gripping on to what I do not desire out of pure fear of having an empty palm. When I ask for guidance, all I hear is LEAVE. When I let go, I know that all possibilities will immediately open up for me.

What in your life do you grip onto for fear of having an empty palm? Are you ready to release the grip, to be open to receive?

Create the space in your life for new creations to rise up.

Chapter 2

Signals & Soul-level Self

The instant I saw the timeline out to March on the calendar in my mind, I knew it to be right. If I'm honest, the signals reminded me of what I sensed at a deep level, far below my thinking mind. I had come to realise this is the very point of signals.

At a deep level sits all the knowing of our soul-level self. We often experience it as inner knowing, or intuition. It is beyond what the thinking mind can grasp. Indeed, an untamed thinking mind would prefer to walk all over soul-level self. Domination is the mind's number one forte. But the whispers of soul-level self are so much more valuable than the screams of the mind.

Soul-level self embodies our oneness with universal energy. The signals we receive from universal energy attempt to catch our attention. The signals never tire if we are blind to them, they never give up on us, and they are *always* in alignment with our soul-level self and why it came into this life. Always.

Answer the Call to Align

Over the course of the coming year it became clear to me that we all choose the lives we come into. By that I mean our souls choose, and our souls are not the aspect of ourselves that we associate most closely with. You and I didn't choose this current life we came into as the people we know ourselves to be, not with our minds, our bodies, our names and our personalities. Rather the highest part of ourselves spiritually, our soul-level selves, chose it.

Soul-level self is higher self.

Soul-level self is infinite and timeless.

Soul-level self is not bound by the three dimensions we know as our reality, experienced in mind and body.

Soul-level self is not who you are in name and personality.

Soul-level self is a divine and ethereal essence of energy embodied within you. It breathed into form through your body when you were born and it remains the underlying embodiment of you until you leave.

When you leave, that end is in fact also the start of a new beginning, a new chapter. A new chapter in your soul's journey.

That is because soul-level self has many lifetimes, in different places and times, playing different roles. For now it is here, as the you that you know yourself to be.

Soul-level self retains all the knowledge, wisdom and memories of previous lifetimes. And, most importantly, soul-level self always knows *why* it came into this lifetime in particular.

A soul willingly comes and goes over lifetimes, each life offering the soul new opportunities for the growth and expansion it seeks. We just forget this fact when we are born, when our thinking mind kicks in and overpowers our soul-level self, and we then spend most of our lives trying to figure out what's missing. It's when we reconnect to our soul-level self and experience our connection to universal energy firsthand that we find what was seemingly missing.

This spiritual journey I have taken, and continue on, has led me to understand that all the hungering, seeking and questioning emanating from me was, and is always, simply soul-level self calling out for growth in alignment with its intention for this life.

Soul Intention

There is *always* soul intention. The fact you are alive denotes that your soul-level self had intention; otherwise it would not have come into this life. That is, it would not have incarnated.

The soul chooses each life for making specific contributions, having particular experiences and learning certain lessons for its growth, as well as to contribute to the experiences and lessons for the growth of other souls. These are the agreements souls willingly, and perhaps lovingly, make with each other. It is hard to understand from our earthly perspective how this can be, when the learning and growth at times seems to involve challenging, or even abhorrent, circumstances and interactions in our world.

There exists a complex tapestry of energetic agreements that weave together in order to support what we might call karma. My understanding of karma is that it is a balancing of learning and understanding at a soul-level for the betterment of each soul and thus for the betterment of "the whole"—that is, the connected oneness of all.

We are each going through the school of life, over many lifetimes. We play different parts in each lifetime, in order to have the opportunity to learn from what we might, from our limited perspective, call "good" or "bad" experiences. This is so we can all grow at a soul-level through and from such experiences.

Signals have the potential to guide you to fall into the slipstream of your soul intention, depending on your level of awareness and your willingness to unfold. Signals guide you toward balance. They allow you to see what is standing in your way so you can break through your blocks and expand yourself. This is all in order for you to be your contribution, that is, to be your unique expression into the world.

Unique Expression

You were born with a gift, and that gift is *being you*. No one else has that gift. Only you can be you. Gifts are for expressing. If *being* you is the gift, then *expressing* you is what you do with your gift. Expressing yourself fully, without inhibition, without fear and without limitation. You are not here to judge yourself, to judge your value, to compare yourself to others, to do what you think you should do or to meet expectations.

If we do not open ourselves to the magnificent truth of what we can offer this world just by *being* who we are, honouring the whispers of soul-level self, then we will come and go from this world and our unique expression will be suppressed and lost forever.

There is no need to work out your unique expression. Just acknowledge that you *are* a unique expression, be willing to allow yourself to unfold and flow with the current of life, and be open to signals as you do so.

When you hold a vision for your life that is as strikingly simple as fulfilling your unique expression, and you then let yourself open up to your own unfolding, magical things happen. This is a conscious choice, living in awareness. This is when signals most fluidly guide you into the slipstream. When you get out of your own way, you're helping universal energy immensely.

Being in the slipstream doesn't mean everything is easy, but what it does mean is that you're living on purpose and you flow *with* challenges not against them.

Of course a broader vision, with goals and dreams beyond simply being your unique expression, is beautiful and juicy, and is the essence of how we go about playing with our expression. Underneath it all, however, the simplicity of being your fully expressed self is fundamental.

How are you showing up in the world? Are you showing up each day with the intention of fully expressing yourself? Shoulders back, head up, heart forward?

Does the world around you know the real you?
What are you hiding?
Who are you appeasing?
What would it feel like to be free of all of that?

Give the universe the impression that you are here for expression. Open yourself to life.

The Design for Awakening

If you have ever asked yourself where you came from or why you are here, or you've ever felt like something was missing, then congratulations. Celebrations are in order, because that is just one way your soul-level self calls out to say, "Hello—don't forget what you came into life for." These questions emanating from you mean that you heard your soul-level self calling; you are in communication!

We first *feel* a disconnection from source and soul-level self, and then we experience the results of that disconnection in the world around us. When experiencing the results of disconnection, some of us seek answers. When we seek we find. When we find we reconnect. This is the design for awakening.

Chapter 3

Lingering Longing

Back in Bangkok, when it was nearing time to go home to New Zealand, the signals about abandonment, children and orphanages had continued to bombard me for weeks.

This one lyrical signal did not give me closure: " ... and it's no coincidence I've come." [5]

It gave rise to lingering questions that leaving Bangkok, and the children, was somehow not complete. It felt like there was something more, something I was not getting, and I could not put my finger on it.

My being in Thonburi was of course no coincidence. My hearing the word Thonburi whispered to me in the middle of the night back home had not been random. I had been led there. The experience with the children had been no mistake either. It had taught me many things. Part of me wondered if it had been just for the obvious lessons I had learnt; of facing situations that felt completely and utterly unacceptable to me, of making peace with such situations and feelings, of being in the middle of what I could not fix, knowing I was not responsible for fixing anything. Perhaps it was about releasing past hurts, of seeing strength in little eyes that by all accounts should have been void of strength, seeing love in the places I thought it could not exist and the opportunity to give love equally in return. The lessons there were innumerable.

But had it been for more than these lessons?

As a childless married woman, it goes without saying that I have been asked by all and sundry whether I am intending to have children or whether I am going to adopt a child. I would be lying to say that I didn't think about how to bring Noname home with me. I would be lying to say I didn't think about what it would be like to have him in my arms at home in my haven on Waiheke, to nurture and love him, to be the one to reach into his cot every morning and free him, to give him what he needed and what he was not currently getting. I did not share this with Aaron at the time and he knew better than to ask, because we had already decided that we did not want to have children.

Aaron could sense the strength of my conviction and feeling about the "not okay-ness" of babies being abandoned. If he had even remotely indicated that adoption was something we could have looked into, part of me thinks I would have succumbed to my incessant need to fix things and started the process right then and there, sprinting to the nearest adoption agency. Mortgage up the house, get on the waitlist, whatever it took. Aaron may have felt it necessary to check my luggage before leaving Bangkok to ensure I had not snuck a rescued orphan in there!

This was my old "fix it" curse. Something I was guided to break free from.

I had cried as the taxi carried us away from our Thonburi apartment for the last time, making its way over the river en route to the airport. Some distance away the children were still there, and I was leaving, alone, without them. Me leaving. Them staying alone. It didn't seem right. But what was I to do? A woman able to have her own children, from a different country, just standing up to say I've decided I want one of these little babies? I could have, but in all honesty I knew it was not my path. Something didn't feel at all right about it. I felt the strongest impulse ever to help them yet that help was not to mother them. I followed my feelings as an indicator.

Thwarted Plans

So, I had signals leading me to the children, and yet I had a strong feeling that it wasn't about me having children of my own, naturally or adopted. I'll fill you in on why.

It was back in that session I had with Augustus, back before this entire signal following adventure started, aka back in my half-happiness.

Part way through my session with Augustus he blurted out a message from my grandmother, "What about you and babies?"

My voice went quiet like a mouse and with a hunger I squeaked out, while looking down at tightly clutched hands, "I desperately want babies."

He told me, "Don't be desperate about it. It's there if you want it. There are three children in your aura if you want that. You've got lots of years in front of you. But ... "

Argh, there's always a BUT. What does he not understand about DESPERATELY want?!

He said, "But don't you think you've got some more growing to do? And evolving to do? And experiencing to do?"

All I could think was: *What the goddamned heck are you talking about? I'm thirty-two years old, married and this is the next thing.*

He had waited, saying nothing, inviting my response. Answering yes was clearly what he wanted to hear, clearly the right spiritual answer given a wise old spirit was asking me this question. It was most definitely a rhetorical question; I was clear on that much. He was not genuinely asking me because he did not know. He was posing this like a gold nugget hovering in the air waiting to be plucked by me.

Before I answered, it felt like time stood still. The gap was perhaps fifteen seconds. It felt like a lifetime. My body was there in the room with him. But my mind drifted off into what had been a quietly fitful, long-running nightmare that went something like this...

I am lost.
I am unfulfilled.
I don't love what I do.
I don't know what to do.
I just want to escape.
I need something to help me escape.
I want a baby so I can acceptably leave my career and stay at home and escape all of this stuff that has become meaningless to me.
I need to find meaning in my life.
I want a baby because it will fill the void I feel inside.
I want a baby because I don't know what else to do.
I want a baby because there is nothing else to do.
Having a baby is the sensible, acceptable next thing to do.
Having a baby is the only next thing available to me.

As a young, sensible, smart, loving and caring woman, I desperately wanted a baby not because my heart longed to be a mother, not because my body longed to have one, not because my hormones were driving me to cuddle every newborn in sight in the hopes it would rub off on my ovarian system. No, I wanted one because I saw no other option available to me in order to *find* happiness, and I wanted one in order to escape a career I was not fulfilled in. I wanted a socially acceptable reason to wake in the morning and not leave the house to go and do things I didn't love.

Yes B, what better way to solve a logistical career challenge (which was actually the fancy dress costume for a disconnected soul-level self) than to bring a baby into the already murky equation. This was not my finest hour.

And here Augustus was putting a spanner in the works of my ovarian plans. He was rhetorically asking me whether I thought I had more growing, evolving and experiencing to do. *Bloody hell, he's right*, I thought. Even though it frustrated me to admit it.

The thought of not starting a family and instead exploring my life to better understand this void seemed all too scary and like a lot of hard work. A baby seemed like a far quicker way to escape what didn't work for me, but easy it would not have been. I am confident that my void would have roared louder and louder, in different and perhaps more challenging ways, until I was forced to listen to it.

I know that for many people having a family is one of the greatest joys of one's life. An indescribably wonderful lifelong experience that touches the soul in ways few other things can. There is nothing easy about it, and there is nothing greater than it. Indeed I respect the viewpoint held by some that we are actually born to recreate by our very biological capability. I've considered that closely, alongside the fact that as a species we are designed with the obvious ability to make conscious choices.

I realised through talking to Augustus that a baby at that point in time represented to me (unconsciously) my fast ticket to what I thought was freedom. When Augustus posed the big BUT it stopped me in my tracks.

Granted back then I wasn't able to articulate any of this. Back then I would have told you one thing, "I desperately want a baby," and you could have challenged me on any of the above points and I would have called you a liar and I would have told you again, "I desperately want a baby."

I could not name my feelings accurately. My head was not in touch with my heart. Soul-level self was buried. I was trying hard to think my way out of what did not feel good in my life. In reality, what I needed was to feel my way out of what was not thinking good in my life!

At that early point in my journey I didn't know what my soul-level self wanted. I didn't know what soul-level self was. I didn't know that the feeling inside of me was my soul-level self calling out, asking me to understand it and feed it with what it really needed then. Unbeknownst to me at the time, my soul wanted to grow beyond fear. It wanted to evolve in its understanding of life. It wanted to experience new horizons. It wanted to seek to overcome the challenges that would forever linger until faced. It wanted to flow into the slipstream of its intention for being here.

And so of course, Augustus was right. No surprises there. I did have more growing, evolving and experiencing to do.

Here's the thing. Not long after my *Pinch Me* journey commenced, with greater awareness and developing connection to universal energy, I no longer longed for babies. What had before been foggy glass started to form into crystal clear view.

Strangely, once I accurately identified my desperate-to-have-babies feeling as actually a desperate-to-know my-soul-intention feeling, things changed forever. I adore children; always have, always will. They are the most beautiful gift of life, but once my soul started singing in the way it was destined to in this life, once I experienced my joy by flowing in the river of life the way my soul intended to, then the void inside of me disappeared and I realised that others things were calling to me.

For now I long to share my love, warmth and knowledge in other ways, a different type of love and a different type of contribution perhaps. I often ponder the fact that through the flow of life I met my husband, who also feels the same way. I guess energetically, with like attracting like, there are no major surprises there.

Having said all of that, if Aaron and I have learnt one thing it is to *never* box yourself in so that you rule out all other possibilities and options from your life. I lived like that once before and it was miserable, making decisions and setting the rest of my life in stone like a foregone conclusion. Make a choice, but don't slam the door on everything else. One day we might change our minds and we might feel a calling for children as we evolve and grow. It does not concern me that my clock may tick beyond its expiration date. There are plenty of special souls out there who need love, and I have much love to give. If that day comes, the love I have will meet the soul who needs it and we'll flow in the river together at that time.

Confusion

And yet despite this journey, from longing for children, to greater understanding of my soul-level self and experiencing an inner peace and joy, and deciding not to have children, here I was returning from Bangkok and feeling a pang.

There was a pervading strange feeling that I was meant to do something about this abandoned children situation, but a very certain feeling that adopting/becoming a mother was not the answer. I was confused to say the least.

It crossed my mind that sharing about the children might help to raise awareness in our communities of these children and their needs, of the need for more carers to spend time with them. For it was clear to me that bottles, milk, clothing, toys and shelter were not the core issue. The issue, from what I had seen, was love, engagement and bonding. Hands to touch, arms to hold, smiles to engage them, and love to envelop and develop them.

Meanwhile, slotting straight back into life at home it was like I had never left in the physical sense, but I felt forever changed at a deeper level. One evening leaving the office, as I marched along in high heels walking faster than the four lanes of jammed up rush hour traffic, I was thinking about Malee and Noname. Head down, I watched the pavement as I walked, lost in thought. I was wondering how long before they would be going to a home in some other country, to a wonderful new family. Looking up, there right in front of me stood a monk. A saffron-robed monk. Right there in the rush hour traffic in Auckland's busy central city.

Arriving at the ferry terminal I stood waiting in line to board. The man behind me, deep in conversation with his female companion, raised his voice to exclaim "Unforgettable!"

followed by murmurs that I could not decipher. "Unforgettable" was a signal word that had popped up repeatedly before I left Bangkok, in relation to the children. One instance had been when I noticed the Frank Sinatra song "Unforgettable" randomly playing in my head. The lyrics were powerful indicators that the children would always remain unforgettable to me.

The next morning a very strange thing happened. I reached up to grab a sweater off the shelf in my wardrobe. As I lifted it, I saw the spine of a book facing out at me ... a book sitting on the shelf in amongst my clothes. *How odd.* I had only recently unpacked my clothes from storage and suitcases after Thailand. The wardrobe had been empty. I had hand folded and stacked every item in that wardrobe. Chills went up my spine.

I reached for the book. A woman holding a baby adorned the front cover. You can imagine my reaction, I'm sure. I could only assume the book belonged to Anne, the lady who had rented our house when we were away. The question of how it came to rest in my folded clothes would never be answered.

It was a book about the importance of reading to babies, for their development and nurturing. My little signal-interpreting mind went crazy. Maybe it was about the children. Maybe it was about mothering and me. Maybe it was about the particular publisher of the mysteriously appearing book (as I had been asking for signals about how to publish *Pinch Me*). I had no doubt that the children back at the nursery desperately needed people to read to them, but my gut instinct was that this was not a literal signal. When I consider something as a possible signal, and interpret it, I am guided by two things. Firstly, I trust my intuition. Secondly, I keep an open mind.

Signal or Not?

By this time I had become reasonably at ease with not always understanding the meaning of signals and in fact being at peace with the likelihood I would never know if some things were or were not signals, or what they meant. I was learning to live with the grey area, reforming myself from a lifetime of black and white "must have the answers to everything" style of living. I was expanding my ability to be with lack of resolution, as I came to realise that some things in life simply cannot and do not need to have neat and tidy conclusions (no matter how much my OCD nature wanted that).

People often ask me how I know if something is a signal. With regards to a song, for example, aside from it either recurring over and over in ways that seem beyond a mere coincidence, or floating into my mind from nowhere, sometimes one lyric or a collection of lyrics resonate so strongly that I just know it to be a signal.

As a result of my *Pinch Me* journey, I learnt that knowing whether something is a signal or not isn't a problem. It is the mystery and intrigue of following signals that I love, regardless of whether I fully understand them.

Following signals is about being aware of, and curious about, the unusual moments and unexplainable phenomena in our life. Why do we sometimes encounter a particular animal repeatedly or in strange circumstances? Why do we hear songs randomly playing in our heads for no reason? Why do we experience helpful moments of synchronicity that seem to be heaven sent? Why do visions or words come into our consciousness out of nowhere? Why do seemingly unrelated things occur in our life that all seem to have a common theme? Following signals is about being inquisitive about life and enjoying the process.

However, there is a fine line between curiosity and obsession! If you spend all day, every day, thinking everything that happens in your life is a momentous and defining message with deep meaning, then you are missing the point. *You* are creating your life, not signals. Yes, the universe loves you dearly but it is not signalling you every minute of every day. Learning that signals exist is a wondrous thing. The feeling of being communicated with by the higher consciousness of source makes us feel loved and connected. It brings deeper meaning to our existence. Signals help us remember those truths and to guide us as we move through our journey in life. Just don't forget to keep living while paying attention to signals.

So, if not everything in life is a signal, then how do we define what is and is not a signal? What is the fine art of discerning what is relevant to one's life path and what just "is"? These are hot questions. It is only through my first hand experience that I have learnt how to identify what *feels* like a signal to me, and what does not.

That doesn't mean I know everything about signals, far from it. No one does. I'm not necessarily getting it "right" either. It simply means I'm following my intuition.

I endeavour, and admittedly fail at times, to live my life with a light-hearted, open-minded approach, which allows signals (if there are any) a clear passage to reach me. That doesn't mean they are coming to me all the time. It may seem that way to a reader who is absorbing one year of my life condensed into this book. Sometimes weeks go by as I live my normal daily life and nothing in particular resonates with me as a signal.

With regards to recognising and interpreting signals, you won't get it right all the time, and that's okay. There are no rules. There is no clear, guaranteed way to identify the signals in your life. No one gave me a handbook or whispered a secret in my ear about how signals work. I've had to play with the signals in my life to understand what they are, why they come to us and how to interpret them. I've also spent a long time tuning into my intuition, strengthening my connection to my spirit guides and developing my relationship with source, in order to seek clarification when I want to better understand the way in which the universe communicates with me, and with us all.

The way we identify something as a signal, and derive meaning from it, is most often because it resonates with us. When we consider a potential signal, we notice that it somehow relates to a personal goal or dream, a challenge or circumstance. We have an emotional reaction to it. It just *feels* like it is important somehow. Our feelings are a guidance system that helps us to interpret and understand life and ourselves.

As with many aspects of life, signals are completely open to interpretation, which is subjective. No one can prove something to be a signal or not. It all comes down to how we perceive the world. There will always be a large grey area when it comes to living a signal-led life. It is not something we can make black and white, and attempting to do so would risk limiting the potential scope we have for benefiting from this guidance.

If you are genuinely interested in harnessing the guidance of signals, I encourage you to consider ways to develop your intuition. Quiet the thinking mind and bring inner stillness and presence into your daily life. One such way to do this is through meditation.

Without cultivating a space for that inner sense of knowing to be heard and felt, it can be difficult to discern what is or is not a signal, just as it can be difficult to navigate many other interpretations and decisions without your intuition. That is because ego and fear can overpower you when you are not in touch with, and trusting of, your instincts. Ego and fear can lead us to force meaning into things that have no meaning, or to easily overlook or ignore things that have meaning if the message is one that we do not welcome. We all exercise our free will and personal accountability when we decide to interpret anything in life, and being open minded and willing to receive whatever guidance serves us best, is paramount. Open up to life and let yourself be divinely guided, even if at times it means shining the light where you would rather not look.

Aside from forcing meaning or obsessing about signals, the other potential trap when living a life led by signals is to risk thinking that signals tell you what to do. That is surrendering your life to signals, whereby you refuse to act of your own accord and take responsibility unless the universe confirms it is "okay". This leaves you powerless and operating from fear and/or avoidance of responsibility. Signals never tell you what to do. Rather, they prompt you. It is you that decides how you respond to and participate in life.

While signals are magnificent, they are not the be-all and end-all of living a conscious life. They are one divine guidance system that we can use to navigate through our life journey. Enjoy witnessing the magic of signals occur in your life and if you do not know what they are suggesting to you, or you're not even sure if they are signals, simply let go of the need to work it all out immediately and let your intuition guide you. Your thinking mind may not understand. You may not even be able to sense your own intuition. However, if signals really want to reach you, they will. So relax and flow with the unfolding of life.

Energy Straggling Behind

A few days after finding the book hidden amongst the clothing in my wardrobe, I was signalled by these lyrics.

"It's just a little crush ... " [6]

I became more aware of the fact my heart was lingering back where I had come from. Our bodies might have moved to another time and place, but our heartfelt feelings, indeed our energy, can continue to linger back momentarily or longer, carrying our thoughts out of the present moment to rewind into the past.

The stronger an emotional attachment to a past moment, an old connection or another place, the more likely the chance of our energy literally straggling behind us. At some point you have to let the past go and live in the present. Choosing to be fully present in each moment brings your energy hurtling back to where it needs to be—right here, right now. There's no point in missing the only moment you ever have access to. It takes no more than a conscious choice to make this so.

I reasoned that my heart could feel the way it did. It was natural, and it did not mean I had to recreate my life path in order to accommodate those pangs I felt for Noname and Malee. The time to be there with them was then. The time to be at home living my life was now.

For a Reason

So there I was thinking I was so mature about boxing that emotional reaction away. Putting a lid on it. Unfortunately, I realised my feelings about the situation were not so easy to put a lid on. I had emailed the nursery supervisor a few weeks earlier to see how the children were and to send my love. A reply came back. Sitting on the bus I heard my phone beep to announce the incoming email.

The summary was: "Malee fine. Family confirmed. Going new home soon."

A wash of relief and joy came over me knowing that she would be embraced by the love that she deserved and starting out on a magical new stage of her life journey with a family to belong to.

Further updates filled the body of the email: "Noname gone. Sent north, another orphanage."

I felt upset rising and all I could think was: *What? NO! Why? Why did you send him away?!*

If I am honest, I actually felt angry. Like Noname needed protection from yet more change. I felt protective of him. Instantly I emailed back to ask if he was okay and where he had been sent. On sending the email, I quickly realised I had no right to ask this. I had been as fleeting in his short life as everyone else had been. But the supervisor knew how much I cared about him. She replied later to say there had been more room and many more caregivers where he had gone, assuring me that it was a wonderful place and he would be well cared for. I ached for that little boy. But still I was confused.

This child had a profound impact on me, but was always slightly unreachable to me somehow. I never quite got his name. I would peer into the cots each visit to the nursery looking for him and several times I could not see his face as he lay asleep tucked away below blankets, indecipherable from the babies either side of him. Now, they had moved him to another place and I could no longer even imagine him in the nursery that I could see in my memory. To me he was now nameless, placeless and still homeless. A little more than I could bear as I tried to adjust to being back in "normal" life at home. So I meditated and asked for guidance:

"Something in my heart cannot forget him. Is it in my best interests to somehow adopt/care for Noname?"

"No."

"Is Noname the reason I cry?"

"No."

"It is about me or him?"

"It's you. Let go."

"I don't know how."

"You are holding on. It's not him; he's not for you. You can't fix it. Other things for you to do. Now is not the time. He is not the child."

Silence.

Now all I could think was: *Is there some other child? But we've decided not to have children. I'm so confused ...*

A whirlwind of unresolved emotion, but greater certainty nonetheless. *At least I'm clear on one thing—it's definitely time to let go and move on. He is fine.*

I remembered that old saying that people come into our

lives for a reason, a season or a lifetime. Noname had come into my life for a reason. To teach me how to be with him, to not need to fix anything, and to learn to love and let go.

Truth Uncovered

As it would turn out, Noname had taught me much more. He had gifted me something, and that little baby would never know how he touched my life.

It would take more time passing and reflection to suddenly glimpse what all of this was about, and to accurately name not only the emotions that had been gripping me, but also the reason for them. As clarity cut through the fog again it was like the clouds parting and the sun shining down for an aha moment.

I felt protective of abandoned children, at least until I knew that they were chosen. Chosen in a way they would know connection, love and would never be alone again.

This aching for Noname was in fact my passion. A passion disguised as upset and longing. A longing aimed in the direction of the trigger that had allowed the passion to rise up in the first place.

That passion that I eventually named was to have every person know they are chosen; that they fill a sacred place in this world, are connected, never alone and loved beyond measure. That is the truth of every person.

No person is alone and no person is unloved. Ever. Even if a soul comes into this time and space we call life and every person leaves them, and they have nothing and no one, my passion is for them to know this truth. I came to realise, baby, child or adult, we should all know and be reminded that:

The way you are loved is not measured by how many hands hold you, by how many people surround you or by how many things you have.

The way you are loved is forever, beyond measure, as the divine soul you are.

These words above are my message to Noname, wherever

he is and to every other Noname. My signal following experiences helped me to distinguish my deepest soul intention to help people know this truth for themselves. How do you thank another soul for giving you a gift of this magnitude?

So often we believe our emotions are caused by an external experience, circumstance or person that has created this reaction within us. We look outward to point to the cause. They may be a trigger, but they are never the cause. We are the cause. The cause always lies within and the cause is further access to your own unfolding.

Chapter 4

Expanding Understanding

My love for signals is primarily due to the wonder of their existence, full stop. The fact that they help us to navigate through life is a bonus.

I find it mind-blowing when universal energy reveals itself to me through signals. It brings acute awareness to life when you know that the universe is communicating with you.

The beauty of following signals lies in the presence they bring into your life, that joy of connectedness you feel, the peace that comes from knowing you are not alone and that you are wondrous and loved beyond measure. Signals remind you that there is a very good reason you are here and that the entire universe is collaborating to support your soul intention. That is, to support your unfolding.

After my *Pinch Me* adventure, following signals in my life, I thought I had a fairly good handle on how the whole system worked. Analytical perfectionist tendencies at play. Miraculous how one could be so confident to assume that the nature of the universe could be understood in eighteen months. Little did I know but the continuing adventure that lay ahead was to greatly expand my understanding. The synchronicity of what was to come was perfectly designed to aid this expansion.

I had broadly categorised, for my own purposes, the types of signals I had recognised. These included synchronicities/coincidences, song lyrics, dreams, animal totems, inspired thoughts, people, as well as other written, visual and audible forms. I also had one last category broadly termed "out there" signals, as a catchall for things that just couldn't be categorised.

BTFA

The core principles that I operated from, as written

throughout *Pinch Me*, were based upon the widely discussed premise that human consciousness impacts upon matter and therefore has the power to create change in our life. I personally refer to this as the BTFA equation. That is:

Beliefs + Thoughts + Feelings + Actions = Outcomes

Through our beliefs, thoughts, feeling and actions we are consciously or unconsciously creating everything in our life. We not only *create* our outcomes through our beliefs, thoughts, feelings and actions, we also then *interpret* those outcomes through the same filter. Of course this is then what we accept to be our reality. Our consciousness plays this twofold role in how our life evolves.

In the first way, we can positively direct our consciousness to influence shifts in matter that create improvements in our life. We most easily grasp this in the context of shifts in our external circumstances.

In the second way, our consciousness is directly responsible for the interpretation of our circumstances and outcomes. We are solely responsible for how we perceive reality. This is best demonstrated with an example ...

Two people could be faced with exactly the same circumstances, and yet interpret them differently through the filter of their unique beliefs, thoughts, feelings and actions. As a result, they would each experience completely different realities from the same set of circumstances. In this way, a shift in your consciousness (a shift in your beliefs, thoughts, feelings and actions) literally can shift your reality, that is, the way in which life occurs to you. This is an internal shift—a shift in perception.

This process of creating, seeing results and interpreting what we see, goes around and around in a cycle.

We are the only tool that we ever need. Everything that arises in our experience of life is a direct result of our beliefs, thoughts, feelings, actions *and* our soul intention.

Free Will or Higher Order?

Many of us are only familiar with our mind and body. We work on and through our beliefs, thoughts, feelings and actions, but we do not understand that our soul also intends for us to have opportunities for growth along the way, throughout the process of creating our life and turning our dreams into reality.

Soul intention may sometimes bring us those opportunities via what looks like, from our three-dimensional life perspective, challenges, delays or obstacles. Why? Because the soul longs to evolve and it came to learn particular things. A soul cannot grow without stimulus.

Soul-level self wants you to raise your awareness, that is, to lift your consciousness higher; the universal energy (aka everything in our world, tangible and intangible) supports this process. Now, if you don't know you have a soul-level self, can you see how stuck you might become? Like part of the jigsaw is missing.

Life challenges begin to look very different in the light of your soul-level self and its desire to evolve. That is why bringing the light of soul-level self into your consciousness is the most wonderful gift for inner peace and joy in the face of the ups and downs that we go through over a lifetime.

The idea of free will versus the idea of soul intention would come to be an investigative pet project for me, soon to be played out in a case study in my own life. I became intrigued by a sense that a higher order existed within the universal energy that played out *in conjunction* with our own conscious creation. This curiosity about a higher order seeded within me what would soon grow to be a deep respect for the universal energy, and the way it weaves.

My Soul Would Not Choose Something Negative!

You might think that your soul would never choose negative experiences. In fact, soul-level self does not choose these experiences for the experience in and of itself, but for the gift of evolution that comes *out* of that experience. For example:

Soul-level self does not come into life for pain. It may come into life to learn how to overcome pain through love.

Soul-level self does not come into life for grief or illness. It may come into life to learn how to overcome grief or illness through healing.

Soul-level self does not come into life for regret, guilt or anger. It may come into life to learn how to live in the present moment without judgment of self or others and with forgiveness for self and others.

If you experience challenges in your life (and we all do) then you need not succumb to the illusion that this is your burden to bear, that it is your destiny to evolve by living within that burden. The design for soul evolution lies within moving *through* that burden into the light.

What light? The light of consciousness, awareness of how our world really works and why you are here.

Reasons Signals Come

As we move through life, signals come to us for primarily four reasons; to guide us into and along a particular path (literally or metaphorically), to confirm a path we are already taking, to support and encourage us in times of need or to intervene when we beach ourselves on the muddy, grassy riverbank.

The beautiful thing about the four primary purposes that signals serve, is that it ensures we are always getting signals right when we need them, for just the right reason, uniquely based on where we are at in our journey.

At times we may receive an array of signals for more than one of these reasons. That is because we are complex beings and we can all at once be focused on what we want and taking action towards it, but also holding negative beliefs, thoughts and feelings, encountering our own blocks, learning lessons through life challenges and at times putting brick walls in front of ourselves. We may be on track in some areas of our life and off track in other areas. Signals come to provide guidance, confirmation, support or intervention as and when we may need it.

When you recognise a signal, notice what purpose the signal might have.

What could it be telling you about the way you are being, what you are doing, how you are going about it or where you are heading?

Flashbacks

There were a series of supporting signals that had given me one last tremendous push forward on that day of the call to Stephen. It started when I was absentmindedly brushing my teeth that morning. I had a flash of two memories. I have these memory flashes/senses from time to time. I'd never really paid attention to this phenomenon before, until I learnt about signals and soul-level self. It always seemed to be so random as to why these memories would pop up from nowhere like a slide show interrupting my thoughts for a split second. I've come to pay a lot more attention to whatever the memory is and how I'm being/feeling at the time I notice it.

The first image was the road I grew up on, of me as a little girl walking along to the school bus through the countryside. The second image was of me sitting next to my grandmother who was lying in her coffin placed upon the bed in her house where she had lived her entire adult life. That moment sitting beside her had signified to me the one reality we can all be very sure of—that we all leave at some point and there is no stopping the sands of time.

I wondered if these flashes were either a signal to remind me that my grandmother was with me in spirit, willing me forward and/or a reminder that this is life ... it has a start in childhood and an end when your time inevitably comes to leave, and what you fill the middle with is entirely up to you.

A song that I recognised in my head that same morning was supporting me to jump the fence and have faith in the river I was flowing in ...

"Hold me, like the River Jordan ... carry me, like you are my brother ... but they told me, a man should be faithful, and walk when not able, and fight till the end, but I'm only human." [7]

I was asking the universal energy to support my decision to step out and it was telling me to have faith. What you may or may not have gathered by now is how many times I said, "But ... " leading up to this decision to jump the fence.

Amidst any lingering doubts, this song made me stop and question myself: *How much longer will I use the but rebuttal for?*

In my session with Augustus all that time ago, the soul of

my grandmother had said, "But you always have a but!" To which I had felt like replying, "But I'm only human!"

In this supporting signal, I realised that while I'm only human, so are we all. When would I allow my soul-level self to rise up and be all it came to be? When will you let your soul-level self rise up to do the same?

And so, just like that, I said c'est la vie to my known form of security. I held onto the message coming to me in another signal song: "It's hard to feel the rush, to brush the dangerous, I'm gonna run right to, to the edge with you ... " [8]

New Carpet

With the deed done, I was now standing on the yonder side of the fence. It felt incredibly liberating and bloody uncomfortable. I'm not going to lie and tell you otherwise. I'm not some winged angel who flounces around with a smile on her face and not a care in the world sprinkling angel dust. Quitting my career in order to create my dream with no clear "how" was both terrifying and empowering. Faced with the vacuum of endless opportunity before me, it felt like someone (namely myself) ripped the carpet out from under my feet. When you do this in an endeavour to achieve something of greater possibility for yourself, you must focus on the belief that there is a better carpet just around the corner, one you can plant your two feet firmly on, a carpet that is much better for you.

If you had told me back then what was to come in the following year, I'm not sure I would have resigned. I had no idea what inner blocks I would face as I went about creating my life in new ways, from a vision so big it bamboozled me to even remotely try to work out *how* it would come to pass. I came to see very clearly that whether we like it or not we are simultaneously taking two journeys in life—an internal journey and an external journey. The sooner we recognise this, the easier it is to ride the waves.

Chapter 5

Two Journeys

Life is absolutely about taking two parallel journeys, internally and externally. If we allow them, signals can assist us on these two journeys.

Seduced by the Secondary?

In a world dominated by the tangible, many people first awakening to signals become primarily interested in what signals can *give* them in terms of their ability to create their life in the physical, material sense. Indeed, signals can guide you on that external journey to create the reality that you desire in the physical environment in relation to the goals and dreams you envision for your life.

Yet this is secondary to the primary journey we are here to take. The signals guide you on an internal journey within yourself, to develop and grow as a person by unblocking yourself of limiting ways of being, in order that you may flourish into all you were born to be. What greater dream could you have for your life?

The internal journey can be both wonderful and challenging at the same time, and the external journey is predominantly a mirror of how the internal journey goes. Of course this directly speaks to the fact that your beliefs, thoughts, feelings, actions and soul intention (internal) create your life outcomes (external), just reframed to make the linkage clear.

The Linkage

Here's the trap that some of us fall into ... we are seduced by the secondary, spending all our time focusing on taking the external journey (on what we want to achieve, accumulate and experience in the physical, tangible world). If it doesn't work, we might eventually gravitate to awakening and come to the primary, our internal journey.

However, when you focus on your internal journey just as passionately as you do on your external journey, looking honestly at yourself and unblocking your limiting ways of being (beliefs, thoughts and feelings), then you reveal the person you were born to be, and the external journey to create the life you desire then becomes a *natural flowing consequence* because you have aligned yourself so fully to your soul-level self. From this space, your energy vibration is powerful as a point of attraction in relation to the external journey you are taking.

The universal energy knows that your power lies within, not without, and it is designed to guide you to unlock that power on the internal journey, using signals to communicate with you. So yes, the signals help you on the external journey, but the miracle really lies within the fact that signals guide you first and foremost to unblock yourself, to know yourself, to unfold.

As people come to the end of their life, what were once before quiet whispers of soul-level self suddenly become clear and unmistakable. The thinking mind shifts to the back seat and things that seemed important throughout life now seem far less so. It's no surprise that deathbed regrets are very rarely about the external journey and almost always about the internal journey.

Are you courageous enough to look honestly at what is blocking you, and to step forward in your life to take both the internal journey and the external journey concurrently? There is only one answer to this question. The answer is yes, you are courageous enough, because this is what your soul intended, and your soul-level self came into life with everything it needed to fulfil it's intention in this life. Don't deny your courage, for in doing so you deny soul-level self.

Let the Energy Flow

Universal energy is like a flowing life force. While we are inherently part of the universal energy because energy is what we are, for simplicity sake we could say that the universal energy flows *through* us, or not, as the case may be. We either allow the flow of energy or we block the flow.

Universal energy is divine and it seeks to manifest into the world as you and through you. When you allow yourself to be all that you are, uninhibited, infusing all you do with love, you are allowing the energy to free flow.

This might seem like semantics, but my take on it is that we don't *make* things manifest (from the sense of forcing it to occur or taking the kudos ourselves for what is divinity playing out in our reality). Rather we let energy flow according to the laws of the universe and doing so results in manifestation. Both interpretations denote us as powerful creators of our reality, the latter however speaks to the heart of manifestation—*allowing*.

If you block yourself up with limiting ways of being (limiting beliefs, thoughts and feelings), you block the very channel through which energy seeks to move. You are the channel. What happens when we block energy? Energy blockages cause all sorts of problems, from ill health to relationship issues, from material carnage to emotional unrest.

The people who seem to manifest effortlessly are not those that have accumulated more tools than you or layers of special secrets they apply to make things happen. They are people who have *shed* layers of accumulated, dead weight beliefs, thoughts and feelings, and they are allowing the energy to free flow. The answers lie not in gathering more tools and wrapping your arms around the secrets to manifestation, but rather in shedding and letting go of what you don't need. When you do so, what is left is a clear channel for the universal energy to flow unhindered through you, for this divine life force to spark into creation through your unique expression.

The Greatest Variable in your Life

The good news is that *you* decide whether to allow or block the flow. As the outcomes of your life stem from your beliefs, thoughts, feelings, actions and soul intention, the greatest variable in your life is you. Unblock your mind and body to let your soul-level self shine. You are the greatest tool you have to create your life. It goes without saying then that you would want to understand and master the use of that tool in order to live the life you desire and deserve. This is the way in which you have control of your life.

In my *Pinch Me* journey, I was ecstatic to take control of my life and feel, for once, that I had true control over how my life played out. At least that is what I thought. As my journey continued, however, I came to see the difference between creating your life circumstances through the influence of your beliefs, thoughts, feelings, actions, and attempting to control your life.

Learning About Control and Influence

As a rough rule of thumb, we like to control our lives. It's pretty natural and in fact largely encouraged and celebrated.

However, we can't control *everything* in life. For example, we can't control the ways of being and doing of other people and things. And, we can't control the signals we get. However, we can control our own energy (through our beliefs, thoughts, feelings and actions) and we choose our reaction to life moment by moment. And our energy does have influence over other people, things and circumstances. It is this influence that contributes to manifestation and shapes the creation of our life. This distinction, between control and influence, is important to understand. Both are possible ways of living, and therefore consciously or unconsciously creating your life. However, one blocks the flow of life force energy and one allows the flow of life force energy.

The universe won't support your attempts to control (i.e. dictate, micro-manage or force) your life.

The truth is that this ability to manage our own energy, and our reaction to the experiences of life, is all the control we need. It is what we were gifted with when we came into life, and we must trust that our souls came into life with all that we needed. Divinity does not make mistakes.

For those of us who like to control exactly how our life plays out, it can be a difficult transition. Learning how to manifest change and live a life led by signals can be frustrating, and involve lessons hard learnt. You absolutely influence and shape the creation of your life. You absolutely choose how you interpret your life. You absolutely call the signals to assist you. Influencing, shaping and creating do not mean you control everything.

What I hadn't fully appreciated when I wrote *Pinch Me*, is that we have this miraculous ability to create our lives and to see life through whatever lens we choose, however, that doesn't mean that we won't be thrown curve balls that the soul will benefit from experiencing. From great adversity can stem powerful insights, incredible courage, deep appreciation for life and closer connection of mind and body to soul-level self.

What happens when we influence the creation of our life is that we sing a beautiful song and a dance takes place around us where all possible paths to our dream open up around us. This happens when we focus on what we want and allow the universe to guide us on how to achieve it. What happens when we try to control life is that we put a straight jacket on possibility, paths shut down and the universe has no choice but to align to our controlling energy vibration, as we dictate how and when things must be done.

Relationships

It is easy to become lost in thinking that we need to get other people to "play our game" if we want to achieve our goals and dreams in life. Whether it is your partner, boss, work colleagues, family or friends—if only they would just change somehow and do things your way *then* things would be different and your life would transform. Right?

Not so. That approach is not going to serve you well. As long as you feel the need to control life, including changing other people, you will be highly likely to experience pain in the form of disappointment, confusion, helplessness, frustration and even anger.

While your beliefs, thoughts, feelings, actions and soul intention create your experience of life, each person you encounter in life is also exercising their free will and experiencing their own internal and external journey. We are not here to change other people; we are here to evolve and expand ourselves, to listen to the call of our soul, and to be beacons of light and love. In doing so we shine bright for others and it is in this way that we influence incredibly positive change in people, things and circumstances around us as a result. Understanding the difference between influence and control in this context is vital if we wish to see the love within us mirrored in the world around us.

If you feel compelled to look at other people and consider what is wrong with them, and what you need to do to change them, I encourage you to consider something else. Will you consider how to be love in the face of what challenges you? Will you consider that within each person is a soul seeking to evolve, and often times people have become so disconnected from source that the only way we can help is to consistently be the energetic vibration of love ourselves? This doesn't mean we need to embrace what they are doing or how they are being. Rather, recognise and love the soul within them, for they themselves may have forgotten who they truly are. In the most trying of situations, when you cannot muster this level of recognition and love for another, remember we do not encounter people in our life by mistake. Your soul knows their soul. Everything is infinitely connected as one. Say within yourself, "The soul in me recognises the soul in you." Never underestimate the power of your *being* love; it is the purest and most healing energetic vibration. Healing for other people you encounter, yes, but most importantly ... healing for yourself. It is through healing ourselves that we are able to be healing for others.

We are all leaders—leaders in our lives, in our families, in our communities and in our work. Leaders do not control others, or tell others how to be. Leaders go first. They model the behaviour they wish to see around them and their influence has a powerful ripple effect that stems from their beliefs, thoughts, feelings and actions, manifesting change as a result. Our energy literally impacts upon those around us. This does not mean that influencing and creating a reality of love is easy. This does not mean that we will have a perfect mirror of our own internal light reflected back to us every day. But then if it were easy, where would be the opportunity for soul evolution?

Start Within

Being predominantly concerned about externality does not benefit you. That only reinforces that life is solely occurring outside of you, which is a falsehood. Investing some time and effort in understanding yourself and being honest about what is going on inside of you will allow you to create change in your experience of life.

Denying our inner workings, including our weaknesses, and hiding that from others or ourselves is simply denying our greatest access point to progress. It is like shooting yourself in the foot. The more you deny, the more life will allow you opportunities to discover what you are denying. The more you ignore feelings that are uneasy, the more life will send you opportunities to further experience those feelings in order for you to discover what you are denying. Again, this is the design for awakening.

The more present you become to what is going on within you, the more easily you will recognise the truth in each moment. How you react, how you perceive, how you feel, what you think – it all lies there in black and white if you are present to witness it. When you witness it you have the instant ability to recreate your experience as something different and more empowering. The external journey will then start to shift into alignment, revealing a new reflection to mirror the internal flourishing.

Challenges for Growth

After cutting the career umbilical cord (straying from what I called the employment mothership) to go and forge a new path for myself, I consciously spent time excitedly envisioning my life, creating it with my beliefs, thoughts and feelings. There were initially only intermittent moments of wondering what would happen in my future, until I realised that of course I was creating that future.

The sneaking suspicion I had that this culmination of events in my life was going to be significant for my personal growth was fuelled by lyrics I awoke to not long after resigning:

"What if you're making me all that I was meant to be ... " [9]

Post resignation, as time crept on, my level of discomfort continued to grow as I nudged the edges of my comfort zone. A quiet anxiousness indicated I was crossing the border into unfamiliar territory.

In expanding your comfort zone, you enter the great unknown. The purpose of this expansion is to turn the great unknown into the known.

Nothing can become familiar unless you allow it in.

Chapter 6

Blaze a Trail

Word to the World

So, the vision was to share the message of signals with the world, not only with my town, my city, or my country. I was overjoyed with the idea of people all over the world awakening to the existence of signals, feeling connected, loved and guided. The vision felt big and beyond me.

Perplexed as I was about how on earth to do this, it was nonetheless the vision that always came to me whenever I asked myself what I was passionate about creating. When I closed my eyes and let myself feel my calling, I would see the same thing—the impression of a person sitting quietly alone with unrealised potential, inhibited self-expression, with fears and doubts blocking their goals and dreams, and ultimately without the road map to the peace and joy that lies within. Quite possibly this person was anywhere in the world. That was where I wanted my message to go.

Unknown Territory

I started by doing the things I felt guided to do. Thus, a large amount of my time post-Thailand was spent on a project which I was extremely passionate about and which I dove headfirst into with great zest.

The project began with a question. How does one publish a book?

This was a question I asked myself a hundred times as I sat there staring at my hefty *Pinch Me* manuscript. A document that was quite possibly meaningless to someone else, which represented everything meaningful, heartfelt and important to me.

Your task, your project, your circumstances and/or your questions will no doubt be different. Regardless, embarking into unknown territory is quite often baffling. What I share in this chapter has little to do with publishing a book, which was simply the particular logistical task facing me within my greater vision. What I share here is not about the task at hand, as your tasks and vision will be different (these are just vehicles for playing out our unique expression in life), but rather it has everything to do with the signals navigation system that we can all use. Signals can guide you through whatever baffling unknown territory you may be facing. I invite you to read on with your own tasks and vision at the forefront of your mind ...

How to Do What You Have No Idea How to Do

150,000 words. A hash first cut at a book by someone who had never written a book before and at least 60,000 words too many as I would eventually discover. A dilemma.

As I prepared to share the manuscript with objective third-party eyes for assessment and editing, I knew I would be receiving a lot of critique, good and bad, for that was the point of the process. Aside from the logistical value of critique for the project to ensure the delivery of a readable story, I knew that the overall message of my journey was truth and any barrage at that greater truth would not dent it. My job was not to convince anyone of anything, but rather just to say what I had experienced. People would have their own valuable views and opinions, filtered through their own beliefs, thoughts, feelings and actions. There are so many endless versions of reality existing in our one world all at the same time, all due to the paradigms we choose to live through. At a surface level, critique could certainly graze me, because I'm not made of stone, yet something deep within me felt more solid than ever before.

Realising that I would need to slash the word count, I became so attached to my words that I went around and around and around in circles. I sought advice from others on how to edit and what to cut out. I didn't like any of the answers I got and so became more entwined in my mess. Not to worry, as lyrical guidance came to point out the issue ...

"I'm a hazard to myself, don't let me get me, I'm my own worst enemy." [10]

Guided Business

Considering this editing dilemma, I thought it wise to ask for more signals. I asked to be shown how to bring my book to readers and this is what I heard:

"Navigate business like you navigate everything else now—heart led, guided."

It was the first time that I really got that signals come for all aspects of our life—personal, business, relationships, health, financial ... you name it and we are guided on it. Guided business decisions would turn out to serve me well.

When you infuse your heartfelt love into whatever you do, including projects, business, vocation or career, and you allow yourself to be guided, then impossible odds become possibilities, and, moreover, possibilities become a reality. I truly believe that the reason for this is because infusing your love into what you do, brings the vibration of love to that very creation, and that very creation vibrating as pure love energy attracts back to it what it requires to flourish within the world. The universe is designed this way. Everything you create has a vibration—your business, your products, your services, your words, your relationships, your processes, your thoughts, your home, your office ... everything. Not only are you yourself an energy vibration (a unique frequency with your own energetic point of attraction), but everything that you create in the world is as well. Lest we forget, *everything* is energy.

In relation to how to navigate publishing then, I thought: *Fabulous. I'll wait for signals.*

It's Not a Waiting Game

Hang on ... fatal mistake. Waiting for something to happen to you is not the way to create your life. If you are waiting, and you believe you are waiting, and you think you are waiting and you feel like you are waiting, then you are slapping a big flashing neon sign on your forehead that vibrationally says, "Hey universe, no need to deliver what I need, because I'm waiting." By their very nature, waiting people do not have what they need, because they are waiting. They have chosen to be waiting. Waiting denotes not having/receiving yet. Waiting is like having a carrot on the end of a stick—it doesn't matter how many steps you take forward, if your beliefs, thoughts and feelings all point to your waiting status, then the world around you will just mirror your waiting, obliging by leaving you waiting until you decide that you are done with waiting. Hilarious, right?

Life is about co-creation, you and the universal energy working in synch. It's all energy after all; you are conducting the orchestra of energy with your beliefs, thoughts, feelings and actions. The signals come in response to your vision, and they come to show you how to achieve your desires when you're actively flowing in the river, not when you're standing on the sidelines, or riverbank as the case may be. Showing your intent and taking purposeful action is critical. Life happens in action, not inaction. When I talk about action, this doesn't mean physical movement. It means being purposeful in what you do, aligning what you do with your goals and dreams. For example, you can be in action in the quiet and still act of meditating, because you know that meditation will help you to connect with your intuition and with source.

In this instance with the project to publish my book, to extinguish the neon "I'm waiting" sign, I thought: *What action do I take? Where on earth do I start?*

In the coming weeks I did the most obvious things I knew how to do. I investigated and read online about the basics of how to submit work to publishing houses and how to self-publish. It was as simple as that. There were only two ways to do this, and it was all there online. In this age of instant information, there is almost no question that remains unanswered if you are willing to seek out that answer.

The Perfect Untainted Vision?

Perhaps many of us don't seek the answers that are there for us at our fingertips because knowing the "how" to our goal or dream would then require action, and action brings a whole new dimension to that goal or dream. Here's what I noticed as I moved ahead ...

It's safe to hold a goal or dream as a vision only, because it remains perfect and aspirational, completely untainted and completely achievable in its current unachieved, and as yet uninitiated, status. In that space we can say we are a person with a beautiful goal or dream. It feels both exciting and admirable, and we hold it up on a pedestal with eager anticipation.

There is something about acting upon a goal or dream that instantly changes the scenario as far as our thinking mind goes, in both wonderful and not so wonderful ways. The moment we act upon it, the perfect and aspirational nature of our goal or dream *can* (depending on our chosen paradigm) turn into what feels much more realistically like a challenging logistical task, with steps to achieve it, and with the very real prospect of what we might traditionally label as success or failure. Suddenly the joy of aspiring to something can turn into uncertainty, underpinned by fear.

> ***What do you aspire to, but resist acting upon in order to avoid the steps to create it and/or the possibility of failure?***

I had not spent all that time discovering this hidden realm of life, being completely enthralled with signals, changing my life and passionately writing about it to share with others, to then approach my project with anything other than a success mindset. Failure was not on my radar. This is what happens when I have a fire of passion lit under me.

Your Paradigm

We all have a choice as to the paradigm we live from and we have the ability to intentionally shift our paradigm instantly. Through whatever paradigm you see the world and life; you will reap whatever comes from that.

Here are some examples of choices you could make to shift yourself from unconscious conditioning that might have shaped your paradigm, into new perspectives that better serve you.

We live in a society that largely conditions us to say, "I'll believe it when I see it." You could choose the perspective of, "I'll see it when I believe it."

We live in a society that largely conditions us to say, "If it seems too good to be true, then it probably is." You could choose the perspective of, "If it seems too good to be true then pinch me because I must be free flowing in the river as my dreams are turning into reality."

We live in a society that largely conditions us to say, "Don't talk too much about your successes. Blowing your own trumpet is tasteless." You could choose the perspective of, "I'm living my fully expressed soul-level self. I will not silence the singing and I will allow myself to swim in the joy I experience because it is fun, infectious and it is so much more life affirming than spreading doom and gloom."

Good Enough for What and for Whom?

I mulled over the pros and cons of each path. To traditionally publish or self-publish, that is the question.

I had a series of what I thought were signals all pointing me towards two mainstream publishing houses; household names, big kahunas. Yet for a long time, for reasons unknown to me, I had felt like I might end up self-publishing my book. I hadn't consciously decided that, but it niggled at me, partly like a challenge asking to be tackled, and partly appealing to my preference for control.

Publishing with a traditional publishing house sounded a lot easier. I wanted easy. After a year of writing there was a part of me that wanted someone else to step in and do the rest of the hard work. After all, what the heck did I know about publishing? The answer to this question was zilch, zippo, nadda, nothing!

Despite that sneaky suspicious self-publishing feeling inside, I discovered I also wanted the validation of a publishing house saying my writing was good enough.

Ah, the old plague of seeking to be "good enough," a plague that at times had bent my confidence. It is one of the widest spread limiting beliefs in our world, buried deep below even the greatest of bravados. At times hiding at a subconscious level, others times bubbling at the surface, it's a puppeteer that invisibly influences how we behave. It can take a variety of related forms, including:

I'm not good enough.
I'm not enough.
I'm nothing.

I'm alone and nothing.

I'm unworthy.

I'm not valued.

Any one of these sneaky little limitations can often result in other layers of limiting beliefs like, "I have to prove myself." Sometimes we come into life with this plague, a hangover from a past life, and other times we unknowingly get infected with this plague by interpreting an experience in life as meaning something negative about who we are at our core.

Some people play it out by walking through life literally telling themselves that they aren't good enough, hanging their heads down. Other people play it out by living life as a process to prove themselves, to other people or to themselves. No amount of validation will ever quench the thirst of the plague though. However it plays out, the belief is running the show until you recognise it and choose to kick its annoying butt to the curb.

In relation to this particular logistical task I was facing, I supposed back at that time that a lot of writers wanted that type of "being good enough" recognition. I had initially fooled myself into thinking I didn't care what anyone else thought, but that ended up being a big fat fib. I realised that I did care. The reason being—I wanted to know that what I had created was of value. But, it would turn out later that I was seeking that value validation in all the wrong places ... because what do we really mean by value?

Was I talking about making a valuable contribution to those people I wanted to reach or was I talking about commercial value? Looking closer at my vision the answer was clear.

What Is the Real Driver?

After a lifetime of doing whatever I did for commercialism, this was the time in my journey to do whatever I did first and foremost for contribution. The vision I had was not going to be a values fit with anyone or anything driven primarily by commercialism. I had written this book to help people. My career job had been my "real job" and writing at that time had been a passion project on the side.

As I set forth, people asked me, "How many books do you

need to sell?"

I reacted with a sort of stunned shock and thought: *What do they mean? How many do I need to sell in relation to what?*

They were of course referring to how many books I would need to sell in order to see a return on my investment, in order to make a living off the writing I had been doing. In fact, the truth was I had only invested my time and passion and had never thought about the supposed cost of that. I didn't care about the cost of my time, because it had been joyful and fulfilling to do it.

Of course, to reach the people I was passionate about helping, I would need to get the book to them and it was part of my wider vision to write and sell books after leaving my career. But volumes sold or profits made had never been the motivating factor that sparked the inspiration in the first place. People benefiting was the real driver. The former felt like an empty enterprise akin to the tasks I had previously engaged myself in, that I eventually realised were meaningless to me. Hence, going forward, my vision always held my true end goal of doing meaningful things as a service to others with what I needed in life flowing to me as result. That flow would be from wherever the universe best deemed that would come from.

Why Do You Do What You Do?

Why do we do what we do?

Why do you do what you do?

Don't answer emphatically with your first reaction. Instead write it down. Now, tease it out. Follow it through, asking why at every step and you will eventually get to the real reason you do what you do. That real reason is, hopefully, what makes your heart sing. That real reason is what your vision is at the core foundation, or not, depending on whether you are listening to your heart singing.

Here is the clincher—heart singing is soul-level self singing! That is the truth that lies in the often heard phrases (which we may have become numb to understanding) "follow your heart" and "listen to your heart." They are simply saying follow and listen to your soul-level self, and ... signals align to soul-level self, always.

The reason to live as fully expressed soul-level self, is to live as fully expressed soul-level self. That's it. Expressing who you are for the joy of being expressed is the fundamental from which all else flows.

Have big, audacious goals and dreams, including whatever types of specific measures and outcomes are logistically important and meaningful to you. What isn't motivating for me may indeed be very motivating for you. We're all unique. But always be clear on why you do what you do at the heart level. Getting lost in believing that you are doing what you do for some surface level payback will never be enough to keep your heart singing.

> *External motivators eventually burn out over time.*
> *Internal motivators glow brighter over time.*

Let your expression, in all that you do, be led by soul-level self. Invite all other considerations (such as measures and outcomes) to be valuable and necessary to support your expression (not the *reason* for your expression).

Passion first, necessities follow. If you are living for necessities first, hoping to find that passion follows, here is a trick ... find *something* in what you do that you can be passionate about. Let that passion lead. Even if it is to say that through whatever you occupy yourself doing you will be passionate about smiling at people while you do it, or that you will infuse what you do with love stemming from soul-level self. Honour yourself enough to *be* your expression no matter *what* you are doing, even if what you are doing is not your goal or dream right now. Who you are being while you're doing it is what allows the life force to flow freely, that is what creates the "clearing" for inspiration and new creation to arise.

Eyes Wide Open

My first approach to a publisher came after a series of signals I followed. A conversation with someone led to a meeting with another person in the industry, which led to an exchange of contact details for a publisher. Having emailed off my manuscript, I was like a little girl the night before Christmas. My tummy churned with nervous butterflies and I could hardly contain my joy for life, joy that was squashed like a pancake when I received my first rejection.

Another valuable lesson—joy is *never* derived from something that relies on other people playing your game. That is temporary happiness. Joy is something that resides within, a peacefulness to just be and allow life as it is, no matter how the game goes. Exceptionally good lesson to learn, even if unpleasant at the time.

I'll be honest; I was a crying pancake. Comically tragic scene ... new writer, first rejection, stake through the heart. *Ground swallow me up, blah blah blah.*

I was grateful at least that the first rejection (ah yes, just the first) came with extremely useful feedback. The publisher kindly gave me their opinion on what would have to be fixed in the book in order for it to be marketable. The things that appeared wrong were listed off, with thoughtful comments and consideration given to the changes I should consider making. Aside from the disappointment, I was ecstatic to receive such insights. Every part of me wanted to dive in and make every single change they had suggested, to quickly make those "wrongs" into "rights." After all, they were experts and I knew zilch, zippo, nadda, nothing.

I wallowed in rejection for a day or so, not at all taking my own advice, until a signal song snapped me out of my funk.

Clasping a hot coffee between both hands, I sat at the dining table with my legs tucked up under me. Gazing out at the mishmash of vibrant ferns in the garden, I went over and over in my head what to do with all the recommended changes they had given me. I was confused about how to move forward. Lyrics played in my head, but I didn't realise what was happening:

"Keep drinking coffee, stare me down across the table, while I look outside ... " [11]

My thinking mind was far too busy trying to work out how to fix my manuscript, too busy to recognise the wise signal.

Do I make the editorial changes they've suggested, or do I wait to see what other publishers think? Is there any point changing what they suggested, given they're not interested? God only knows how this whole process works. I wish there was a manual for navigating this industry!

The song continued bubbling away in my mind, buried below the thinking:

"You've got opinions, man, we're all entitled to 'em ... who cares if you disagree, you are not me, who made you king of anything?" [12]

Once I started to hum the tune I realised I was being given something. Looking up the lyrics, I saw that I made this one publisher, the first one to consider my writing, the king of everything. I was placing so much emphasis on their opinion that I had lost faith in my own decision-making ability. This was a tiny blip and I was stumbling already. I needed to remember that plenty of moments like this occur in life, and not to invest so heavily into the opinions of others.

Naturally, we all interpret life through our own lens and it's a fairly subjective lens. The most empowering thing we can do for ourselves when faced with challenges, is to stand back and look as objectively as possible, as if it were someone else's situation.

In this situation lay an opportunity for me to learn the fine balance of absorbing valuable informed advice, weighing it up and then allowing myself to *feel* what resonated about the input, following my own guidance and signals forward to the next step in the project. Sounds easy, right? Mmm, I was a work in progress.

Watching a movie one night, the name of another publishing house was bandied around in one particular scene where a woman was joking about an upcoming meeting she had scheduled. That same publishing house name came up twice again in other situations I found myself in that week. Signals for certain I thought, approaching publishing houses was my path for sure. Buoyed by all of this, I prepared the manuscript, printing it in hard copy for the first time. Aaron captured my ear-to-ear grin for posterity, as I proudly stood holding all 400+ pages of double-spaced typing.

Fast-forward several weeks to when Aaron returned from the letterbox and slammed a self-addressed return courier bag in front of me on the kitchen bench. In the instant I realised it was my beloved manuscript rejected and returned, he looked me in the eye and said "Don't worry B, the universe sent you a big fat signal just for this special moment."

Heartless! I said, "How can you ... " and then on top of the courier bag he immediately placed a bright red marketing brochure that was sitting in the mailbox with it.

The septic tank cleaning company brochure read: "SHIT HAPPENS ... Deal with it."

I looked at the rejected manuscript lying under the brochure. I looked at Aaron, and I couldn't help but laugh.

The amusing thing was that this second rejection also came with brief advice from the publisher, including one suggestion to do the direct opposite of what the first publisher had suggested. They disagreed with each other and here I was playing clueless piggy in the middle.

I had followed what I thought were signals. I had no idea at that time why it had not worked out, seemingly a dead end. Or was it a detour?

However we choose to react to situations not panning out as we anticipate, for whatever reason, there is one thing we can always rely on knowing ...

It is what it is, and everything is always just as it's meant to be by the very nature of it being that way in the first place! There is no other way it can be. The present moment is fact. You can't argue with fact. The present moment is always perfect, from the perspective that we are here to evolve, learn, expand and we can only do so through setting a vision, creating our life and encountering hurdles and opportunities as we do so. If we didn't, we'd all be sitting stagnant, living bland lives until we died. Where would the growth be in that? Life gives us opportunities to learn lessons, sometimes little ones, sometimes big ones, and sometimes lessons we didn't even know we needed to learn. Well, at least our mind didn't know. Our soul-level self, on the other hand, knows exactly what is happening.

My sister Ella reminded me of something I had apparently been preaching so many times that she parroted it back to me perfectly without skipping a beat. It was just what I needed to hear at the time. Perhaps it will be useful to you, for whatever your vision is ...

"Don't forget what you've always said B. The people who *are not* well placed to leverage you towards your vision, and are not aligned to your energy, will say no. The people who *are* well placed to leverage you towards your vision, and are aligned to your energy, will say yes. There's nothing else you need to know."

Contrast

And so I took these moments of rejection as learning opportunities. To know success we must know "pending success" (my new preferred term for failure). To know joy, we must at some point have known what joy was not. There is no black without white. There is no day without night. It is in our world of contrast that we come to have experiences and to know what it is that we are experiencing and whether we like it or not. We have circumstances in our world to create this contrast.

Divine Timing and Detours

We may not always understand why signals come to us when they do and why they lead us where they do. This ethereal fabric of higher consciousness that is the universal energy operates beyond our understanding.

We may be in a position where we want signals to guide or support us and it may feel like there are none. Signals don't arrive on demand, but they come to us when it is right for us and in our best interests. There is a great level of trust and faith required when following signals to know that the signals will be there when needed, and all the while our job is to live our life as fully and expressively as we know how to regardless of the existence of signals.

There is a significant difference between soul-level need and mind/body want. Signals are primarily about getting what you need when you need it, not what you want when you want it.

Moreover, that *need* is determined at a soul-level in connection with universal energy. This might not be what you want to hear if you are so intently focused on your destination that the journey is merely a means to an end, which you'd like to expedite.

There Is No Destination

Yikes, no destination?
I know! But it's true.

In relation to life, to following signals and turning your dreams into reality, the journey *is* the point, not the destination.

We are conditioned to think there is a destination and moreover to have expectations about how everything should be on the way to that destination and upon reaching that destination. So conditioned in fact that from the day we are born many of us miss the entire point of human existence (the journey) and get to the end and exclaim, "Is that *it*?" And the answer will always be, "Yep, that's *it*." And on that note, remember life is always what you make of *it*.

Imagine you are driving a car. There are three children in the backseat. They are all simultaneously asking nonstop, "Are we there yet? Are we there yet? Are we there yet? Are we there yet? Are we there yet? Are we there yet? Are we there yet? Are we there yet?"

You cannot understand why they would ask this question over and over again. Are they trying to torment you? They can quite clearly see they are not there yet. Why are they not there yet? Also a tormenting question, because the answer is quite simple, "You are not there yet because you are not there yet, because you are on the journey."

Life is nothing more than a series of moments. Enjoy those moments lest they pass you by unrecognised as the very destination you think you are seeking.

Are you being like the children, tormenting yourself needlessly? Are you missing all the scenery on the drive? Are you frustrated with the magic of the journey and all it is allowing you to experience because you want to get "there"?

Just to consolidate a point, let me ask another question ... What will you do when you get *there* anyway?

You will start another journey, because in life there is no standing still. Energy flows by its very nature. If it is not flowing, it is blocked and we all know what happens when energy is blocked. You are energy. Your life experience is energy. You are either taking a journey or you are no longer here.

Being at peace with the journey, and being present in each moment of the journey, is the point of life. It is the access point to joy, the only access point. The fact we get to create awesome stuff along the way is the cherry on top as we dance and play with our unique expression.

To embrace the journey, just live with awareness. As I wrote in *Pinch Me*, we all have the ability to be aware. That awareness can be turned on and off, much like a tap. Turning our tap off happens unconsciously. The stream of awareness dries up and we go into auto-pilot mode, a default way of living. How do we turn our tap back on? We bring attention to the fact that we lost our awareness in the first place, thereby becoming aware again. So, turn on your tap! When you do so, you are present to the wonder of everything, to the magic of nature, to the fragility and therefore the value of life, conscious of the signals you are receiving, attuned to your heart singing and following that feeling, flowing freely. Don't drive yourself bonkers by asking the question that needs no answer, "Are we there yet?"

So while setting a vision and creating it is the extraordinarily compelling process of a life lived on purpose, it is the process not the reaching of the mountaintop that is the joy. I'd found this out for myself one too many times in my life, and it would be this *Going Out On A Limb* adventure that would teach me, finally, what it meant to really learn to be without a place to get to. For switching lanes in life, only to continue behaving the same way in your new lane as you did in your old lane, will still yield the same underlying unrest. This I would discover.

Hindsight

It wasn't until many months later when a publisher and an agent simultaneously showed some initial interest in my writing, that I realised there was a reason I had experienced a series of rejections, suggestions and advice to do this and that with my manuscript. It was all for necessary learning, lessons that signals gifted to me. I had gained greater understanding from the experience, leaving me at the end of the process with a different perspective than I had had before. From this point of view the journey was invaluable, despite the outcome not fitting my expectation.

Signals are not there to fulfil our expectations. Expectations are our demands upon life to be a different way than it is, one of the key reasons many people live in dissatisfaction. Having a vision combined with willingness to be open to *all* paths that may lead you there, is very different from having expectations.

It was the filter of my beliefs, thoughts, feelings and actions that interpreted those signals as meaning one of those publishing houses would say yes. In reality, those signals were leading me to gain valuable insights from those publishing houses. I set myself up for expecting something different (through my beliefs, thoughts, feelings and actions) and then reacted badly when it didn't fit my expectation (as filtered through my beliefs, thoughts, feelings and actions). Signals were perfect, life was perfect, and the universal energy was perfection. I was blocking the flow.

My signal following adventure into rejection was constructed so that I could see that everyone has a different opinion and opinions are just that ... opinions. It was a detour to show me that there was no one way or right way in this industry that I was so unfamiliar with. There are endless ways in which any one outcome can be created in any area of life. I had to feel what it was like to have a stranger suggest my story be changed and my book commercialised in order to make sales the primary driver. I honour the publisher's reality because that is their reality and the way energy flows in that path. It took all of this for me to realise that both creative and logistical ownership of the publishing project were vital to me, so I could fulfil my vision of reaching the people I intended to reach for the reason I intended to reach them. This was heart-led work for me. The signals were showing me that at a deep level it was critical to me, and for me, to infuse this project with love from end-to-end.

Had I not followed those signals and ended up in particular conversations, interactions and with those rejections, I would never have been able to come to these conclusions and my project would not have flourished the way I envisioned it would.

Look at what signals you might have followed that didn't

lead where you expected. Broaden your perspective, unblock your filter and you may start to see the gifts of life that remain invisible otherwise.

> *Some signals lead us to what appear to be dead ends, but indeed there are no dead ends in life, only detours with valuable scenery waiting to be understood.*

In addition to these valuable lessons learnt, following those signals also ended up leaving me synchronistically placed for the timing of coming unforeseen events. Events where the people who could leverage me toward my vision, who were aligned to my energy, would say yes and give me the support I needed.

Right time, right place? Or rather what I refer to as Divine Timing, the platform of synchronicity.

By following what seem to resonate clearly as signals, even if you do not end up where you expected, it may all be part of the Divine Timing of how the universal energy weaves all manner of people, things and situations to your benefit. Quite simply, having a little faith in the universal energy goes a long way. Give it a chance to do its part.

Flowing to the Yes People

I paid close attention to suggestions, to conversations, to anything and everything I encountered that even remotely related to books, writing and publishing. I investigated, asked questions, noticing what resonated with me. All the while I held my vision.

More signals flowed, I confidently followed, and they led me directly into contact with several inspiring and experienced people. I looked a few times to see if they had wings on their back, because it was clear to me that my being in connection with them was a direct result of the universal energy responding to my focus. They seemed to willingly, almost without question, offer me priceless wisdom, contacts and leverage for no other reason than they believed in what I was doing.

Through showing my intent and taking purposeful action following signals, I became aligned with people generous in spirit. They may say their momentary passing words were nothing. But as we all know, what one person says in a passing moment may be nothing to them, and everything to us.

The outcomes of my project were not because I'm a manifesting machine. None of us can take full credit for what is the universal energy expressing itself into form through our heart singing. We are the vessel that allows energy to flow. Our job is to unblock our filter (our beliefs, thoughts, feelings and actions) and experience the results.

Self-belief

When you don't believe in yourself, your energy draws out the doubt of others. It's all too easy to fall victim to living from a limiting paradigm that includes, "I'll believe in myself when others start believing in me." Rather, believe in yourself and your vision knowing that energetically it becomes much easier for others to believe in you as well. Creation starts within, not without. The energy of your self-belief draws out the confidence of the yes people, because like attracts like.

Here's the gold—have faith that the universe is doing you a gigantic favour when you hear no from the no people. It's not in your best interests to hear yes from the no people. Do you get my drift? Don't push up against the flow. Go where the flow takes you.

I blazed my own trail by self-publishing. I also decided that I wanted the book published by the time I left my job. Aka—in a lightning fast timeframe. I wanted to launch into the next phase of my life with gusto. I knew it wouldn't be easy to meet such a timeframe as I traversed that big area outside my comfort zone called "what I know that I don't know" and, as I was soon to discover, another area beyond that zone called "what I don't know that I don't know."

There were plenty of times in the process where I was up to my eyeballs in question marks with no idea what exactly to do next or how. I let myself overthink and lose my connection to guidance. This resulted in multiple intervening signals, including one minor car accident and one incident in which I got a black eye from Cash! In an exhausted bad mood one evening from a day of too much doing and not enough being, I wish I had remembered the old saying to "let sleeping dogs lie," because sometimes when you grumpily nudge awake your sleeping dog while bending over him, he sits bolt upright smacking into your face.

This is all just energy. It's not bad, sad or punishment. It's just how the system works. Isn't it great that there are so many ways we get woken up to be who we came to be, and to not linger in anything else?

The signals supported me to have self-belief all the way. Seeing a bee in my mind's eye while meditating one morning I reflected on its meaning as outlined in my favourite animal totem book, *Animal-Speak: The Spiritual & Magical Powers of Creatures Great & Small* by Ted Andrews:

"The bee reminds us that no matter how great the dream there is the promise of fulfilment if we pursue it." [13]

The book also noted that bees are useful insects, without which many flowers and fruits would never blossom. They are pollinators. This would remain meaningless to me until much later.

Your Movement Forward Reveals the Path

As you traverse the unknown, you only need to know the next step. I only knew the next few steps (actions) at most throughout this project, sensing my way along as I went. The road beyond that remained somewhat a mystery. Each time you step forward, more of the road ahead becomes illuminated for you to follow. Here is the absolute key to remember—your forward momentum *is* what reveals the path. Your action is what calls in the next phase of signals. Your action is what opens up the path for you to see the way forward. You are unfolding and signals react to that unfolding to show you more of what you need to know, when you need to know it.

The system of life, how universal energy works, really is so logical when we stand back and consider it outside the confines of our limited perspective. The system of life is designed to show you that:

To know more you must seek.

To achieve more you must act.

To see further ahead you must step forward.

To succeed you must have faith.

Common sense, right? But why is it designed this way?

Because soul-level self cannot expand if you do not seek, do not act, do not step forward, and do not have faith. Soul-level self came to expand. That is the point of life.

How does the system of life show us this truth? By not supporting the non-expansion of soul-level self. Put another way, it will not support your goals and dreams if you do not support the expansion of your soul. Simple as that. It knows you want your goals and dreams, and it wants you to experience your goals and dreams. The optimal way you do so is through your awakening.

Perplexed

Despite what was a single-minded focus on my publishing project at that time, I had been acutely aware of what I will call a "family of signals" that left me intrigued but perplexed. Each signal seemed to be related, with a common thread. I deduced that due to the recurrence and the theme, there might have been some meaning.

The pattern indicated there was someone I needed to be in contact with or something I was meant to be doing. I gave thought to it over weeks as I recorded these signals in my notebooks but I was never quite able to put my finger on what it all meant. I trusted that eventually it would become clear to me. The signals came to me primarily through song lyrics.

Firstly it started with: "Old friend, why are you so shy? Ain't like you to hold back or hide from the light. I hate to turn up out of the blue uninvited but I couldn't stay away ... don't forget me." [14]

I pondered the literal and not so literal meanings: *Who is this old friend? Am I hiding from the light? What is the light? No one has turned up out of the blue that I can recall. Is someone going to materialise from my past? Who I am forgetting? What am I forgetting? Some part of myself?*

It would be months before I would get answers to these questions, a very long time to wait for clarification on signals for someone with my level of impatience. So long, in fact, that I forgot all about it.

Chapter 7

Happy Place

Those first few months after returning from Thailand felt like living in a blissful bubble. You know that feeling you get when you return from a holiday or transformational experience, and nothing can ruffle that good feeling you have, that happy place.

There was a sign erected over the doorway to my happy place. It said, "Unhappy people need not apply within. Unhappy stuff not welcome. Thou shalt not pass!"

Bubbles, by their very nature, have a tendency to burst. It's not that easy to guard your happy place as I would soon realise. Unless you run away and live in the middle of nowhere, extracting yourself from life completely. Rather than not letting in "bad stuff," the trick lay in making friends with it (or at least making peace with it).

I'd observed and experienced this happy place bliss phenomenon over the years. Typically the bliss would slowly but surely dissipate over time, with a fall back into the everydayness of unconscious default living and doing, until such time as the next holiday beckoned on the horizon. It seemed like the only way to get over post holiday blues was to plan some other project or holiday so there was something to look forward to. A future focus in this context seems like avoidance of the present, declaring "where I am now is not okay". This is the clouded cycle of expecting peace and joy from things outside ourselves or living for a future moment. Another lesson beckoning to be learnt.

My post-Thailand bubble was filled with a peacefulness and joy that seemed unshakeable at the time. As I navigated my way through the city to the office on my first morning back, cars zoomed and tooted, people dashed here and there, the bus driver had a fight with a passenger, another would-be passenger started bashing the side of the bus with their hand when it wouldn't open the door while idling at the traffic lights. Someone cursed at another person as they pushed past to find a seat. I watched it all and saw it with fresh eyes. Default living. Unaware. Disconnected. It's all well and good to do, be and have what you want in life, but what if we're all cursing and rushing, hitting and pushing, frowning, judging and demanding in the process, then what type of life is that?

I became acutely conscious of the fact that creating goals and dreams, and/or following signals is not at all about desiring things, places, people and/or experiences if we spend our time pushing to get "there" while degrading ourselves and everyone else in the process. Even if that degrading is a subtle, almost unnoticeable habit. In fact, all we're likely to receive in that way of being is a whole lot of intervening signals.

If the people bashing the bus and pushing past others and arguing were all aware of what they were doing and aware of the impact it was having on them and others then at least they would be using their own free will to choose that. Though, it would seem only insane people would choose to behave that way. After all, banging, bashing, pushing and arguing aren't very enjoyable pastimes.

It didn't seem there was much consciousness going on that morning at all. I silently hoped I would never fall asleep again and get lost in chaotic doing-ness with no awareness of what I was creating.

But ... oh how the mighty shall fall.

Enlightenment

When I came home from Thailand, I think part of me *thought* I'd become somewhat enlightened. Which is hilarious, because after another roller coaster twelve-month journey following my *Pinch Me* story, I looked up the definition of enlightenment to see what illusion I had been swimming within. I particularly liked this definition offered by Buddhism: " ... a final blessed state marked by the absence of desire or suffering." [15]

You may not be laughing yet, but by the end of this book you will be. Let me give you a synopsis; I had not reached any blessed state and I'm not sure I ever will, given I'm an ordinary girl creating her life, learning all the traps as she goes along.

There was no sainthood waiting and I was most certainly not living in the absence of desire or suffering. No, there was to be plenty of desire and plenty of self-induced suffering in the journey I took after I returned from Thailand. If enlightenment was a sliding scale, then maybe it was more accurate to say I'd moved further towards it from where I was before.

If you profess yourself to be enlightened, it's most likely ego talking. I have a sense that enlightenment doesn't need to profess its own state. Ego, however, likes to profess itself to be all sorts of things, and is the polar opposite of soul-level self. Yet the wonderful thing is that when there is more to learn on your path (i.e. you are not fully enlightened), then life has a way of offering you opportunities to see this clearly for yourself.

I promise I don't have a penchant for sharing my deepest darkest truths that paint me in a less than enlightened light. There is no upside there for me, unless you consider honesty a virtue, which I was reliably told in Catholic Sunday School it is.

The other humorous notion that I discovered was that I thought I had overcome my fears when I returned from Thailand, like they were singular, limited, one-off. I also thought once I "found" joy then it would be something I could own and hang on to, just like all the other things I had accumulated in my lifetime. Ah, the lessons we learn. Life has a special way of showing us when we are trying to hang on to something (blocking the flow). It allows us to see our attachment disorder, in order to let go. It allows us to allow ourselves, and to allow life.

Trajectory

It was not long after finishing my publishing project that I decided to experiment and test out doing a "future reading" for myself. I'd read numerous spiritual materials that indicated asking for a glimpse into the future is possible.

I strongly believed, at that time, that my future would solely be created by my beliefs, thoughts, feelings and actions, that I was directing my path even while taking guidance from signals. We experience a delayed, and sometimes not delayed, effect of however we are being and what we are doing as energy whirls in response. I was intrigued to know whether it was possible to glimpse the potentiality for my journey based on the trajectory I was currently on.

I like using the word trajectory, as it sounds like the path a missile takes ... if you fire it in a certain direction it will end up at a certain point unless you intercept it. In many respects, a missile was probably a fairly accurate way of describing my ingrained way of being, even post-Thailand with all that serenity and bliss. It was common for me to lock my vision onto something and then intend to fully hit my target, in an achieving sense, not an obliteration sense of course. And it would tend to take a military-sized intervention to stop me once I set my mind to something. This resulted, not surprisingly, in good times and bad times depending on two things. Firstly, where my vision was locked and secondly, how willing I was to deviate from my path when the signals came to show me more expedient and magical ways of being and doing.

So, I asked for a glimpse of a future based on my trajectory and in my mind's eye a sense of ... movement, walking down a narrow corridor, passing people one by one. It felt like I was transiting. And then, one clear word ...

"Hiatus."

Hiatus? Mmm, I'm no wordsmith but I'm pretty sure that means a period of stagnation.

Jumping online to find the meaning, I frowned at one definition offered: "A break or interruption in the continuity of a work, series or action." [16]

In meditation I asked: *"Will this be a self-selected hiatus? Like an awesome holiday somewhere?"*

"No."

Mmm.

"Is this hiatus in my best interests for the vision I have declared for myself?"

"Yes."

I wondered: *When will this hiatus materialise and why? Surely I can control this hiatus?*

In time I would learn my lessons firsthand about control. Until then, I left this transcription in my notebooks, soon to be buried below months of other hand scribbled notes. Left forgotten in the pages.

Further Preparatory Indicators

A series of dreams added further food for thought to the path I was on. I'm sure everyone has a nude dream every now and then ... you know the one where you're happily going about doing something only to realise you're stark naked and everyone else is staring at you. I was glaringly aware, after this dream, that I was conscious of people watching me, someone watching me, maybe of being judged and of being seen in all my vulnerability.

In the same dream I was carrying a bottle filled with something like stones, shaking it up and down. I considered a literal interpretation ... perhaps it meant things were about to shake up.

Glide Time

Then in the weeks to come I would hear two random messages as I tossed and turned in the early hours of the morning. That time when you're not fully asleep and not fully awake is what I call Glide Time. The thinking mind is not running on full acceleration and yet you have not given over to deep slumber. I liken Glide Time to listening to a radio. If you pay attention you can tune in and notice signals that might otherwise just drift through your consciousness like static noise. The two messages, days apart, were:

"Ned Kelly."

"Pioneer."

I knew Ned Kelly only to be some type of Australian outback outlaw who wore a very strange looking, and not at all fashionable, lead helmet. I'm not one for going against authority (with my obey-the-rules-at-all-costs modus operandi) and while I know for sure I'm no fashionista, the lead helmet was just not going to happen. I preferred the pioneer signal, but what was I pioneering? Perhaps sharing the joy of signals with people. I could only assume this was my version of moving in a pioneering Ned Kelly kind of way, minus the bad helmet and the outright disregard for lawful authority.

On top of all of this, I could not deny the constant signal songs that indicated someone or something was with me or waiting for me. Who or what I could not tell. All I could do was be aware and marvel at this continuing intrigue.

"I knew you were waiting for me. With an endless desire, I kept on searching, sure in time our eyes would meet." [17]

Chapter 8

Akashic Light

Convergence of Signals

It wasn't until I looked back at my signals recorded in notebooks that I saw not only multiple references to this someone or something being there for me, but also repeating signals about light.

"Lights will guide you home and ignite your bones ... " [18]

"I'll be the light to guide you ... " [19]

I had always associated the idea of light with the concept of the higher realms or source. I was so busy with work and publishing that, by default, I didn't put further thought into what all these references might have meant, and I reasoned that if there were something for me to know it would become more apparent.

The songs continued to come, weeks turned into months. The pattern consolidating:

"Wherever you go, I'll be with you ... whenever you need someone ... I will be the flame." [20]

"Come back to me, I'll be waiting here patiently. Light will always shine in the heart of you." [21]

"She was blinded by the light ... " [22]

Something was definitely up with this light business, but I had no idea what. It really does blow your mind when you notice a melody in your head, having no idea what the lyrics are, only to discover mysterious themes emerging across your signals even if you don't understand what they are telling you.

Gardening one afternoon, a dragonfly darted around me, hovering long enough for recognition.

Huddled on the couch later that evening reading from my favourite totem reference book, the point that resonated was, "Dragonflies and damselflies are often depicted in Japanese paintings, representing new light and joy ... life is never quite the way it appears ... dragonfly can help you to see through your illusions." [23]

Again, for the hundredth time a song that was actually stalking me now: "Old friend, why are you so shy? Ain't like you to hold back or hide from the light. I hate to turn up out of the blue uninvited but I couldn't stay away ... don't forget me." [24]

The signals were unrelenting. I dreamed I was driving a car to get somewhere in the dark of night. There was also a buffalo on the roadside. I love the peculiarity of dreams. I scoured the Internet piecing together information to understand what the heck was being fed to me via the subconscious, a portal for all things weird and wonderful. What was this symbology telling me?

Travelling/journey—A message about how we move forward in life.

Night—Allows us to create fresh beginning with dawning of a new day, period before fresh growth, dark before rebirth or initiation.

Buffalo—Teaming right action with right prayer, honouring the Divine's part to play in the physical.

I was up for the Divine playing a part in my physical reality. The idea of dark before dawn didn't appeal; I was hoping to just stick to the dawn segment. Perplexed as I was by these things that felt so strongly like signals, I guess the next signal was just to tell me that rather than be perplexed, it was time to get ready to see through the mystery of it all and be ready to see truth.

"Didn't you show me a sign this time ... there he goes turning my whole world around ... can you see what I see, can you cut behind the mystery. I will meet you by the witness tree." [25]

Akashic Records

There was still some time to go before leaving my job and my sister Charlotte called to tell me about a woman she had been in touch with, Rosanna.

Rosanna had for many years been providing spiritual readings of a particular type, Akashic Readings. As Charlotte explained about her chat to Rosanna, I remembered the spirituality course I did with Meredith. She had briefly mentioned a book written by Kevin J Todeschi about a man called Edgar Cayce, a famous Seer who accessed information from what is known as the Akashic Records. Back at that time I had stared at Meredith with a blank expression. The child in me was off in imagination land, visualising a large library with rows of books sitting on a cloud in the sky. It was all a bit of a stretch for my constrained thinking mind back then.

The Akashic Records apparently hold all information regarding all souls that have been and ever will be, for all of time. A repository of soul information, clearly not of this time/space dimension we live in, so I supposed it to be somewhere "out there," in some other dimension. Intrigued by these claims that such records existed, I trotted off to the local library. Finding myself in a far-reaching corner, attempting miserably to work through the Dewey Decimal Classification system. Funny ... my fear of institutions actually stemmed to libraries. I hated not knowing how to find what I needed and worrying that I would get lost in the bowels of these mammoth, imposing and eerily silent places ... like I didn't belong there and I was insanely stupid to not be able to work this 78132457.149 ABC system!

I made my way along the bookshelves, hoping that a simple looking for author names starting with "T" would suffice as a strategy to find what I needed in the spirituality section. Hoorah! By design or luck, Todeschi's book about the life of Edgar Cayce sat right in front of me. Absorbing the pages of this book would educate me about his life accessing the Akashic Records, including helping people by drawing upon information about their soul journey through lifetimes.

Facing the massive change with leaving my career, and feeling nervous about how it would all evolve, I wondered if the timing of this conversation with Charlotte was no mistake. While a small part of me felt like there had been enough seeking answers, another part of me knew there was much more yet to uncover. My thirst to know truth was palpable. As Charlotte is a trusted and like-minded soul in my life, the way in which Rosanna had resonated with her meant I immediately felt comfortable with proceeding to request a reading for myself.

Given the opportunity to ask whatever questions you wish

about your life and overall soul journey, the challenge is ... what questions do you ask?

I figured it would be wise to use this opportunity to go big picture, a holistic view of my soul rather than to delve into unimportant but all the same perplexing mysteries like, "Why at thirty-three years old do I still get pimples and will this torment ever end?"

There was a certain way to ask questions in the Akashic Records I was told. It was not possible to ask closed questions that would seek to elicit yes or no responses, the records were not to be accessed for the sake of ascertaining whether something was right or wrong as a decision or path. For there is no right or wrong, rather merely an inclination towards paths that serve better, towards the highest plan for your soul journey. That made sense to me and happily aligned to my free will jurisdiction within that bigger picture.

Compiling the questions felt reminiscent of job interview training. My perfectionist self reviewed my questions very carefully before sending them off to Rosanna. My questions went like this:

Why did my soul choose this life?

What is there for me to know as I embark on this next, very different stage of my life journey?

Why do I feel such crippling fear about moving away from what I have previously been doing?

I emailed Rosanna my questions. It seemed the process was as simple as that. Several days later I received my Akashic Reading by email, a two-page document. Somehow, information from this ethereal place, this repository of splendour, had made its way from "out there" to right here on my very computer screen. The wonder of spiritual connection meets the wonder of technology.

Let's get to the juicy bit ... the answers. I'll give you the highlights. It's certainly worth letting you know how I was feeling when I sent the questions to Rosanna. I was seeking certainty. I was seeking assurance. I needed to know that I wasn't launching myself down a path to certain devastation by having quit my career and deciding to create this new life. Despite all the signals and my heart telling me I was on track, my head still kept intervening by screaming "What if ... " statements. This is the curse of incessant thinking overriding intuition. I wanted to know I hadn't taken it all too far.

From this woman whom I had never met and did not know, came my soul choices, indeed my soul's very intention for this life, relayed from the Akashic Records.

Soul Intention

"You wanted to be here at this time to assist ... help embrace consciousness ... supposed to work as a light worker and healer."

It went on to say, "Listen to the promptings of your heart and follow your heart. Do not doubt yourself and your journey ... You have chosen to come to be of service to others and this is the work you must do ... Follow your inner guidance in all things, connect with spirit ... You have a vision that is closely aligned with your purpose. See this vision, breathe in this vision, believe in this vision and you will soon live it. You are a sensitive soul and the fear you are picking up on is the collective fear on earth ... feeding feelings of self-doubt. As a soul you have no self-doubt ... deep down you know this and now must live and believe it."

It was through this reading that the feeling of resonance and connection with my soul intention continued to grow. Doesn't it make you wonder ...

> ### *What was your soul's intention coming into this life?*

How I would now choose, in mind and body, to play out and live that soul intention was going to be my own doing it seemed. This matter of soul intention is a lifetime's work, a highest path and plan for expansion. For some of us we may flow with that intention from very early in life, others of us may not awaken to that intention until partway through or even at the end of our life.

I find it fascinating that prior to this Akashic Reading I recognised and followed mysterious signals in my life, even when they did not seem to be the path to my bliss (leadership, healing, Thonburi), and my life number had pointed directly this way too, and it had all led me straight into the path of my soul intention. What this reading offered me now was greater faith. Faith that I had not gone mad and faith that my heart-led guidance system was perfectly on target. It was all adding up.

Muting with Stimulus

What causes us to not trust our heart-led guidance system, to think that we don't have an inner knowing, or access to greater wisdom and higher consciousness? What causes the knowing that we all have within us to seemingly sit dormant or active but unheard?

After all, you're guaranteed access to your inner knowing because it's inherently part of who you are and what you are a part of.

Life after Thailand involved new insights about following signals as I continued to discover more through practical trial and error. My paradigm was shifting as I continued to learn in practise and as I observed those learnings and reflections in the world around me.

One of these realisations came to me as I sat chatting with a new friend, Linda, over coffee in the sun on Waiheke. The insight arose just through chatting. It never fails to amaze me how we can have profound new insights if we have the conversations that allow them to come. Many of my own life-changing moments of realisation have come about through conversation with both my trusted loved ones and with complete strangers who do not know those conversations flipped a switch inside of me.

Allow yourself time to engage in conversations that go beyond the surface level of life—to places, times and corners of yourself that don't always see the light.

While I had always known that my corporate life had been full-on—high-octane striving and achieving, I had never realised there was a reason for this. It was a world that I had solely created in my head and dutifully played my part in. In retrospect, I can see it is not the reality of all people; rather it was the paradigm I was living from. In my conversation with

Linda, it came from within me:

"So many of us live muted lives. We have stuff going on within us, unresolved and uncomfortable stuff, and we mute it. It can seem too hard to listen to what is going on inside. Sometimes it hurts. Sometimes it scares us. Sometimes it makes us angry, upset or worried. We push it down and mute it. I muted myself from as young as I could remember, because there was a void inside of me that just seemed to roar louder the older I got. Questions about life, death, about "what's the point?" filled me, along with my fears. I had no idea ...

"Oh! I've just had an insight. I've just realised from what I've just said ... that my being busy and racing around and filling my life with striving and achieving, that was all just my attempt to mute myself, to mute the void. Stimulus is a perfect way to dampen the uncomfortable flames that flicker inside calling out for answers and resolution. Keep busy and you don't hear the roar. Of course we mute ourselves ... who wouldn't mute feelings of dis-ease!"

What things do we do to fill our voids or suppress issues that linger inside?

Do we work every given minute available to avoid being still?

Do we overeat?

Do we drink ourselves into oblivion?

Do we drug our bodies to numb the numbness?

Do we trance ourselves with brain candy?

Do we shop in excess for things we don't need?

Of course the longer we mute whatever it is that is going on within, the more likely we are to slowly (or sharply) end up out of the river, on the muddy riverbank.

Unmuting

I like to relate the process of unmuting to that of gold mining. Let's be honest, there's got to be some type of incentive to unmute, and the pot of gold is a worthy analogy to pique the interest of anyone.

Unmuting involves slowing, reducing or ceasing the stimulus that causes the muting. It involves stripping back layers that have numbed whatever lies beneath, in order to fully see and dissolve that which is ugly enough to need such muting in the first place.

You start to break through layer after layer of bedrock. Each layer of rock represents challenges, and new insights arise from understanding those challenges. What sorts of challenges?

Perhaps a layer of questions that pester you.

Perhaps unresolved emotions that trigger from time to time.

Perhaps a layer of fears that you do not face.

Perhaps a layer of issues that you hold onto.

Perhaps layers of past hurts that you own and wear like a pair of your favourite pyjamas.

Perhaps a layer of false rationale about what you do and why you do it.

Perhaps a layer of perspectives you've formed which block your view of the truth.

And in all cases, a layer of stories you've created about yourself, your experiences and the world. These stories are your interpretations, as filtered through your own unique beliefs, thoughts, feelings and actions.

Though at the time you're not sure what you're uncovering, any good gold miner knows that as you dig into each layer of rock, it's critical to pan that rock to see what it's made of, to understand the substance and density of what you're dealing with, because ... within the rock lies the gold.

So you get to know the rock layers and formation, you take rock samples and you study them. You place them under the microscope to assess their form, their origin and/or how old they are.

As you better understand the rock, and you remove more and more layers, panning, sifting, understanding, assessing, considering, you gain greater and greater clarity about what lies below.

Eventually you hit the jackpot, the deposits of gold—your true self that lies beneath all the unresolved layers of rocks, that lies beneath the stimulus that muted those layers. When you find the gold it's a great relief. It makes all the digging well worth the effort.

We think muting our lives is resolution. Muting is not resolution. Gold mining for your true self is resolution.

It is a fairly well accepted fact that humans will do more to avoid pain than they will do to gain pleasure. Essentially pain is a greater motivator than pleasure. This is why, in the majority of cases, muting wins over gold mining. Pain wins over pleasure. Sad but true. Here are two things that most muters don't realise.

Firstly, most muters don't realise they're muting. Secondly, a cost benefit equation that I discovered ...

A lifetime of relatively easy but ultimately destructive muting = unhappiness.

A short time of intriguing, albeit slightly uncomfortable goldmining = inner peace and joy.

Familiarity Wins Out

My insight into this for my own journey is that while people might have one or more areas of their life where they are in pain, unsatisfied or generally uncomfortable, they know how to live comfortably within familiar discomfort. Familiar discomfort is the existence of unrest accompanied by the known outcomes that come from that discomfort.

On the flip side, there is stepping out to create change in one or more areas of life, which involves reaching into uncertain territory with unfamiliar outcomes. Unfamiliar discomfort, as a rough rule of thumb, appears to be a much greater deterrent than familiar discomfort.

There is no doubt that going out on a limb in any area of life involves a level of discomfort, whatever you are creating. What then motivates those people who decide that the unfamiliar discomfort is worth the journey, rather than sitting in familiar discomfort? The answer is what I call the Pain Pivot Point, when familiar discomfort becomes so unacceptable in one or more ways that unfamiliar discomfort actually starts to look pretty darn good!

If you are sitting at the peak of your Pain Pivot Point where familiar discomfort is becoming too much to bear in any aspect of your life, I want you to know something ...

The people you see who step out to unmute themselves and step forward to create different outcomes are not immediately moving into some glory land where the second they decide to shift an aspect of their life then everything turns roses. To tell you that would be to keep you stuck. For when you step forward and you feel a new type of unfamiliar discomfort (being outside your comfort zone) you might then think you've done something wrong, possibly hesitating and even more likely turning back and deciding you're not cut out for it. But in reality, you would have done *nothing* wrong. Stepping out and forward is sometimes uncomfortable. How far you step out dictates how uncomfortable. You're just in unfamiliar discomfort (which serves you well) instead of familiar discomfort (which serves no positive purpose, other than to propel you to shift).

Too often we get tied up in thinking that if we feel uncertain, fearful, uncomfortable or lost then we are doing something wrong and clearly all those other people who created the changes they wanted must have had some lucky strike. No. There is no lucky strike. Creating transformational change in your life, indeed any change, is exhilarating and it is also often uncomfortable.

Discomfort for no gold is just not worth it. That's insane. Discomfort for gold is definitely worth it. That's smart.

So, are you up for gold mining?

Chapter 9

They Came to Visit

After a lifetime of practising, to absolute perfection no less, the art of over complicating things, I decided that it was time to keep things simple.

In relation to my soul intention, to be of service through light work and healing, the reading had also said that when working with people in this way it would be beneficial to "go with the flow."

Mmm, go with the flow? That's not me. I'm more of a control the flow type of person. Probably why it says, "go with the flow" then.

The reading had gone on further to say, "Reconnect with soul knowledge of different healing techniques ... stored within DNA ... You are also closely assisted and guided by spirit so stay open to this and you will work together to help others to the best of your ability."

Aside from a myriad of other messages in my reading, all of which resonated strongly with me and left me feeling no doubt that I was right where I wanted to and needed to be in this life, the above messages in the reading particularly caught my eye.

What does this all mean, how do I make use of this?

I flipped it over in my mind and decided to approach it from the simplest possible angle. I sat cross-legged on the floor at the end of my bed. I meditated and said, *"Please help me better understand this path I'm on. If there is something dormant within me, something my soul knows that my mind and body does not yet, something that will help me to help others, any spirits that want to work together with me, then let's get this party started. I'm up for it. I'm up for transformation for others and myself. So please awaken in me whatever it is that I can utilise."*

The Unconventional Path

I sat silent, waiting. Then my head began tracing a figure eight motion in the air. This was not new, as my body often moved of its own accord whenever I was connected in meditation in this way.

Then the familiar tickles on the top of my head and a feeling like something was with me in the room. I felt presence around my head and shoulders. As my head continued circling around moving left to right, then right to left, feeling light and airy, I thought: *Something? Someone? Information?*

Then it happened. My neck went stiff, my body followed. A feeling of compacting downwards, like something or someone had just come into my energy space. Part of me thought: *Oh, this cannot be good, what the heck is going on here?*

But a quieter and peaceful part of me knew there was nothing to be afraid of. I sat there for a moment, fully aware, wondering what was going to happen next. Then it was gone. I wasn't sure what "it" was, but I knew it was something that had come, visited me, and then left.

I was intrigued as to what this was about. The energy had felt strong, commanding is probably the best way to describe it. Different to my experiences up to that point, more intense. I had heard a lot about how to protect yourself and your own energy space when working with other dimensions, and I had trained in this, ensuring my protection at every step of my journey. This day was no different. I knew whatever had come to visit me had to be in my best interests. Yet, I still considered: *Maybe I should just stick to what I know. Perhaps I shouldn't go here.*

It seemed, though, that maybe the universal energy and my soul-level self had a different idea. Somehow signals had led me to an Akashic Reading, and that Akashic Reading had led me to that night there on the floor in my bedroom, having that experience.

I sat quietly and asked, *"What was that?"*

I heard, *"Jedediah."*

Jede-who? A spirit guide? Where is this all leading?

The signature mark of my spiritual journey so far ... unanswered questions. Trusting without having a clear idea of what I'm doing or where it might lead me. There was no doubt my declared vision held strong, it was simply the details of the finer paths that would take me there that were not visible.

Something told me I might be going there via an unconventional path.

Making Their Acquaintance

What followed over the next few days were a series of meditations where I asked for clarification on who this Jedediah was. I appreciated it was quite clearly something to do with the fact I had called forth whatever was within me to be awakened and any spirits that were there to assist me to make themselves known.

Ever the sceptic, regardless of how deeply embedded in this way of living I now was, I didn't ask this Jedediah anything to start with. I went straight to source, universal energy, to clarify if this Jedediah was here to help me. The answer had been yes. I asked if this was a form of spirit guide and spirit assistance that I was encountering. The answer was yes. I asked finally if this was in my best interests to be fostering a connection with this spirit guide and to be listening to its guidance. The answer was yes.

My first meditation to speak with Jedediah was brief and to the point.

"Who are you?"

"Guides."

"Plural?"

"Yes."

"You're not one person, I mean soul, I mean spirit guide?"

"No."

"How many of you are there?"

"Many."

"Why did you come to me the other night?"

"To help."

"Who?"

"You."

"With what?"

"Your work."

I had encountered what I would soon come to know as a collection of spirit guides, or collective spirit wisdom. I guessed at the time it was like any other spirit guide I already had encountered, like we all have, this was just a merry band of many of them together. They were coming into my life at a time when they could help me, guiding and supporting me in some way I could not yet understand.

This I also came to understand was not unique, which was immensely reassuring for my desired normality. We all have guides; sometimes several, sometimes many, sometimes they come individually, sometimes they come in pairs, trios or groups. As it is for me, it is for you.

At first I was uncertain as to whether Jedediah was the name of one of the guides, or the name of the collective. Over time it seemed that the name represented their collective wisdom.

The more I connected and asked, and the more I researched, the clearer I became in my understanding that spirit guides come and go, or come and stay, for a reason, a season or a lifetime, just as people here in our physical world move in and out of our lives.

Whether this particular guidance, Jedediah, had always been there poised at the ready for me to awaken and call them forth, or whether they had aligned to me based on the particular path I had flowed into, I was not yet entirely sure.

I'm obsessed with googling everything even if I have no idea what I'm looking for, so I googled the name Jedediah. It made me feel somewhat better when I saw the name was derived from the Hebrew name Yedidya, meaning friend of God. Well, surely any friend of God has gotta be a friend of mine!

Instruction Manual?

In that first week or so, I attempted to make sense of what was happening. I could hear the communication from Jedediah in a clairaudient way, though for the first time I noticed a sensing that wasn't present before. I could sense what they were communicating with me through images and feelings combined together, as well as words.

In the early sessions, I told them I would call them Jed. I told them it was much easier to call them Jed than a multi-syllabic name, hence why I go by B and not Bernadette. That is where the journey for Jed and B began.

Jed told me they were with me to support my journey, to support me in giving voice to my truth. They were there to share messages and information with me that could help me, and ultimately to help me help others. When I invited them in to be with me, I was still feeling confused about how those messages would be shared with me because I was getting bits and pieces but it was like a radio station going in and out of reception. My chronically overactive thinking mind seemed to be filling all the gaps. I would soon realise it was more than filling the gaps; it was causing the gaps.

Their energy was strong and I started to feel uneasy about how to do this communicating. It had been one thing to acknowledge I had spirit guides hanging around "out there" with my best intentions at heart, watching over me. It was another thing altogether to discover a merry band of spirits had formed together, named themselves and decided to relay messages of support. From day one, I was clear that this was intended to be a relationship of frequency and longevity. This was going to require me to tune in and proactively engage with them in order to receive these messages. I didn't like the idea of being some inter-dimensional communicator. This, I was sure, was social suicide.

Yes, I know. You're probably thinking it was a little bit late to be backing off from being too weird. After all I'd long been out of the spirituality closet, was living my life led by signals against all logic and using energy healing on a regular basis. Many considered this in itself weird. But I wanted to hang onto my last remaining vestiges of normality if I could. B and her merry band of spirit wisdom wasn't really part of the vision I had created for my life. You see I liked to think of myself then as a mainstream hippy, not leaning too far to the extreme and with no intention of doing so.

As weeks went by, I had no idea how to clearly receive these messages from Jed. I went around and around in circles trying to figure out specifically how this was going to work.

As my mind continued to interrupt any attempt at having free-flowing conversation, I felt more and more inept and uncomfortable. No one had given me an instruction manual to explain how to receive and relay messages from spirit wisdom. Learning how to do energy healing—a cinch. Three days training, a handbook, instructions, lots of practise, done.

Jedediah wanting to relay messages for me, through me, to me? *I have no idea what the heck I'm doing!*

I constantly asked for information to clarify what was happening, trying to label it in a way that made me feel more comfortable. I would get the same answer over and over again, no matter how many times I tried. So in the end I stopped trying and accepted what I was hearing.

"Sharing information. Label it what you will in your human way. Guidance, divine messages, spirit wisdom, whatever makes you comfortable. It is through sharing information and insights that greater consciousness emerges. We are helping you. There is a new generation coming through that is lighter in energy and more open to the ways of the universe. There was a time of scepticism and resistance. That time is not now."

Shutting Them Out

I did try to play my part. However, I was concerned I was losing my mind and it was all just too unpredictable for me to comprehend. I didn't consciously decide to shut them out, but I didn't make the effort to invite them in. I thought about it. It stayed in the back of my mind as I went about my life doing other things.

I continued to diligently record my signals, more notebooks piling up. As I inadvertently blocked Jed out, I did not reflect back over the meaning of many signals, which were primarily songs popping into my head left, right and centre. I didn't want to know what they meant, because in all honesty at a deeper level I think I knew what they meant and I didn't want to admit it. They meant, "Come back to us."

"But you didn't have to cut me off." [26]

"I know you're somewhere out there, somewhere far away, I want you back ... trying to get to you, in hopes you're on the other side talking to me too ... they say I've gone mad ... but they don't know what I know." [27]

Standing By

I initially only told two people about what I would come to call the "Jed situation." You guessed it, Aaron and Charlotte—from whom I was most assured of not receiving a raised eyebrow.

Staying at Charlotte's for a few days of family fun, she questioned me on why I was resisting it. For I had gone straight to source to appease my concerns and Jed had told me that they were only there to benefit me. But then of course they would say that, so could I trust them?

I realised that of course I could filter any information using my own judgment, listening for what resonated, which in essence is no different to how we filter the bombardment of external messages we encounter in our world every single day. There was no reason not to do this, if I was using my discernment while doing so.

In all honesty, the whole thing felt like hard work trying to figure out how to receive the guidance and constantly questioning whether it was just my mind playing tricks on me. I preferred to ignore it. I told Charlotte I needed fresh air to think, so I went wandering down the road through the countryside near her house.

Leaning on a fence post looking out over the pastures with the range of hills rising in the distance, I spoke aloud to the universal energy (something I only do in sparsely populated places where I am sure no one will hear me). I spoke of my desire to be of service to others and to live a meaningful life of contribution. A monarch butterfly flew past me and settled on a nearby fence post. It felt peaceful. I didn't acknowledge or speak of Jed. I just asked for signals to guide me on the vision I had set for my life.

I walked back to Charlotte's along the roadside verge, enjoying being in nature. The long grass was almost knee-high. Something lying in the grass to my left caught my eye, a flicker of something white. I stepped sideways and bent down for closer inspection to discover a tiny little paper booklet of four pages, no bigger than the palm of my hand. The title in black bold capital letters on the front cover read, "STANDING BY."

I stood in that grass and read the booklet in astonishment. It was a Christian teachings pamphlet, the kind the door-to-door knockers leave at your house when they wake you on a Saturday morning at some unearthly hour, as you stumble to open the door in your pyjamas with your hair standing on end. Here I was happening upon a discarded pamphlet just after asking for a signal.

The pamphlet told of a lifeboat that sailed out in stormy seas to help a ship. The captain of the ship, intent on doing his job the way he saw fit, refused the help of the lifeboat, preferring to forge ahead unaided. The captain refused the help even though the lifeboat had everything that the captain needed. The lifeboat remained ... "standing by."

It could not have been clearer. Jed was standing by. I would come to discover, soon enough, that they had been standing by for a long time. And after we connected, I had forced them to continue standing by through my refusal to participate.

The power of signals never fails to make my jaw drop, for imagine my surprise when I realised the parallel to a song that had been cropping up a little too frequently of late: "If you ever find yourself stuck in the middle of the sea, I'll sail the world to find you." [28]

Exasperated I told Charlotte, "I don't know what they want from me and I don't know what they expect of me. What if I don't know how to communicate with them? It feels like my mind keeps interrupting all the time."

"Why don't you type what you hear? You're the fastest typist I know."

She had a point. Jed would confirm it was a great idea, as typing would allow my, and I quote, "busy little brain" to focus on the message rather than on interrupting the flow.

The typing would end up forming a collection of notes that I entitled "What Jed Said."

On the first day of typing communication with Jed, the first page looked like this ...

"Give over. Give over."

It would seem that giving over was the first point of order. This was not something I did easily in life, and in this case, it would be something that most parts of me would resist for some time to come. One thing was for sure; I was no pushover, whether I liked it or not.

Little Words, Big Impact

This time in my life was teaching me some valuable lessons. Perhaps these lessons, by-products of my new relationship with Jed, were no mistake and all part of the intended help they were giving me.

I found myself using variations of two particular words often—should and try.

I shouldn't do this because it seems abnormal and absurd.
I should do this because I'm guided to.
I shouldn't worry about this so much.
I should give more time to this.
I'm trying to work it out.
I've tried to hear them.
It doesn't matter how hard I try ...

The Shoulding Syndrome

The very popular word should is often used to, "Express obligation or duty ... to express probability or expectation." [29]

Unfortunately, while this word can be a useful and important part of our vocabulary, many of us have become addicted to using this word to corner or trap ourselves or others by applying the word as judgment, expectation, unnecessary comparison, blame or even when giving well-meaning advice.

It *should* be this way.
It *shouldn't* be this way.
You *should* do that.
You *shouldn't* do that.
Life *shouldn't* be this way.
I *should* be better.
I *shouldn't* be so XYZ.

I call the overuse and detrimental use of this word the "Shoulding Syndrome." Every time we say "should," in the most commonly used forms I have personally encountered, it immediately denotes a non-acceptance of what already is, or a forcing of something into existence. The expectation that something be different than what it actually is creates immediate discontent with the reality we are experiencing. If we go to the effort of saying it should be a particular way, we are just going the round about way of saying it currently is not that way, or that any other variation of it is not expected or accepted.

Should is often used in relation to expectations. We see something that isn't as we expect and we say it shouldn't be that way in terms of how it aligns to those expectations. We give and receive advice, looking at what we expect, and then we should others or ourselves into a corner with how something needs to be. Shoulding often boxes us in.

> **Bring awareness to how you hear "should" used and when you use it yourself.**
>
> **Notice—are you being limited or limiting another with should'ing?**

Doing or Not Doing—No Trying

It was Augustus who originally called me out on my frequent use of the word "trying," after he heard me say with great commitment, "Well, I'm trying really hard."

Which was met with an immediate rebuttal, "Well don't try hard, just do it."

Nike says it. Augustus says it. So B, just do it!

Looking back at my life, I could see that I'd been a frequent user of the word trying.

I pondered this "doing it" versus "trying." Same thing right? Just different mindsets.

Nature is possibly the best example of just doing it, not trying.

Nature doesn't try. Trees don't try to grow. They just do. Flowers don't try to bloom. They just do. Waves don't try to ebb and flow. They just do. The sun doesn't try to rise. It just does.

People love to be around nature and I surmise it to be because the energy flow of nature is effortless, natural, undisturbed and unaffected. Pure free flowing life force, energy flowing just as intended.

When we allow ourselves to just do, instead of trying to do, we are in fact still doing the same thing, but how we have chosen to go about it, our state of being, is different. The person who is trying is taking the same action but has consciously decided it takes effort and the outcome is unknown and to get the best outcome they must try hard. The energy vibration of the person changes when they choose to try. Our energy vibration is our point of attraction.

As you go about creating your life, whenever you are in action choose to do, versus try it. It's all about mindset.

Asking for Proof

I continued questioning if somehow my mind had tricked me into thinking Jed was real. It felt small and weak to ask for proof that what I was experiencing was real, but at the same time I was ever the seeker of evidence.

I sent a text to Charlotte, "I'd like more proof that it's real."

The text reply said, "Ask."

In all the communication between Charlotte and I, "ask" had always referred to connecting to source for guidance. I texted back, "Of course. I always forget the simple answer. Thank you, I'll ask."

Charlotte called me immediately. She said, "What was that text you just sent me about?"

"You just texted me 'ask' didn't you?"

"No I didn't. I'm sitting right here with my phone and I didn't text you."

Nevertheless, there was most definitely a text message reply and it did say, "Ask."

In meditation I asked, *"If you are real, how come I don't see you or sense you physically. Show me somehow, let me feel or see something."*

Nothing at all. Well, at least not that day.

Two days later Aaron was in the city. I was at home working on my laptop at the kitchen counter, tapping away. Cash was doing what Cash always does best, lying in the sunshine sleeping. The house was peaceful, until I heard a loud noise that made me jump clear off my seat. Something knocked over in the bedroom at the other end of the house. My heart started beating a million miles an hour and with a lump in my throat I couldn't move. This was a "someone is in my house" invasion freak out moment.

Thump, thump, thump, thump. Steps moving up the hallway towards the kitchen. I could hear the footsteps on carpet slowly getting closer. I yelled at Cash to get up and I grabbed the only thing close to me off the kitchen bench, a plate. God only knows what I thought I would be able to achieve defending myself with a plate! Note—B does not possess the power of logic when under threat and is also not a good thrower so the chances of me hurling that plate like a ninja star to maim an intruder were slim to none.

The steps came closer and, forced to defend myself, I leapt out in front of the hallway and yelled, "GET THE F*%* OUT OF MY HOUSE."

Nothing. There was nothing. No one there, nothing there. I was certain someone was in the house and so I grabbed Cash and ran out to the driveway. Standing there for what seemed like an age I wondered what to do next. I knew it was energy in my house. Part of me had known that when I heard the noise and the footsteps but I went into fight/flight mode.

Was it Jed? If so, I had just cursed blasphemously at them.

Once my logic returned, I meditated and did an energy clearing of the house. As a now slighter calmer version of myself, I went back inside.

Putting Cash to good use, I sent him ahead of me through the house room to room just to ensure there was no actual intruder there. Part of me knew he would probably only lick an intruder rather than actually bark at them, but he was certainly more useful than a plate.

There was nothing. Well, nothing more than a lamp knocked over in the bedroom where the noise had come from. I didn't know what had caused it, but I had a sneaking suspicion something or someone had come to visit me.

I was so unnerved that I pronounced, "Whatever that was, whoever that was, you are not allowed to come into my space or my house uninvited ever."

The next day I sat in meditation and asked for guidance. The response:

"Thank you for bringing us back. We were sad to be sent away but we understand that you were afraid of what you

experienced. You had invited us to make contact with you in new ways and we thought you were ready for that; it is okay if you prefer not being able to connect with us using your other senses and we can remain audient only. There is no danger to you. You are afraid that what you get told isn't right, and questioning it all only makes it more challenging for you as you go around and around and around in your head. We only wish to give you clarity and guidance if you will trust that we are here for you and here to serve you in the way that will support you on your journey."

I had asked these beloved guides who were giving to me and supporting me to show themselves to me, and then I had bluntly told them to leave. This was the equivalent of playing the awfully confusing game, of "come here, go away, come here, go away, come here, go away, come here, go away."

I thought I was ready to see them and hear them in new ways. I wasn't and the only reason I invited that experience was because I was doubtful and felt like further proof would help me accept their presence in my life.

"There was no danger yesterday. You are simply fully attuned to what has always been around you; you just couldn't sense it in these ways before, now you can. How do you want to work with us going forward? We want to connect more regularly with you because we can be of great benefit to you if you will allow this to happen. We recommend that you do this once a day, and make this a key part of your 'business' if you like, connecting with us as your advisors. That way we don't have to startle you to get your attention. When life itself wants to get your attention it does all sorts of strange things to get you to stop and question what is going on. When 'things go wrong,' like when your phone wouldn't work yesterday, the website crashed, the dog misbehaved, you panic. It is all just to get you to stop and ask the question, 'what is happening and why?' You resist asking us why because you don't think you will get a clear answer and then when you do trust look what happens—answers flow to you so freely that you can only know that we are here with you wanting to give you all the guidance you ask for. There is no need to prove ourselves as being present with you; you know that we are here. You only want to know that you are safe and can manage how this happens and you can, but if you

open up just a little bit more you will receive so much more that can benefit you."

"What do you want me to do in that regard, to allow you to communicate more freely with me?" I asked.

"Allow. Allow this to happen. Allow this free flowing typing of messages to take place. Allow us to support you and invite us to be with you; there is no harm that can come from this. Please trust yourself, you are one with us and we are one with you. There is no separation and for as long as you continue to believe you are separate, that belief will hinder you. Know this oneness for yourself fully and you will reap the benefits of guidance."

"Okay. I think I'm ready then. I guess I have nothing to lose. I am inviting you to be with me and to guide me, but if you want my attention please do something subtler than moving objects or walking around my house like that again."

"So let us work together. We can help you remain grounded, in balance and intuitively connected to source."

"Is there anything more that I need to be doing in order to ensure my vision for my life and that what I need flows to me?"

"It's all about your being—be trusting, be confident, be the person you came here to be and that you know you are, and all that you envision will be your reality. Flow and take action as a natural consequence of the momentum. It is so now, you just can't see it with your physical eyes yet, as your time/space dimension doesn't show it to you."

A few days passed before they showed themselves to me in gentle, subtle and reassuring ways.

The tip of my nose tingled. I swiped at it, assuming it to be a twitch. It did not go away. My tingling nose was to become my new call button for Jed wanting to converse. It would also be the signal that I was off on a tangent or remiss in connecting to my stillness and to them. This nose tingling became our way of interacting in the physical sense.

It was a few days after the nose tingling started that I walked past the glass doors to the dining area and noticed something white and wispy floating in the air. It drifted down and then disappeared. I bent down to look from a different angle. Nothing. It had looked like a cobweb floating in the air, or a piece of white cotton.

It next appeared above my hand as I moved my mouse while working on the computer. A white wisp, almost like the slight trail of smoke after extinguishing the flame on a candle or match. There for a second, gone the next. Bending down to open a drawer, it again appeared in my peripheral vision. The wisp happened on and off for weeks.

I must admit that if I had been more diligent I would have set a routine for how I communicated with Jed, such as connecting daily, or every second day, at a particular time. I didn't though, I just connected when I had time and when I felt the need or urge to. Whenever I did connect, it was always in a quiet place in the house with my eyes closed and my laptop resting on my knees. Being an extremely fast touch typist has its advantages! I would meditate, ask Jed to share with me generally or in response to questions I had, and I would type whatever I heard, sensed, saw or felt come through me.

Chapter 10

Time Warp

Once I let go of the curse of thinking so much about the Jed situation, and just let it be, I came to benefit from the light they brought into my life.

Light is the only way to describe it really. Amusing, given the signals preceding their arrival all alluded to being guided by the light.

It started with them showing me that I was living with a warped sense of time.

It's Time to Talk About Time

I wish I had more time.
I don't have time for that.
I would if I had more time.
I'm running out of time.
I can't slow down; time is of the essence.
I have to hurry, time waits for no man (or woman).

These are just some of the sayings that regularly came out of my mouth for the first thirty years of my life. I wonder if I was a busy little Baby B crawling around telling my mum that I didn't have time to listen to her. Most probably.

My obsession with going fast was not just a personality trait where I liked to do things fast. No, my need to do things fast, usually multiple things at once very fast, came from a non-negotiable need to have everything completed and perfect. Any new task or project on my to-do list felt like a scar on a perfect landscape that had to be cleared away promptly. And so I would go about my life on a mission for completion. There were no ifs or buts that would get in the way of this, for I would work and work at the expense of resting, eating and drinking in order to have completion.

Naturally, because life is life and not a game of completion, there were many times when I felt I did not have enough time to meet my own expectations. For many years of my life that "pushed to the limit" feeling had resulted in me carrying particular health problems. This was most visible in the way I pushed myself in my work.

Now listen to the humorous story I continued to tell myself even once I was semi-awake and had jumped the fence to align myself to my new vision. You may have heard this from people in your life, or from yourself, in relation to the old "one-day" scenario ...

When I finish the publishing project I will have more time.

When I finish at my job I will have more time.

When my new business is up and running I will have more time.

Tomorrow I will have more time.

Next week I will have more time.

Next month I will have more time.

Unfortunately, and naturally, I would always get to that place in the future and realise that the moment I had been waiting for was of course no different than the moments that had gone before, and of course I had no more time than I had had before. Not surprisingly, every day and week has the same amount of time as the last one.

Charlotte had tried not to laugh as she listened to me exclaim every not-enough-time statement in every given situation during my stay with her in the weeks after I left my job. She said, "This whole time thing really has a grip on you, doesn't it? Do you think it might be *time* to kick that in the butt? Have you asked Jed what it's all about?"

Guess what I said? "I haven't had time."

Freaking hilarious! I even laughed after it came out of my mouth.

"Okay, I know. I have a terrible addiction to thinking I don't have enough time. I just don't know what to do about it and I can't seem to quiet my mind enough to connect clearly for guidance."

Charlotte sensed there was a paradigm shift possible for me. She forced the issue, as only Charlotte can. In fact she offered to ask for guidance on my behalf. For over a year now Charlotte had also been communicating with her own spirit guides, typing messages she received from them. The first time

Charlotte meditated and asked to hear a message on my behalf from Jed, with my blessing to open the way, the following message came through:

"She is funny about this time thing. For of course no time exists, she in fact does not exist. We are all constructs of one form or another. And she is there in a body and so certain laws do apply, gravity and the like, but time is not a law of the universe. She would do well to remember that the laws of the universe are the only things by which she is bound. Look at the laws. Is there one about time? No. She creates not enough time, or the feeling of not enough time because she says she does not have enough time. This has always been the way of her, she has always said this, and she has worked furiously fast because she believed the only way to do it all was to go fast, fast, fast, because time was in charge and she had to fit it all in. She has been in battle with time. This is big for her. Her speed is a battle with time. Why? Because understanding that time is a construct and that she can manifest enough time is the key to her achieving what she wants now. That is why it has been big in the past. The Law of Attraction applies to time. She attracted not enough of it and that is what she has had—not enough of it. If she were to attract all the time she needs, that is what she would get. And she need not start with the buts and ifs and so on. She knows this herself. She is just in a long held negative belief and habit of thinking about time. So stop it now. Not enough time sucks the joy out of her. Instead—always enough, more than enough in fact. She would do well to create more than enough for then she will have time to relax too. No need to manifest just enough—go for the best she can, the best she can imagine. She will have to imagine concertedly, because she has been imagining, and so manifesting, busy, busy, busy, too much to do, too many people to please, travel, work, writing, doing, doing, doing for so long. She must manifest how she wants it to be. But enough of this already too, she knows this. She gets it. Hurry up now, wait for it ... it's TIME to do something about it."

It was a few days later that I recalled an earlier message from Jed, of a similar nature. One that had obviously gone right over my head. I was sitting in the public Rose Gardens sunning myself in meditation, asking questions of Jed.

Disturbed by the slashing blades of a ride-on lawn mower, I opened my eyes to see the garden caretaker whiz past me on his four-wheel mower. He U-turned at great pace and shot past me in the opposite direction, grass and twigs flicking up as he continued his speedy lawn cutting mission. Mesmerised watching him, I heard:

"He is in a hurry. Everyone is always in a hurry. Always rushing. Always obsessed with time, not enough time. Lost in the paradigm of time. Not enough time is not real. Indeed time itself is not real. There is a need to break the false paradigm of time."

Suppressing Expression

I processed all that Jed had said, shifting my limiting beliefs about time and directing my energy to a belief in more than enough time.

On returning home from Charlotte's, I noticed a song repeating over and over. The melody in my mind triggered me to ask where this time obsession had come from. Over and over again, the lyrics swirled: "You're out of touch, I'm out of time." [30]

The fact this song referred to time, after what Jed had just told me, was too coincidental. I knew it was guiding me to understand something.

I meditated asking, *"Why have I always felt like I'm running out of time? Where did this come from?"*

I saw two images for a fleeting moment, as clear in my mind as a photograph. I had the desire to understand, but I had no desire to dwell. Here is why:

Firstly, I was standing imprisoned in what appeared to be a dark stone cell. Secondly, I was being led toward gallows.

When the images left, I heard, *"Heresy. Stood for beliefs, but couldn't clear your name. You ran out of time."*

I didn't need to hear more. I didn't want to know more. I had been given exactly what I needed, when I needed it. What I needed was clarification on my obsession with running out of time, in order for me to fully put this behind me.

I had been signalled toward truth. These images resonated with me. One meaning of "resonate with" is, "To produce an emotional effect on someone." [31] In reaction to these images and this message I felt physically ill and it instantly moved me to tears. Somewhere in me that past life memory had stayed and now it reverberated in my energy, within my soul-level self.

I could see how this had played out, it had driven me my entire life. Ask anyone who knows me and they will tell you, "B is the most driven person I know. She does so much in so little time. How does she do it?" I'll tell you how ... because I've felt (at a soul level) like my life depended on it. And at one time, quite clear to me now, my life did depend on it, and I failed to save myself. I ran out of time. Failure is a surefire why to drive someone incessantly in the hopes of never failing again, whether consciously aware of it or not.

Which leads me on to the next massive realisation to come from this episode. In relation to speaking my truth of these evolving discoveries about how life and our world works, about the universal energy and the very real signals it sends us, and our ability to heal ourselves of blocks ... at first I felt like I could be attacked for saying these things.

The thought of being challenged about my beliefs by people from all quarters, made me fear that I might have to defend myself as if my life depended on it. It may sound odd to you, but whenever initially questioned about my experiences I felt a defence mechanism within me that at times was so visceral it made me want to hide, and at the very least to stop and ask why I would react that way. Standing for my beliefs had once, quite clearly, landed me in very hot water. While standing for my beliefs again might not have ended in the sad state of affairs of the past, it still created an intense, albeit illogical, reaction within.

In my *Pinch Me* adventure I had overcome strong illogical fearful reactions, and I was determined to do it again.

I was encouraged by the signals to move through any barriers to speaking my truth. If it hadn't been for signals like this next song I heard, I may have turned the other way and retreated to what felt safer ...

"We have the chance to turn the pages over, we can write what we want to write ... you're the voice, try and understand it ... we're not gonna sit in silence, we're not gonna live with fear ... " [32]

If this wasn't enough, cicadas showed up everywhere. They

were all over Waiheke at the time. It was clearly the season, but it was their persistence to make themselves known to me that surprised me. Five cicadas altogether on the front door mat one morning, a cicada inside my shoe, cicadas lined up one by one along the banister on our front deck and a cicada inside our car on the dashboard. Then sitting on the ferry, carrying some one-hundred-plus people, I heard the unmistakable crackling, flicking noise of a cicada's wings and where did it land? On the glass window next to my face.

One cicada totem reference online said that people who have the cicada totem are apparently, "Driven to understand their personal soul journey, they always feel like they are running out of time and will stop at nothing to discover their true self." [33]

Cicada also teaches about communication and the ability to "shed one's skin." It calls out to say, "Emerge as something new and different in life ... come out from hiding, to break free of what restricts you ... use cicada's wisdom to inspire you to share your own voice." [34]

And so despite my blocks, the kinds of challenges we all have in one way or another, my desire to share my message prevailed. Maggie Kuhn famously said ... "Speak your mind, even if your voice shakes." [35] I decided my stance on truth would be—voice shaking, doing it anyway.

Chapter 11

Called to Write Again

It would be an understatement to say I have an aversion to spiders. I considered it punishment and ghastly that the universe would send me signals by way of these little beasts. Indeed, I found it necessary throughout my life (until that point) to always have a can of insect spray handy at all times in case of the need to obliterate any eight legged blighters that strayed into my path. Since recognising their prevalence as a recurring signal, I decided it was probably not karmically wise to harm them.

In those early days of self-employment, it seemed whenever I turned around, looked down, up or sideways, there in my direct line of sight would be a spider. I knew the meaning of spider well by then. The part that resonated most with me was:

" ... spider is considered the teacher of language and the magic of writing ... spider can teach how to use the written language with power and creativity ... " [36]

It made me laugh how surreptitiously the spider totem came to visit. One such time I was sitting on the deck in the sunshine at home chatting by phone to Charlotte about writing. I was asking her advice about creative writing and the challenge of weaving words and ideas in a way that takes it beyond transcribed events into a story that steals you away. Charlotte is gifted at doing this. I was ready and willing to let any bit of that talent genetically rub off on me.

Cash meandered around the corner towards me with a leaf hanging out of his mouth. My thoughts were off in the distance as I listened to Charlotte, and in an absentminded move I reached out and took the leaf from his mouth. I played with it in my fingers as we chatted. Flipping it over, I saw a tiny little spider curled up on the underside.

Standing in the shower the next morning, as the hot water

pelted my back, I realised there were words in my head calling to me.

"Staring at the blank page before you ... let the sun illuminate the words that you could not find ... today is where your book begins, the rest is still unwritten." [37]

These lyrics dancing a melody in my mind were an obvious call to put a blank page before me, in order that I would fill that page with words. As someone who writes their experiences and observations of life, I thought I would need to have a little more life in between books in order to have something to write about. *Could I actually start writing another book already?*

The stack of notebooks recording all my signals had been growing. I considered that perhaps they were ready to be woven into a story. All I had to do was give myself the opportunity to sit and write without self-induced distractions, and to give myself permission that it was viable and valuable to do so.

I proceeded to shampoo, and as I touched my head something fell out of my hair onto the shower floor. *Is that a leaf? No. A spider? What the heck is a spider doing in my hair?*

You know the reason that spider was in my hair. Just like I knew. As it would turn out, I was going to have plenty more life to inspire my desire to write again but it wasn't to be in the way that I anticipated.

Jed had suggested to me numerous times that I was to write regularly, that it was a key part of my work at that time. I was dilly dallying, aka I was not writing, because it seemed indulgent to launch into writing another book straight away, without even waiting to see what happened with the first book. I *thought* I *should* have been doing something more immediately akin to "real work" in order to support the growth of my new business.

You might have noticed that I *thought* instead of felt (head over heart) and I should'ed myself into a corner. The facts were—I loved writing and I was guided to write. Yet still, I was not writing.

The appropriate objective questions to ask in this situation were: How much did I believe in the vision I had set for myself? How much did I believe in the truth of my signals?

Was I willing to follow my heart?

Cut it Off

When Jed later suggested to me that it would serve me well to consider stopping my 1:1 coaching work, I felt like they'd slapped me. They were asking me to consider focusing, from the outset, on the broader vision of sharing my words, written and spoken, with those I wanted to reach around the world. My reaction ...

"Cut it off? Are you insane? I've only just left my career, to be Author, Coach and Healer B. What am I if I'm not doing coaching and healing? And more to the point, where is my income coming from if I don't accept 1:1 work at present? And when will I do that work again? Ever?"

I was torn between (a) not knowing *who* I was if I wasn't those things and (b) not knowing *what* I was doing if I wasn't doing those things.

It felt like I would be unanchored in many respects if I took this suggestion onboard. Just write? For how long?

When I sat quietly with my eyes closed, I could see the rationale and I could feel the potential within it. It didn't seem sensible, or logical in many respects. Yet, here's the humorous part—despite my fear, I cut it off just like that. I trusted the signal and I adjusted my course.

I knew then that words had the ability to reach people in special and very effective ways. So this suggestion did make sense in alignment with my vision. Jed highlighted that I could not achieve that vision if I was to stay working 1:1 all the time in the way that I had been up until that point.

Being analytical and by now very at ease with confidently rallying with Jed in our communications, I did of course bluntly yet lovingly ask, *"Why was this not suggested to me before I left my career?"*

To which they replied, *"Because you would not have left."*

Touché. I had to agree. I wouldn't have leapt into an even less certain future. It was at this time I started to see the first glimpses of my inability to be with complete uncertainty.

Feeling out of my depth, a song would come to reassure me: "Tonight, we are young. So let's set the world on fire, we can burn brighter than the sun." [38]

Step Away from the Spreadsheet

In the face of that income stream instantly being cut off, by me, I now had to face the inevitable task of re-budgeting. I am a genius with money management. I know how to manage money like a human calculator.

So I sat there with my budget spreadsheet, which now looked like this:

Definite, reliable, no-brainer income = $A LITTLE.

Definite, reliable, no-brainer expenses (same as before) = $A LOT.

How do you balance the books, adjusting a budget to make it work, when there is little to rely on in the income line? I got an A grade in accounting at school and so I feel well enough qualified to tell you the answer is ... YOU DON'T!

And so I, the girl who had kept a spreadsheet to reconcile every single expense for her entire life (ask my long-suffering husband if you want confirmation that this insanity is true), closed the spreadsheet and sat staring out the window. I wondered what on earth would happen next.

Aaron marched up and announced, "I've been getting this song in my head all day."

"What is it?"

"That song about being young and setting the world on fire."

Sharing signals. Priceless.

Chapter 12

Aloha

Setting aside my broader vision for one moment, I had one particular specific goal that occupied my mind. Seemingly at the time I thought it was a goal completely unrelated to my vision. Not so unrelated, as it would later pan out.

This was a dream asking to materialise and one that inspired me endlessly. Yet my circumstances, particularly as they were evolving, pointed to this dream being nothing more than a fluffy cloud that was floating out of reach.

In the weeks before leaving Bangkok we had set our mind to "what" for the year ahead in 2012. Sitting in the white-walled box in Thonburi, both of us tap tapping away on our keyboards working, we had thrown around ideas in response to this question ...

"If we could go anywhere in the world for another three-month sabbatical, where would we go and what would we do?"

Sitting at the end of a three-month excursion in Thailand, I knew this was more than a game to play and was actually a very real possibility.

Aaron and I had become clear on the fact that if we both desired something from a place of joy and for our betterment, and we aligned ourselves together powerfully and we believed it to be attainable, even though we had no idea how, and if we focused our thoughts positively, consistently and frequently on it, then it was a very real possibility it would come into our lives.

We were willing to take action, to trust in our signals and know that we would be guided on how. It would come down to guidance and Divine Timing.

Sounds easy right? Maybe not so easy ...

The challenge lay in each powerfully aligning our own individual beliefs, thoughts, feelings and actions with our dream while also *moving in tandem* together, energetically speaking. For Aaron and I both like to describe ourselves as determined people. Do you know what happens when two determined people join together? You either get one massive ball of enthusiastic energy on target or you get two determined individuals walking their own paths singing Sinatra's "I did it myyyy wayyyy."

For anyone who has another person (be it a business partner, spouse, companion, friend or family member) to consider in a shared vision, this is my contribution to you regarding what I learnt about aligning together.

Moving in Tandem

During my time with Augustus he had, mid session, blurted out quite abruptly, "What about you and Aaron?"

"Um, what do you mean what about me and Aaron?" *Is he questioning the peas in the pod? We're very happy peas, what is he on about?*

"Are you working together or are you working in opposite directions?"

Augustus had very intuitively picked up on an undercurrent in our river that went like this, "I want what I want, and you want what you want, and together we also want what we want. You do what you do and I'll do what I do, and hopefully it will all work out awesomely."

Aaron and I had been quietly aware of it for some time, the fact we both had a penchant for independence. We had a shared vision, roughly speaking, to the extent we wanted the same result of a healthy, happy and balanced life together, it's just that we had certain ideas of the details of that vision and how that vision would come to life. Our shared vision at times became slightly morphed into two visions that were trying to meet in the middle. Augustus knew this instantly.

He told me that it was critical to be collaborative, feeding our collective plans by communicating openly throughout the journey. I figured it was no big deal, because any wavering from a shared vision from time to time just seemed like hitting little speed bumps along the way, not a mountain. What I didn't realise was that any tiny speed bumps experienced when your shared vision deviates, add up over a lifetime to not getting very far ahead with what you want, aka your shared vision, and presumably therefore not making for a happy pod. The speed bumps amount to a mountain the longer they exist.

Augustus then managed to leave me at a loss for words, when he asked me, "Why have you permitted this to happen please?"

This question was met with silence. I had no idea how this had happened. I didn't even consciously realise it had happened. I was living in a happy pod, in love with my fellow pea.

Maybe unconsciously I had allowed our visions to go in different directions but thinking somehow we were on the same path? After all, how do you know where the other goes inside their head, as to the details and the "how" of the life they desire? It's not like we held weekly "manifestation of our dream life" meetings to exchange notes.

The clincher was that we had both wanted the same outcomes, but what drove us and how we wanted to do that sometimes differed. That made sense to me, because we're different people. That's the point of life; we're all driven by and operate from different motivators.

Yet the guidance had been clear about moving in tandem. Augustus was definitive; "You won't get your goals if you don't work collectively together better. The reason is that you are angling at it too differently."

Augustus explained that aside from each person being an energy vibration, the relationship in and of itself is a vibration too. You have to feed the relationship vibration to strengthen the collective possibility.

Augustus told me that Aaron and I had been together several times before, in different lifetimes, in relationships of a different nature. This is common for souls to weave in and out of lifetimes together, intersecting time and again. The fact we were together in this life was just testament to the fact our souls had made an agreement again to be together for whatever reasons fed our soul intentions.

"Create your options together powerfully. If you don't work together better you won't get the results you want in your life, and at the end of the day you want that. The potential is enormous."

The choice was ours. The balance of our love for each other and our passion for our vision meant that we did align, and the result was our *Pinch Me* adventure.

> ***Who are you moving through life with in love, family,
> friendship and/or work?***
>
> ***Do you hold shared visions?***
> ***Do you communicate to support the shared
> vision and collective possibility?***

Rendezvous in Paradise

So, in a world where anything is possible *if* we moved in tandem with a shared vision and clear communication, what might we do next? Where might we go next? This was the conversation we had in our little box in Bangkok.

Paradise is, Aaron reliably informed me via Wikipedia, "a place in which existence is positive, harmonious and timeless." [39]

To me that sounded like a place I wanted to be. Positive people, positive experiences, positive energy. Harmonious equilibrium of people and nature, all energy in balance. And timeless ... I wondered if that meant it was so blissful that you forgot the manmade construct of time.

What better place to put my time-obsessed self. What better place to write. What better place to exist.

So we had daydreamed about all the places we would love to go in the world and various locations came to mind. We chatted, laughed and imagined. Within twenty-four hours we had received three home-swap requests on email. We had not had any requests for months, then out of nowhere three all at once via the home-swap website we were members of. Our intention was set. However, it was not any of these places we would end up setting our hearts on. No, our beliefs, thoughts, feelings and actions would instead align to paradise in the Pacific Ocean ... Hawaii.

Neither of us woke in the middle of the night to hear a message about Hawaii. We did not see signal after signal about Hawaii. There were no dreams about Hawaii. We just knew that was a place we had both always felt compelled to go. And, *then* the signals started and did not stop for several months ...

Two weeks after returning to my job in New Zealand, I had a meeting with a client. She told me she had not long returned from a holiday herself. While we were in Thailand, she had been in Hawaii.

Watching the sports TV channel, a programme about surfing came on. Surfing in Hawaii.

A documentary on TV, about a particular northern region of New Zealand, and randomly the narrator mentioned surfing in Hawaii.

On and off over the coming weeks, my mobile phone and laptop both showed my location on the Google search page as Hawaii. Bizarre. Then my Twitter profile settings randomly showed my time zone as Hawaii.

Advertisements for "Flights on Sale" to Hawaii on email and TV.

Sitting on the ferry, daydreaming off into the distance, my eyes refocused on a pile of bags at the side of the seating area. White bold capital letters on black canvas ... HAWAII.

In conversation during a barbeque evening at our local beach on Waiheke, our friend Rick was visiting the island after more than a year away overseas. He said, "You can't beat Waiheke huh? It's like the Hawaii of New Zealand."

Sunbathing at our local beach, a surfer dropped his long board down beside us, with "HAWAII" plastered across the base of it.

Music TV was playing in the background one Saturday morning as I cleaned the lounge. A music video came on. In the video Ben Stiller was driving along talking on his phone, telling the caller that he was on location filming for a Jack Johnson music video, in Hawaii.

I knew I would be there one day. I just didn't know when and I certainly didn't know how. Divine Timing and signals knew the answer. A line from a song playing in my mind one day told me: "You're gone from here ... " [40]

I had long been intrigued by Hawaii—the aloha of the islands, the culture, the beauty and diversity of the landscape, not to mention the tropical climate and lifestyle. I did not realise at the time that Hawaii, particularly Maui, was a place beloved for its special energy. It drew people from all over the world to be in that energy, something indescribable, something ancient perhaps. Was the energy there more tangible than elsewhere? I hoped I would soon find out. I had also not consciously connected the very close links historically and culturally between New Zealand and Hawaii.

Upon returning home to New Zealand from Thailand, facing a busy six months ahead, I knew one thing I could do right away to set my intention. So I showed the universe what I wanted. I scoured through images online looking for a beautiful photo to inspire me. The decision of which photo to use was instinctive, because the picture was strikingly similar to a vision I had during a meditation when we had first set our hearts on Hawaii.

My laptop desktop now displayed a vast cove. A long stretch of golden sand swept around in the distance to a point, which enclosed deep blue water hosting crested waves. Wild, untamed Ironwood trees hung at the edges and majestic peaks with clouds hovering like white frosting rose up in the background. Maui.

No Answers

As soon as I told anyone about my goal to go to Hawaii, after the first obvious question of, "Why?" came the second question, "What about Cash?"

What does one do when one has forty-five kilograms of dog that one loves beyond words, that one most certainly doesn't want to leave at home?

Leaving him with Kelly and Brent (pet-sitters, who then became very dear friends) had been manageable when we went to Thailand, but I couldn't stomach being away from Cash again.

When I called to get a quote from the pet freight company, rather than quote me the price, their simple response to my enquiry was, "It's not worth it." I thought they were joking but they really were suggesting that they didn't think it viable to even quote the cost.

I said, "Humour me."

I could hear tapping on the keyboard and a few minutes later, "$3500."

"Well that's certainly a lot!"

"That's one-way, Miss."

Oooooookay.

$7000 for Cash to come with us, flights only. I had a small coronary on hearing this news, and I went straight into my analytical mode of working out why on earth my dog was $7000 when I'm not that much bigger than him and my return fare was more like $1500. I looked Cash in the eyes and remembered the promise I had made to him when we returned from Thailand ... "I will never leave you at home again. Wherever I go Cashy, you're coming with me." Granted I didn't mean *everywhere* I go, but for longer excursions.

And so, the "how" of Hawaii just got bigger and more ambiguous. I added "$7000 and one large dog" to the list of questions that I needed guidance on.

I couldn't quite resist trying to work out how we might end up being able to go to Maui for three months, and how we would sustain ourselves financially while there. My need for answers drove me to look at contracts in Hawaii. I found several corporate consulting opportunities I could do while there. Not the type of work I wanted to do, and not aligned in any way to my vision but work it was all the same. Just to see what would happen, I thought: *What the heck, I'll apply.*

I prepared the contract application, filling in forms online. I tried three times to attach the necessary documentation but it wouldn't accept it. I then tried to submit the application without the documents. My computer froze and then crashed. I rebooted it. I tried again to submit the application, the website froze and my Internet browser suggested I reload the page. To no avail. Frustrated, I thought about trying one more time, and then I heard, *"Take action, but not that action."*

There would, in time, be action that was more guided and less forced.

Chapter 13

Forming Connections

Connecting & Collaborating

Scrolling through my contacts list, I came across Corin, a friend of a friend who lived in the United States. I had met her once years ago when she visited New Zealand and had since heard that she was living in Maui. I emailed her to share about signals and my intention to go to Hawaii. The response to my message was overwhelming.

She could not believe that I was also a signal follower. Somehow our understanding of signals created instant unity, as we rallied back and forth sharing how astonishing signals are and the power of following them. Corin, unbeknownst to me at the time, had been following signals for some years, at times flying in the face of logic as well. She offered to put me in touch with all her contacts in Maui, in whatever way she and they could help me when I arrived. This connection was uplifting.

Days later an email arrived which caught my attention. It was a promotional marketing notice for a series of events overseas. Rather than delete it, I felt like perusing. The advertisement within contained the details of three events, in three locations, with three speakers. The photo of one of the speakers caught my attention. Something about her face felt familiar and warm. It was like I knew her, but I didn't know her. I had never seen her before in my life. Reading on, it was a surprise and yet no surprise at all, that she was the speaker for the event held in Hawaii, in Maui. Her name was Marisa.

The date of the event was only weeks away and I knew full well I was not going to Hawaii for that event. However, there was something else I couldn't put my finger on. I just felt compelled to reach out to her.

I wasn't sure what to say or what the point of making

contact really was, but I emailed anyway in response to my gut instinct. The email explained who I was, the way I followed signals in my life and the fact that I had set a dream to go to Hawaii. I said that I felt compelled to reach out and connect, and that was all.

Forty-eight hours later her reply arrived. She suggested that we Skype. I had not asked anything of her. She had not asked anything of me. A date was set.

The morning of our chat arrived. With ten minutes to spare before logging in, I headed up into our garden first to collect a bowl of lemons and limes. Bending down to pick the limes, I noticed one was lying underneath the little tree. I put my hand on the lime to collect it and was mesmerised by what I saw—a monarch butterfly sitting right next to it.

The butterfly moved its delicate legs and attached to my finger. It was not at all flighty. There was no flitting up, down and around like they normally do.

Wondering how many minutes until my Skype call, I moved my hand out from under the tree and upwards for the butterfly to fly away. It didn't move. Its legs were glued on. So I walked back into the house and my new friend came with me.

Logging into my computer was delicate with this butterfly perched precariously on my index finger.

Twice more I put my hand out the door, shaking it, so the butterfly would fly free. But it wouldn't let go.

So began my Skype meeting with Marisa. This woman did not know me and here I was about to unveil myself as some strange Pied Piper of butterflies, or I could hide my hand for the entire meeting. After a pleasant exchange of greetings, I said I needed to tell her something so she wouldn't think I was too strange during the call. I said, "I have a little friend with me who doesn't seem to want to leave." I lifted my hand in front of the webcam. When I moved my hand away, Marisa had a wide smile and glistening eyes. We both looked at each other, stunned and yet not surprised. She didn't have to say anything and I didn't need to say anything. Something had drawn us together.

That butterfly was our common thread. She was in her own metamorphosis of sorts at the time, she explained. The butterfly was a beautiful totem that resonated strongly with her. She had felt compelled to connect with me when she received my email, not knowing why either. What followed was a two-hour discussion that blew my mind.

It turned out that Marisa had recognised the signals in her life much like I had. Not only had she recognised them, as many people have, but she had also followed them wholeheartedly, just as I had. She understood them to be the mysterious and divine navigation system that they are. In fact, she had walked out on a limb many times with trust in signals, beyond logic, beyond reason and with absolute faith.

Two strangers across the world had been brought together through an inexplicable compelling desire to connect, perhaps energetically linked by a shared passion for followings signals. Never have I conversed with a complete stranger in such an authentic and soulful way as I did with Marisa that day. With the butterfly perched on my finger, I got full body shivers several times during the call.

Here's the thing—at that time I'd been feeling like I was so far out on a limb with how I was interpreting and approaching life now, so distinctly different to how many people around me were living, that in moments it felt a bit isolating. I had been asking in my meditations to connect with people who lived this way, people I could learn from and be supported by as I moved ahead. I had said: *Please send me guides.*

It was of course no coincidence that Marisa was now in my life. It would turn out that the most wonderful part of my initial, and then ongoing, contact with her was to be her unwavering belief in me. She believed in how I was approaching my life and her encouragement of me to continue this heart-led journey was invaluable. She knew what it meant to be guided through life by signals, and to act upon them. She knew what it meant to allow yourself to unfold, to show up with the intention of being your fully expressed soul-level self and what it meant to face complete uncertainty while doing so. She knew what it meant to leave behind the old ways of thinking; the paradigms of an old way of living that would no longer serve us in our evolving world. We both intuitively felt that the world in which we all live is calling *all of us* into a new paradigm, into a shift to higher consciousness.

It did not escape my notice that Marisa was vastly experienced, personally and professionally, in speaking her truth. She spoke without inhibition of her beliefs and without concern of judgment. She had lived for many, many years as one who reached out to help where help was needed, one who was allowing the life force to flow through her freely. I knew with certainty I was meant to be in connection with this type of energy at this time. We agreed to meet in Hawaii, to spend time together, whenever that might be. Marisa offered to help me in whatever way she could, with anything I needed for my time in Hawaii. The door was open for whenever I arrived.

The second that we ended our Skype call, the butterfly that had been perching on my finger throughout the call literally pinged off. It didn't lift off and fly away gracefully like a butterfly normally does; rather it flung across the dining room like it had been fired from a slingshot. Alarmed, I raced over to peer behind the dining table where it seemed to have ricocheted off the wall to then land on the carpet! It was peacefully sitting there, with its wings slowly fanning in and out. I gently picked it up and its legs clung to my finger. This butterfly encounter had been wonderful, but I had housework to do and it was time to say goodbye to my winged friend. Alas, when I put my hand out the door and shook it multiple times, the butterfly did not budge. Amazed by the whole scenario, I put the butterfly on my shoulder and continued on my day. I literally laughed out loud as I vacuumed the house with this beautiful creature perched on my shoulder. Like a pirate with a parrot, I was a B with a butterfly. An hour or so later, it flew away.

As I later sat marvelling about the conversation with Marisa, I mused our Hawaii dream. Only days earlier I had sat on the ferry into the city and overheard a man behind me talking exuberantly about the United States, and specifically about Hawaii, to his travelling companion. I had been on my way to meet a new business contact, Jennifer, at which time I had shared my Hawaii dream with her. Her response:

"I met this woman called Laurie at a dinner party a few months ago. She's a friend of a friend. I don't know much about her, but I think she said she leads retreats to Hawaii. I'm not sure where in Hawaii she goes, possibly Maui, but it may be worth connecting with her. She's a neat woman."

I saw this as a possible signal, so I followed it. I searched for Laurie online and in response to my introductory email she invited me to her home one evening.

Through various degrees of separation I found myself sipping tea in Laurie's living room. She was so welcoming and encouraging of my dream to go to Hawaii, a place she held dear to her own heart.

"Where in Hawaii do you go on retreats?"

"Maui. I've been many times. It's magical. You would love it."

And so proceeded several hours of conversation and sharing about Maui, particularly about places of significance, spirituality, history, sacred energy centres and much more.

"B, why are you going?"

"To write. To be. To meet new people. To be out in the world. To be in action in and around areas, energy, history and people that resonate with how I want to live my life and the contribution I want to make to the world. I feel drawn to go there. I can't think of any better place to be right now. Though I have no idea how on earth I am going to get there."

"You'll get there, I'm sure. When it's your heart-led path, divinity moves in ways beyond what we can understand."

Unexpected How

I believed anything to be possible. I knew that if I were open enough then a way would be shown to me. The how would come, perhaps not in the way I anticipated, but I was sure that it would. Would I be willing to accept the path of least resistance when it showed itself to me?

At home the next afternoon, replaying the conversation with Laurie in my head, I thought to myself: *How on earth are we going to afford to go to Hawaii? How is this going to happen?*

"Sell your house."

Clear as day it came through and not at all what I wanted to hear. I could not pretend I hadn't heard it. They were the clearest three words. Unmistakable.

I was not in some sleepy state with words echoing in my mind. Someone or something had just put an ethereal loudspeaker against my ear and boomed the message.

Aaron was only a few steps away, peeling carrots over the sink. I said, "Do you want to know what I just thought and what I heard in response?"

I relayed it. Then he turned to me, carrot in one hand and peeler in the other, and said, "What the heck, let's sell the house and go then. Bring it on. Who cares? It's just a house. We can always get another one. Follow the signals, B!"

Part of me wanted to say, "It's not just a house, this is our life here, isn't it?" But it had been almost two years since we'd arrived. That time had flown by. Before I could reminisce about all that we had created there and my fear of letting it go (because it felt like my security and what defined my foundation in life) I remembered what Charlotte had told me the week earlier ... "Don't forget your vision B. You needn't stay in one place forever. If you want to reach out to share your message with people, there might be times when you need to physically get out into the world. This might be one of those times."

Sometimes you need to let go of what you have, in order to receive what you desire. This exchanging of energy moves you through the phases of your life journey.

I became distracted as Cash was barking up a storm outside. Leaving Aaron to the carrots, I went to quiet Cash down and realised he was most distressed because there was a man lurking in the bushes of our property. I called out through the bushes to ask who he was and what on earth he was doing.

"Sorry, I'm helping Richard next door. I'm trying to find the boundary pegs to measure up his boundary line." The property next door was for sale. *For sale. Mmm.*

Laughing to myself I walked inside to mention this to Aaron but the phone rang before I could speak.

His mother started the conversation with, "Hi B, how are you? Hey, I've been meaning to ask you, did you sell the house?"

What the?! On clarification, I discovered she was referring to our old Wellington house, which we had indeed sold some time earlier. I got the whole body shivers.

I laughed and told Aaron. He added, "Do you think it's any coincidence that leaving the supermarket this morning we

drove past the real estate agent that sold us this house?"
I called the agent. I wasn't quite sure how to explain that
we might be going to Hawaii and we thought we might need to
sell our house. There were a lot of mights in there. I didn't
know what would happen. I was following the signals, and
talking to the agent was a clear intentional action to show my
commitment to my dream, without any actual commitment,
yet.

And so the games began.

At that time I did not make the connection about one
particular line of a song that I'd been getting in my head for
months. On and off it had floated in and out of my
consciousness. It was not until much later when I looked
through my notebooks that I made the connection.

" ... but we still pay rent, 'cause you can't buy a house in
Heaven." [41]

How is it that the universal energy can weave such
synchronistic little miracle moments? How is it that I would
hear this line in my waking moments for months before I
would hear this "sell your house" message, on this day
amongst other house-selling signals, when I could not have
conceived back then that I would even remotely consider such
a thing.

Here's what else I hadn't consciously understood or made
sense of. In the weeks leading up to hearing this "sell your
house" message, I'd been experiencing a slight sort of
disconnection with my surroundings. It was no less wonderful,
no less beautiful and no less dreamy than before. Yet as I had
wandered around the property lately, I had this strange
sensation that I wasn't meant to be there.

This may sound odd, but in the coming weeks this is how I
would describe my situation in conversation with those closest
to me. It went like this, "Have you ever been somewhere, doing
something, seemingly settled but then had an eerie feeling like
you're not meant to be there anymore? Not at all like it's
wrong, but that you're somehow meant to be somewhere else?
Like something is calling you forth."

No Plan

I'm such a homebody and that's why it involved so much

fear-facing and courage-raising the first time I moved away from family to relocate from Wellington to Waiheke. Reestablished in a new life two years later, I was feeling compelled to uproot again. I didn't know exactly where I felt called to be, but for the meantime it was Hawaii. Perhaps after that I would be home to settle again. That I could not foresee. At that point all I had was a vision, and no clear plan beyond Hawaii, in fact not even a clear plan of how to get to Hawaii.

I always had a plan. For some people, it's growth and evolution to develop a plan and execute it, to be more definitive and organised in their life. At that moment in time in my life, it was growth and evolution for me to *not* have a plan. Doing so was asking myself to be okay with a blank canvas for a while, against every instinct that had driven my life to that point. This was no mistake; it was all pointing me towards a major learning curve.

Letting Go

I couldn't help but consider that the direction of my life at that time felt like a culmination of proverbially letting go of parts of my life that I had previously felt were highly important in making me feel good, secure and successful. Indeed, "things" that I felt were responsible for my joy. I could see what life was reinforcing to me, that joy and peace within has little to do with the external circumstances of your life and everything to do with your perception of it and your inner state. That was all in good in theory.

This signal following adventure seemed to be pointing me in a direction where theory might become practise, a point where I would perhaps be in a position of having to let go of not only my career, but also my house, and later, as it would turn out, a few remaining paradigms that just didn't serve me. Hesitation gnawed at me.

The Thing About Things

At the time I deemed a house to be my security, an asset that kept me safe. A house was also a mortgage. A mortgage was a shackle during this time of transition. Money and mortgages had been the two primary considerations in almost everything I had done in my life in the past, and at the expense of joy many times. You can't buy a house in Heaven? Had that song simply been calling me to recognise the fleeting impermanence of material things, in order to prepare me to let go at that point?

I love things; I love having a home and I love knowing where I physically belong. But this all led me to another insight.

While things are great, and I'm up for everything life has to offer including the shiny baubles, fab experiences and delicious comfort that comes from the things we surround ourselves with, this journey I was on had brought me to the glaringly obvious realisation that my mind, body and soul were somewhat out of balance.

It is one thing to love and enjoy things. I celebrate that. It is another thing to need things. I acknowledge that to a certain extent. It is yet quite another thing to say that you *must have* things. If this is you, then I feel your pain, for I have also suffered from this "must have" affliction. Or indeed, better put, addiction.

I self-diagnosed my attachment disorder to physical things, things that made me feel safe. It occurred to me that in order to live my vision and take the soul journey I wanted to take, I would need to sever my attachment to things by letting go of clinging on to "things" with white-knuckled desperation like my life and my personal validation depended on having them. This, for me, was not about status; it was entirely about security, about being okay. By letting go of thinking that things created that okay-ness, I would be able to move forward freely without inflicting this restriction on myself.

It is important for me to clarify for you that when I say "sever my attachment" and "letting go," I mean emotionally. It is the switch from desperation and fear-based "must have" to detached enjoyment without making it mean something that it just doesn't mean. I'm not an advocate of being thingless in order to have a happy life, very far from it in fact! There is absolutely no need to let go of physical things in order to flow in your river of life, to align your soul-level self with your mind and body. It is not the experience of having or not having, it is the willingness to see what the having means to you and the ability to enjoy what you have without adding meaning and limiting stories to it.

Things don't make you somebody, they don't position you and they don't protect you. Things are just forms of energy. Once you can see things as being nothing more than forms of energy for your enjoyment, they lose their emotional straightjacket hold on you, a hold you may not even be consciously aware of.

Those children in Bangkok had no things. They had less than no things—they had no labels, no titles, no money, nobody, in some cases no name. They were almost invisible in the eyes of the entire world. And yet, they were more "somebody" to me than I had ever known before. I saw that my fear of being nothing, dependent and vulnerable had driven me to accumulate.

No amount of things will ever validate who you are. No one else will ever validate who you are. Seeking validation externally is all too common, and so subtle it's almost undetectable, that is until life takes away whatever external source we use to validate ourselves, showing us very clearly what our attachment has been.

Again, there is nothing wrong with accumulating, especially if you're having glorious fun along the way! I'm simply advocating that we understand *the drivers* behind this as a way to free ourselves of negative blocks. From that place, unblocked, we can have inner joy regardless of environmental factors.

Don't Quibble

I talked to Jed after the "sell your house" message came to me. Here is what they had to say:

"What you need will arrive when you need it. Believe it and it always will. When the offer comes, do not quibble over dollars and cents; it will make no difference in the long run. Move forward."

I asked Jed to help me understand what the obsession with money was all about, my desperate need to have it in order to feel valued and secure, and the obsession that ran through society as a whole. The broader human relationship with money seemed to be an all-pervasive issue that had created most of the world's problems from hunger to war.

"At the thought of not having money, or losing money, or

someone else winning out over them, many people feel sick and throttled like the life might leave them. It has little to do with money, as money is just paper and coins. It's not about the money; the money is a secondary concern and not the be-all and end-all. Money is just energy, as is everything. Energy flows. People are making it mean more than it is, it is what people think that money means that is the issue, that is the primary driver. There is nothing to worship about money. It can come and go fleetingly. It is not something to own or have or hold onto. It is something to flow in and out of your life day to day as you utilise it as one means of energetic exchange to achieve your goals. Holding onto it with fear stops the flow of energy."

Shifting Priorities

Jed then said it was time for Aaron and I to hear another message, one about shifting our priorities. They made it clear that the timing was now right for us to hear and receive this message fully, for we would not have been ready had we learnt it any earlier. Perhaps we had previously been too attached to our blocks in order to fully accept the message. The message indeed applies to us all, and it was clear:

"Contribute. Contribute. Contribute. Shine your light and contribute."

I told Jed that the journey Aaron and I had elected to go on, internally and externally, seemed at certain moments like taking steps outside of the norm. At times this only felt possible to me because we had each other to turn to, to understand and support what we were experiencing. Here is what Jed said about that:

"Sometimes two souls come together in a lifetime for this reason, they make an agreement with each other when they come into life to have a kindred spirit to take the journey with. In order to break outside of the tightly held norms of society you have chosen to do this together. It is not easy to do so there in the earth energy that is so strongly disconnected and lost in identification with form and falsehoods of security. You have found a way out, a small window of opportunity to step beyond the illusion and see what else it could mean and what else could exist. Through that small

window you opened up a whole new world, where many other people are living also, but they are still the minority, and to get more people into that new world of greater freedom, love and support, it takes others leading the way. You cannot just ask people to go there, you cannot suggest it or try to explain what it is like. People must make their own way there; they must sense that something for themselves and choose to go there. They are most likely to experience that calling when they see someone else go there and see it as possible for their own journey. Be a contribution."

It seems appropriate to share a dream I had months earlier that resonates in direct connection with Jed's message. The dream shows the simple fact that often what we desire, the light in our life (indeed the light within), is right under our noses if we will only have faith and see it. Instead, many of us never do. If we only knew what was possible by venturing out into the unknown, behind the veil of what we *think* to be true (our perceived reality), to uncover the hidden truth of who we are, what is possible and how our world really works.

Lost in the bush at the bottom of a valley with a shoreline behind us, it was dark and my faceless companion and I were huddled close together. There was no way out of this valley except walking up through the thick forest. The problem was, there was a wailing, screeching, crazy person in the forest. I did not want to take our chances walking through the dark and encountering danger, but I knew we could not stay huddled there in the dark on the shoreline forever, cold and hungry. Lest of all because the wailing, screeching, crazy person might have come down to the shoreline and attacked us. Fearfully and with caution, we set out into the forest. Watching each other's backs, we followed trails through the undergrowth. Then the screeching and wailing noise immediately changed, now it sounded like multiple people. Suddenly, the forest cleared and we popped out on the top of a hill above the valley in the middle of a busy little town. The screeching and wailing noise had just been people, cars and music, surrounded by shops, lights and facilities, i.e. everything we needed.

The dream ended with a sense of ... *Imagine that. We were down there and this was up here all that time. What if we had stayed down there scared, and had never ventured to find a way out?*

Chapter 14

What Jed Said

What follows are further words from Jed. I've always felt like these words were as much for you as they were for me. These words helped me through the upcoming transition in my life that I often find it hard to believe I've made and I'm not sure I would have made if I had known what lay ahead before starting the journey. The old me would have said "Never!" to a suggestion of change like what was to come. Instead, the evolving version of me resisted then gave over, then fell over, then stood up and fell over again, letting fear continue to get the better of me, until courage eventually broke through! Jed stayed with me always. Universal energy and signals, in whatever form they arrive for each of us, provide all the courage we need to flow into our own unfolding.

For Jed's guidance I am grateful. For their bluntness I am forgiving. For their humour I am always amused.

So here is what Jed said, on a range of matters requiring fear-facing and courage-raising, and soon you'll come to see where conversations like these led me on both my internal and external journeys. May these messages also benefit you in some way, small or large, on your journey.

Denying Your Greatness

On a day when things weren't going so great for me, full of frustration, I sought guidance from Jed about it. I must have been wondering if I had one or more negative beliefs that lay below whatever the surface level issue was. What the issue was is not the point. What Jed had to say about denying your greatness and making a choice is the point. Let me introduce you to the blunt side of Jed:

"Little tantrums like that do you no good. There is no need for it so cut it out. It is powerless and boring and we are not

interested in being with you while you behave that way. Your ear is burning right now because we are signalling that you are hearing us correctly. It is not your imagination my dear, it is us telling you that you are a person of greatness and it is time to practise full-blown commitment to yourself and your beliefs through your ways being. If you want to know what you need to do we will say only one thing—be who you were born to be, who you came here to be. There is no distraction from that which is worthwhile. In every moment when you behave out of alignment with what you know to be true, you deny your greatness. You have free will so you have to make a choice to exercise that. Not every deviation has to do with there being a limiting belief you need to heal, sometimes it's just a choice."

Stand Up

Do you sense that it's time to embrace who you really are? Do you feel a calling to be the greatness that you secretly know deep down is in you, and to let go of the ways of being that deny and belittle yourself?

Jed said it's time for all of us to stand up. Let me share with you what they offered:

"People want to overcomplicate things because they think it can't be this simple. There is no need for complexity in a world that has been designed in the simplest way. You believe and feel what you desire and you receive that which aligns to that, the signals are just a guidance system to help you. If you pay attention the signals are everywhere, as many of you already know.

"People are spending much time in their heads and are associated with their minds, like the mind defines who they are. There is an essence in everyone that is their soul, the soul is where the life force flows from, not the mind. If you can disassociate yourselves from your minds, and connect with your core essence, then the monologue that goes on within your mind will cease to control you.

"You must realise that in fact you are greater and more powerful than you know yourselves to be; it is your minds that sabotage your paths and fill you with limiting thoughts and resulting feelings that keep you locked in being smaller

than who you really are. You are all born for greatness, indeed you are born as pure greatness, and over time your feeling of greatness diminishes within yourselves as you fill your minds with limiting ways of thinking. Your brains are reacting to the stimuli around you. If you wish to find a new way of being, a new way of thinking and feeling, you must focus on that which reflects your greatness and which is in alignment with who you really are—beings capable of embodying extraordinary love and producing extraordinary results in your life.

"The role of signals is simple—through energy you are being given a helping hand towards that which is in your highest and best interests to experience. If you are manifesting for something that at source level is not in your best interests, you will not get signals to guide you there, energy will not cooperate to bring it to pass. If you are manifesting something that is in alignment with the greatness you were born as, then energy cooperates.

"Signals exist as an extension of you, because they are energy, just as you are. They are a gift from source to you, a reaction, to help you on your journey. People wish for help but walk around with blinkers on, blindfolded to the extraordinary guidance that has been with them since the day they were born. All of a sudden when they awaken to their signals, they reconnect with what they already knew and have always felt deep inside—that there is greater meaning and that there is guidance there, just for them, unique to them, designed to guide them forwards, and to guide them back to the greatness that exists within themselves.

"Know that the greatness is always there, you were born that way. You don't need to strive for greatness, you simply have to go back to your core and realise that greatness is who you always were, and you may have simply strayed to thinking you were something else.

"We want for the greatness in all of you to shine and for you to believe in yourselves, so that you can create the life that you intended when you chose to come. You were born to shine brightly. Stand up to shout out who you are and what you want in your life. You deserve it. You are loved beyond measure and there is no more that you need to know in your life than you are wondrous and you are a creator with an

extraordinary ability to flourish in life, and you are not alone. Signals are always guiding you and supporting you.

"The world is plagued by negative beliefs that have become so ingrained in the human psyche, such as you all believing you are not good enough, that you are alone, that you are never going to achieve what you want, that it is not possible, that you want what you can't have and so it goes.

"We are here to tell that you it is not so, it is a fear-driven cycle of belief that has been created by humans who have strayed far from their greatness and been fed these limiting messages through generations, and this has been perpetuated by a worldwide focus on that which is not working in your world.

"Stand up each of you, individually stand up and say you want better for yourself and say you deserve it. Say it now and let signals guide you as you step forth to create.

"When you have negative beliefs and thoughts, rather than ignore them, you must shed light on them. For in bringing light to these issues you will in fact dissolve their power over you. These ways of being are not who you are, they are ways of being that you have taken on over time, taken on from the collective fear that exists in the world, taken on from the everyday stimuli around you that you have absorbed like a sponge, which you now own as your ways of being and you feel so connected to being these ways that you have forgotten that you are actually an infinite creator of greatness.

"If you think you are a worried little person with no power or influence, who is at the whim of life, then listen to us now—you are not a worried little person who has no influence and who is at the whim of life. Life is a creation. You are a creator, of your experience and of your own reality.

"Write down what your negative ways of being are, write down how you feel when you are in those bad feeling places. Write it down in a notebook, look at it and remind yourself that is not you, you are not these things. You are a powerful creator of your life. Then simply decide not to be these ways. Decide to replace them with new ways of being. Choose your ways of being. What do you want in your life? Do you want to be a peaceful, trusting, patient and powerful creator? Say that to yourself then, say no to the worried little person who

is at the whim of life, and acknowledge that it is just a false role you have taken on because you lost your way when you strayed from the greatness you were born as. It is not your fault that it happened. You were moulded by the world around you, and you took upon yourself the things you heard, saw and experienced to be truth. You are doing your best, but we are here to tell you that the time to be a little person at the whim of life is over. The time of the powerful creator within you is now. Own it. Want it. Be it.

"We hear you say ... 'How do I be it Jed?' We tell you that there is nothing more to do than to choose it. Stand up now and say it, 'I am a powerful creator of my life and I am greatness.' Write down every bad feeling and negative belief you have that enters your mind—you will feel it, your stomach will turn, your mind will go into overdrive when the beliefs arise, write them down and then say, 'I choose to release this. I am a powerful creator of my life. I am greatness.' Practise this every day. Set your dreams in writing and let the signals guide you."

Negative Stories

Everyone enjoys a good old story, don't they? Well, it seems perhaps we enjoy some of our stories a little too much! Jed is not a fan of our negative stories, because of how these stories dim our light.

"People suffer at their own hands, due to the negative story they tell themselves about what they sense, see, hear and touch. They have a story and that story defines their life and the way they live their life. A story is made up, it is meaning added in response to what has been going on around you. You needn't live by a negative story. You have a choice. You cannot change your story until you can see that you indeed have a story to start with.

"You experience difficulties and challenges (what you deem to be bad things) and you make it mean something negative about who you are as a person, which then forms a chapter in your story. You are now a person to whom that bad thing has happened and it means something about life and about you and about your past and about your future. You then carry that with you into the next experience. This

goes on for a lifetime and at the end of a lifetime you have either awoken to the fact that you were living that negative story or you remain so well embedded in that story that you cannot see the character you were playing out. If you want to learn the truth about your soul, about who you really are, then let go of your negative stories. Notice what it feels like when you let what happens around you be nothing more than opportunities for your soul expansion, with no negative meaning adding about you and your life. When you remove all the negative meaning adding, there is in fact more valuable meaning than you could imagine. You can choose the theme of your life; you can choose how the story goes.

"So we ask you: What stories do you tell yourself about who you are? What stories do you tell yourself about what you desire and deserve to have? What stories do you tell yourself about the things that you do that hurt others and that hurt yourself? What stories do you tell yourself about your ways of being that don't serve you, the things you spend your time doing that you know do not add value to you? What stories do you tell yourself about the people you spend time with who are not aligned with you and so cause you to fall into a bad feeling space? What are your stories?

"Any story can be written down and when you read a story in writing you have more clarity and objectivity than if you think about it. Write your story down and look at what you believe to be true, and then ask yourself how much of that is merely your interpretation of your life. What themes have you extrapolated and decided to live as truth? Do those themes serve you well? Are those themes negative or positive?

"Why, when you know that you can influence your life, do you let yourself believe that you are at the whim of life? You know that you can move your legs and arms and talk in ways that you choose, you can believe, think and feel in ways that you choose, and yet you feel like life is happening to you. You are a creature of creation and the godliness in you can shine out, if you will let it. It cannot shine through negative stories. Negative stories block the divine light within you, negative stories limit you, negative stories are only something you have used to protect yourself and help yourself cope with things that happened in life that you could not make sense of.

"Let your life be a theme of light, a theme of possibility, a

theme of the pure soul that you are, a theme of why you chose to come here, a theme of contribution to others, a theme of greatness. Do not let your life be a negative story about what is wrong and what happened that held you back and the reasons you cannot shine. There is no reason not to shine. You are able to shine when you release negative stories. When you shine, it is the energy flowing freely. Interpret life differently. Rewrite your story."

Pushing the Comfort Zone

One common message amongst manifestation teachings is that by only moving in good-feeling ways we lift and hold our energy vibration at a high level. Our energy vibration is our point of attraction. If something doesn't feel good, then the theory would suggest to listen to that feeling and instead move in directions that make your heart sing. I was still slightly stumped by this, as it seemed to contradict the idea of pushing one's comfort zone to expand and achieve, which to me invoked feelings of fear. Fear did not feel good to me at all. Which is it? Do I only move in good-feeling ways or do I allow myself to feel the immense whirling emotion of fear in order to expand and grow on my journey?

I had pushed my comfort zone so many times that fear had become a regular feeling that bubbled away inside of me. After leaving my job, I woke most days with a feeling of heightened adrenaline, not knowing what would happen next, holding my vision but sitting in the midst of a current reality of little to no income. I suspected this was not good for my body to be constantly on edge. This led me to consider that maybe I was taking the fear facing a little too far, venturing way outside my comfort zone. When you follow your heart, taking risks and stepping into the unknown, the mind has a way of messing with the heart.

As this head versus heart battle grew noisier, I checked in with Jed for perspective:

"Nothing you are doing B is too risky, nothing you are doing will lead you to misery. You are still caught up in your box, but you are letting yourself push further and further beyond. This level of fear will diminish; it will not always be this difficult for you. It is a time of immense inner growth for

you and you will not have to face this level of fear again, this is the worst of it for you in this life. You do not need to resign yourself to having great fear and nerves all the time because you have chosen to do things outside the norm that you were used to. You can face it and move through it and next time it will not be so daunting. Do not be concerned about lack. There is no lack in what you are envisioning for your life. You have a fruitful, abundant and joyful life.

"This period of time now, with this fear, is what it was like for you back in Wellington when you had to let go of your old job and your house, then the time on Waiheke was magical. Now you are letting go of your job and house again, and this time is again fearful, but Hawaii will be magical. Then there will be little else to let go of, you will be moving freely and easily. This is a significant time of your life as far as overcoming blocks, and you are handling it with honesty. It is a hard time, we know that and we are watching and supporting you. Living with signals is requiring you to live in a new paradigm, with new ways of perceiving the world, and it is blowing out old, stale paradigms.

"When you wonder if you are making a difference or contributing, know that people often never see the full effect of their work. When you cannot see the impact, do not be discouraged and do not turn away."

As I heard the message of moving freely and easily, and I felt the draw to be "out there" somewhere in the world, I noticed a melody repeating in my head. The theme became clear, and the old saying "a rolling stone gathers no moss" seemed an appropriate way to sum up the message. The lyrics felt like a story of my move to Waiheke and my realisation that I was going to keep moving, for now at least.

"This city desert makes you feel so cold ... he's got this dream about buying some land ... he'll settle down in some quiet little town and forget about everything but you know he'll always keep moving. You know he's never gonna stop moving ... he's the rolling stone." [42]

A montage of songs by The Rolling Stones also came and went. When and for how long I would be a rolling stone I wasn't sure. It did not matter, for I knew that I would create my life and follow what my heart wanted. When my heart wanted to be in one place I would be, settled and grounded.

When my heart wanted to move, I would move. I committed to listening to soul-level self.

Collective States of Being

Jed also offered me insights on collective states of being. At the times when I had felt most buoyed and joyful in life, I noticed that I was either feeling further expanded as my best self through interaction with others who were naturally bringing me up due to their own high vibration and positivity, and/or that the joy I was feeling was naturally flowing out of my energy space directly onwards to others through my interactions and communication with them, buoying them.

We have the ability to have an immensely powerful impact on the lives of others through our own state of being, our energy. Just as we can bring others up, by a mere smile, a thought, a word, a deed or simply being our fully expressed soul-level self around them, it was very clear to me that the opposite is also true and is a major reason why there is so much unrest in our world. We have the powerful ability to bring others down. By a mere frown, a word, doubt, fear, anger, frustration or general negativity, our energy permeates outward and flows on to others whether we realise it or not.

Consider one person who interacts with, and thus impacts, ten to twenty people per day through their state of being. Then those ten to twenty people, thus impacted and slightly adjusted on their own course that day, go on to impact another ten to twenty people, and so the flow of one person's state of being reaches far wider than they could ever imagine or realise. Much of this happens unconsciously. Why do we feel good around certain people and places, and why on the flip side do we feel bad around certain people and places? We may not stop to give deep thought to this but the effect is real nevertheless. We have encountered individual energy vibrations, literally frequencies intersecting with our own energy.

If we view the entire world as one large ball of flowing energy, which it is, with every living and non-living thing being energy within that collective flow, each with its own vibration contributing to the overall vibration, what would happen if we each consciously tuned our individual flow into being a positive contribution to the overall?

Jed had this to say about the collective energy of humanity. There are collective states of being that, if we individually allow (consciously or unconsciously), can bring us down, or raise us up.

Collective Fear

"Fear breeds fear. To have fear is to be consumed with worry about something that you perceive to be a threat, that you perceive as real, perhaps something that has not even happened yet. You know fear well because you tap into fear from the past, the fear of others, the fear of what you have heard or seen. You have no fear when you do not know there is anything to fear. It is your filter that creates fear. So the collective fear is like an organism that grows and breeds and grows and breeds the more that people join it and feed into it. You all have a role as souls to not become a part of the collective fear for your own journey and not to feed the collective fear that traps others. For when you step aside from that collective negative energy, you serve yourself and you serve others in doing so. Do not play in the collective fear game; it is not a game that aids you well and it adds no value to your lifetime."

Collective Possibility

"Possibility is contagious. If you think that negativity can spread like wildfire, wait until you see the impact of collective possibility. When you put people in a room who are all full of the possibility of human life and the potential for all beings there on earth, you will feel the energy flow so tangibly that you cannot help but be caught up in that collective possibility. People flock to be with other people and places that allow them to tap into the collective possibility, for that energy is good. Others sit on the outskirts of those energy centres and wonder why the people in there have all gone crazy. They think them to be dreamers. They think to them to be living in a dreamland. They think this because they are caught back in the collective fear. Jump into the collective possibility, for when you do you not only feed the possibility of your own life, glimpsing all you can be as the soul you are and what your

soul chose to come here to do and be and have, but you also give others the opening to see the possibility for themselves. In doing so you feed the collective possibility in the world. When collective possibility tips the balance on collective fear, a massive tidal wave of change can occur that will be powerfully healing for humanity. Possibility is not hoping or wishing. Possibility is inner knowledge of the truth that anything can be achieved by the power of human belief. Swim in that possibility and rush forward with the momentum of the collective. Do not forge alone, for in forging alone you are assuming yourself to be separate from the collective. You are not separate. You are one part of the overall flow of energy; you could not separate yourself even if you tried. The ones who try to separate are the ones who become, and behave, most disconnected."

Collective Courage

"Many think that to move from fear to courage is a natural flow, that there is no step in between. But for all who step from fear to courage it is due to the sensing of possibility. To withdraw from the collective fear, one senses possibility for themselves and steps into the collective courage to move forward to be all they came to be. If you stay grounded in fear it means you do not fully sense possibility and so you are lost in the fear being all that there is. Courage is the rising up of belief and the confidence to move ahead powerfully in living soul intention. Courage allows one to move into this space of flourishing. Some of you move through your life journeys with very little interaction with the collective fear; you have always sensed possibility and acted courageously as a natural occurrence. You feed and live in the collective courage. This is not the case for the majority. Many will tell you they are not part of the collective fear, but scratch the surface and you will find a different story. The ones who live courageously will tell you they do not live courageously, for it comes so naturally to them they do not see it as courage. Just as those who live in fear do not think themselves to be fearful. Rather they assume their acceptance of what they perceive to be real and limiting, and their negative state of being, as the way everyone experiences the world. Act with courage in

seeking out, following and living your possibility. In doing so you free yourself of limitation and can flourish. You also give others the permission to live courageously themselves. You show the way forward and you shine a light for others to see the living demonstration of what it looks like to step forward from collective fear into collective possibility into collective courage. From this state of being you are creating, collaborating and contributing to the whole."

Chapter 15

Breaking Invisible Shackles

How & Why You Measure Yourself

In my corporate life I was much like a tightly wound rubber band version of myself kitted out in high heels and power suits, running around like a headless chicken. I certainly have love for myself back then, there were many very good times, and many upsides to that life, despite my pervading half-happiness.

One thing I am certain about is that the previous version of me was highly productive, and highly valued by myself and others based on my level of productivity. Productivity pointed to my ability to create outcomes, my ability to churn like a machine. I would go to bed at night with feelings that, unknowingly, were vague indicators of my self-assessed level of machinelike productivity. Never consciously, but nevertheless somewhere there within myself ... *Did I do enough today? Did I get through all my errands? Did I complete all those meetings? Did I close those deals? Did I meet the targets?*

It was a delusional game of self-measurement for validation. In some ways it was like having a devil on your shoulder telling you that you get so many points for each task achieved, and I'd value myself based on how many points I accumulated, my measures of success. Meeting the points quota never resulted in the joy I anticipated, only an immediate hit of pleasure, the rush of validation. However, just like any stimulant-induced high, the rush would fade and it would never be enough to fill the void.

> *How do you measure yourself?*
>
> *What do you tell yourself that you must be or must do or must have in order to feel worthy, valuable and satisfied?*

If you're not sure, just ask yourself when you feel most deflated. What is missing in those situations that you think caused you to feel deflated? Whatever is absent is most likely what you subconsciously use as a means to validate yourself.

Halfway Between

That was back then, I told myself. *Now, things are different.*

I was sitting there in my house, having yet another day of serenity in the very dream life I had created. Waking when my body woke me, starting each morning with meditation and yoga. Lime and honey tea from my dusky blue teapot. Birds singing outside the open windows. Jogging with Cash for a midday break, perhaps to the beach, or perhaps to the cliff-top lookout point near the house to absorb the view and be reminded of how vast the world is when you open your perspective. The first two to three hours of each day were usually spent responding to emails and helping friends and family—support, coaching, healings and readings. Of course, now none of this was for paying clients, having officially cut off that arm of my business. Then came focusing on connecting to new like-minded people as I reached out through referrals and through signals.

Anytime I recognised a signal, I recorded it in my notebook, assessing the possible meaning, researching and expanding my understanding of this mysterious language of life.

As I sat there one afternoon researching, connecting, following a particular signal, I thought to myself: *What have I turned into? Am I actually insane? I am sitting here, at home, I've left my job, I have no consistent income to support myself, and I'm spending my time connecting with random strangers around the world following signals, and drawing animal totem medicine cards from a pack. Oh god, I'm totally Person A, aren't I? I fit that crazy hippy stereotype I wrote about in Pinch Me, the one I told myself I would not become.*

Half of me was screaming ... *get back to the real world,* and the other half was screaming back ... *this is the freaking REAL world. Unlock the mystery!*

I reasoned with myself: *I must follow the signals, I have a vision and to achieve it I cannot live by logic alone. Logic is not going to work out the "how" of my vision, and logic is not going to work out how on earth to support myself when I've got no job and a fledgling business (other than telling myself to get another job, which is not in alignment with my dream). No, logic will have to play second fiddle to the most primary driver required in this situation ... trust and faith in my heart led guidance, and in the signals. I've trusted them before and they worked every time. Now I'll have to trust beyond measure.*

What was now a familiar song to me kept popping up at the most convenient times. It seemed to be ingraining in me a message that went against everything society had told me ...

"We leaving across these undefeatable odds, it's like this man, you can't put a price on life ... it's not about the money, money, money." [43]

Noticing cockroaches (eek!) and seagulls in unusual ways on and off led me to recognise the theme in these animal totems that further embedded the other messages being given to me at this time—persistence and being masterful at survival. Jed had said that what I needed would come to me when I needed it, if I stayed aligned to my vision in belief, thought, feeling and action.

I was not going to intentionally create anything in my life that was short of having what I needed in all areas. Health, well-being, balance, love, joy, living soul intention, and resources to support myself to flow in the river ... what I needed, when I needed it. I was going to learn that very important distinction between "what I want when I want it," and "what I need when I need it."

If there was to be an interim period requiring my persistence and a necessary juggling and canniness as I got my new life off the ground, then so be it.

New Field—Same Old Game, Same Old Rules

This dreamy daytime living on Waiheke, my new routine, was bliss. The pace of life and the focus of my attention were more aligned to how I wanted my life to be than ever before. I had spent thirty-plus years of my life building habits that had gotten me to where I was, and the type of life I wanted to lead now was more about balance of mind, body and spirit, rather than mind domination, body suffering the consequences and spirit ... what spirit? Consequently, I had to break those habits of a lifetime in order to play a new game of life on this new field I had chosen.

The rules of the old game on the old field had been a work ethic based on working to the bone, striving for results, reaching for recognition, measuring my value by hours of productivity and unconsciously viewing almost everything in life as an opportunity to be perfect and to compete to do well. I thought I could break these old habits easily but I had been terribly mistaken. I only started to see this most glaringly once I was on the new field.

No one told me that the rules of the old game on the old field wouldn't work in the new game on the new field. What a predicament. Don't worry though, because when you try to apply the wrong rules to a game, you soon realise your error because you will quickly start to lose the game, and when you start to lose the game, you ask yourself: *Why?*

The lesson to be learned is that you can't overcome something within yourself by ignoring it and skirting around the outside. You are better to traverse right through the middle, see it for what it is and then leave it behind. Let me explain.

False Value Construct

In my new life working from home I was constantly measuring my value each day by how many people I had helped, how many hours I had worked, what results I was producing and how much money I was or was not making. Not a good starting point. I had actually just picked myself up out of corporate life, physically transplanted myself into my home office and tried to continue with the same modus operandi. I felt satisfied when working seven days a week from eight in the morning until eight in the evening, like I had done really well. What a calamity and a complete and utter farce.

I thought moving into this new path would see me more rested and relaxed for my greater well-being. I thought it would help me to bring my intensity down a notch, just like a Palm Reader in Bangkok once told me.

Seeing the Light

It was late afternoon and the Bangkok skyline was a thunderous dark grey. I was sitting cross-legged with my back against the stone wall of a temple. Resting, contemplating and listening to tiny bells chiming all over the complex, after a long day adventuring around the city on my own. I rose to leave and followed a paved path in the direction of the road. I could not help but glimpse through the narrow gateways that lined the path, peering into the inner courtyards where saffron robes were hung over banisters and monks moved silently within. Continuing to meander forward, over higgledy-piggledy cobblestones, something white caught my eye as I passed. I almost kept going, but a feeling of curiosity made me stop. In response to that feeling, I stepped backwards two paces and looked to the right. It was a small white paper notice pinned to one of the narrow gateways. The pin failed to allow the notice to show itself, with edges curling over. My index finger pushed the corner back to reveal, "Palm Reading. English" with a hand-drawn arrow pointing through the gate. Two words randomly scrawled in pencil on the top right corner, "New Zealand," compelled me to follow the arrow.

The arrow took me a few steps inside the gate, to find a rickety little wooden desk, two vacant stools and a withered looking potted plant. A few stray cats minus tails milled around my feet, mewing with hunger. I was about to turn around and leave when she appeared around the corner, stooped over as she made her way towards me. There was little by way of pleasantries, though I detected a peak of a smile for a second as she lifted her hand up in the air as if to announce we could proceed.

My palm was laid forth and so commenced a palm reading that in no way related to the experience with Ava all those years ago when Jessie, Aaron and I had gone together.

I didn't know what this lady's name was. It was all business and concentration as she marked up my hand with a ruler and twenty plus tiny blue pen dots all over the creases of my palm. I tried not to fidget, perched on my stool, as I was eaten alive by ravenous mosquitos. I was under instruction not to move the hand.

She did not make eye contact. She was talking to my hand, seemingly oblivious to there being a body attached beyond the wrist. This was not a question and answer session; rather she was foretelling my path and I was to listen. I found this intriguing. It was another opportunity to balance my prescription to free will with this very real set of possibilities that we each uniquely have etched on the palms of our hands. The things we naturally lean toward, and the reason our soul chose to be here, is marked like a map on the vessel that carries the soul through life.

Short, sharp, definitive sentences coloured the coming hour, as she intermittently stopped to scrawl her findings on a piece of lined paper to her side. Fascinated, I soaked up every word. Not even the bloodsuckers on my arms and legs diverted my attention once the reading began. She changed subject frequently and abruptly throughout the session. After a brief pause she announced, "You live long, die old age." Delightful news.

Then, I kid you not, she literally said, "No tsunami or no knife get you. You die natural, old age."

Then she put a strong and specific caveat on that possibility, with a raised finger shaking in my face, "But *only* if learn how come down" as she then patted both her palms down towards the ground. "If not, you serious health problem after sixty, you die early."

A brief pause, then, "You set mind to something, you no stop. You up here." She lifted her hands up above her head. "Go, go. No calm. Busy. At work … okay busy, make good success. At home, no okay. Must bring down. I teach you meditation."

Thirty seconds of diaphragmatic breathing meditation instruction would prove to be the daily practise I would come to use going forward. This little incident helped me to see the light of what the long term effects would be if I carried on my life at the pace I had been living. The only way of being I had ever known, driven by false value constructs, would be my eventual undoing if I did not change. I had hard habits to break, but ones I had to learn to break if I was to thrive in my life.

This is what Jed had to say about that. The message is universal:

"The only reason you worry about how productive you are is that you were conditioned to think that being productive made you good and worthy, valued and important. And you feel like how much you do is how much you create, and in actual fact how much you do has little to do with it, it's all about your way of being, your intention behind what you do and your level of belief in the outcome. You are moving in the direction of what you wish to create and you are being purposeful about it. No amount of overdoing the action will make any difference to the situation, especially not if you sabotage yourself behind the veil."

On the basis that every way of being has a consequence in the physical body, be that positively or negatively, what messages has the universe (and your body) given to you about your ways of being?

What practises, if any, do you employ to maintain balance in your well-being?

The Promise

Other than feeling compelled on every level to continue this new lifestyle I was creating, and most importantly to learn how to be a better version of myself in it, there was one other reason I would continue—I had promised myself and I had promised Jed.

The phone rang one morning. It was my friend Rebekah.

"Are you okay?" she asked.

"Yep, I'm good."

"Strange. I dreamed of you all night. But nothing was happening, you were just sitting there staring at me. I had to call you to see if everything was okay."

The phone rang again. It was my sister Ella. She sounded

concerned.

"Are you okay?" she asked.

"I'm fine. Why? What's up?"

"Something odd happened last night. Whatever it was, or whoever it was, they wouldn't shut up. All night I saw you in my mind as I was tossing and turning trying to go to sleep. I heard over and over again 'She's going to the beach. She's going to the beach. She's going to the beach.' I have no idea what is going on, but given how this all seems to work now, I suggest you get your butt down to the beach and see what happens. Maybe you are meant to bump into someone there?"

"Maybe it's about Hawaii?"

"No. I don't think so. I have a strong feeling you're meant to go to the beach today. Just go and stay there and wait until something happens."

After a few minutes of bantering about the hilarity of me loitering around the beach like a weirdo, I did go. Like the diligent signal follower and born-again hippie that I am, I left the house and went to our local beach. I wandered up and down, water sparkling like diamonds as a reflection of the morning sun. I saw a lady off in the distance and a man far behind me.

I cannot go and talk to them randomly in case they are the reason I'm here. That is beyond weird. I must have actually gone insane. What am I doing here?

I smiled at the lady and waited to see if she would strike up conversation with me, but alas nothing.

So instead I just sat on the sand dunes cross-legged, like a little yogi. I closed my eyes and waited. A few minutes later it started.

I could feel them around me, the familiar energy around my head and shoulders. Jed had arrived and they commenced by saying, *"We wanted you to come here because you will hear us better here. You will focus more on this important message we have to give you. You have been too distracted at home. Too in your head, caught up. You are part of us. We are part of you. You may not remember where you came from. We are here to remind you and to promise you something, and to ask for you to promise to us in return. We have been waiting for you a long time, to get to this point when you would be awake and ready. Waiting for when you would be open enough to let life flow through you. And that time is now. We will promise to you that we will always take care of you, and in return, you must promise us this. You must promise us that you will not stop and you will never give up and turn away from living your truth. Will you promise us this?"*

I promised.

For weeks after, I awoke each morning to messages of encouragement. There were songs I had never heard before. Tracking them down, often by the melody alone, I found embedded special messages of progress, of movement forth, of continuing with momentum with my soul intention.

"Head under water and they tell me to breathe easy for a while ... promise me you'll leave the light on to help me see with daylight, my guide." 44

"Don't stop me now." 45

"Can't you see I'm just a writer ... taught myself to never ever try to pretend ... got a dream that's bigger than me." 46

Cave Days

As time wore on, each day alone at the house, Aaron and I were both heads down working on our new ventures. It felt like we had gone into some awful cave man isolation. There were occasions when I wouldn't see anyone for days and, at times, weeks.

While I reminded myself it was a time of quiet building of infrastructure and tools, and of learning, doing all the necessary things that had to be done, I still feared that everything I was doing was perhaps not right. The quiet was unnerving. The not having one-on-one clients or a consistent income was leading me to feel like I was suspended in limbo.

My logic would not stop torturing me telling me that sane people don't risk everything and live without certainty of income based on nothing but belief and faith. Weeks turned into months ...

How long can I go on this way?

Jed said, *"Stop your addiction to worry."*

In my short time connecting with Jed, I had come to learn that they would tell me what I needed to hear, even if it meant that the truth hurt. They had become used to me asking the same questions over and over again.

"You ask a question but you don't like the answer. Come back when you are ready to hear the answer. You are making problems where problems do not exist."

This was the not the only time that Jed gave me advice, that while seemingly a little School Master-ish and blunt, was exactly what I needed to hear. Their other gems around this time included:

"You come to us and get what you need and leave. If you listen longer you will hear far more of benefit than if you only ask. One-way traffic does not benefit you."

Charlotte called me each day. My mother often called to check that I was eating properly, sleeping and staying well. Each time I answered the phone, even on my up days when my mood was good and my spirits were high, I would find myself starting to sink down when they asked how I was doing. I would feel a lump form in my throat that would start to ever so slightly ache and throb. My lip would move, slowly starting to quiver and my voice would fail to hide the emotion. I could never hide from my family. It always came pouring out to them. I had been shoving my fear deep down for months. I started to internally berate myself for being a silly old parrot: *Woe is me, for I know not what is going to happen, wherefore art thou security and stability?* A parrot whose wailing was not making any difference to the situation and yet the parrot could not stop herself from crying out.

Fear consumed me. I woke to morning after morning of that uneasy feeling in my stomach. The feeling that niggles so far down that you almost can't see or hear it, yet like a rip under the surface of the water it pulls you left and right, side to side, up and down.

The fear I felt, in truth, was not a fear of *what*. I had this exacting conviction within me that I was on the best path forward. The fear, instead, was of not knowing *how* and not knowing *when*. I had given up everything, or so I thought, to follow my dream and pursue my passion.

Yet, all the same, as a person who had never wanted for anything, here I was facing what felt at times like impending nothingness. Savings dwindling, mortgage rising. Indeed, no different to what many people experience in life, regularly or from time to time.

I called Charlotte thinking I would see how she and the children were and what plans they had for their day. Instead the conversation was to be a breakdown for me. This was on par with the "Blood, Sweat, Tears and Poo" incident, and the Thonburi meltdown. However, this time, much more was at stake. At least it felt that way. At stake now, in my mind, was everything I had built for thirteen years, plus our livelihood, our ability to be independent and self-sufficient, closely followed by our well-being and peace of mind.

Bending Branch

As tears streamed down my face, Charlotte just listened. "I feel like I'm so far out on a limb here that the branch is hanging down and it's about to break. I keep wondering when it will spring back up. I keep wondering when am I going to fly?"

Charlotte waited.

"Am I being pushed to my extreme limits, to the brink of what I can cope with, so that I've experienced this firsthand to know what it is like for people in similar situations, people who go out to create their life and have to live in the grey area where no clear answers lie, with only faith to believe that something great is possible? Is my faith in signals being tested? Is my attachment to certainty being tested?"

There is a trap we can fall into when creating our life, where we set our focus but constantly check to see if the results have shown up yet, checking over and over and over again. Checking for evidence kills possibility. It says, "I'll check again because I'm worried something is going wrong. I'll check again because I'm concerned that it's not working. I'll check again because I don't believe." It was a little challenging not to check for evidence, when the evidence I was checking for was the very means by which we pay our way in life. I was humble enough to admit I was afraid and that I was taking a major leap of faith. I knew I was not so proud as to not take other opportunities to earn income. I knew I could do endless types of work right then and there if I chose it, but I was convinced that wasn't my path. Despite how incredibly uncomfortable it was, and how insane this sounds, somehow being in this experience felt like my path.

After talking to Charlotte, I had a flash in my mind of a particular beach on the southern side of Waiheke. I ignored it and instead pulled a card from an animal totem medicine card pack for guidance. I pulled the Frog card, which said clearly that the medicine of Frog includes the cleansing qualities of water, that water clears the muddy-ness away and brings clarity. The flash of the beach now felt like somewhere I needed to go.

So I did. I went to that beach and sat and let the wind whip through me. I could have stayed hunkered up at home writing, but I sensed that writing from a place of despair was not going to work. I asked the cleansing qualities of water to clear my muddy mind. I walked Cash on the beach and breathed the sea air deeply. Walking back towards the car, I heard, *"Stay longer."*

So I sat myself on the bonnet of the car, looking out over the water, feeling vulnerable. Ten minutes later I climbed behind the steering wheel and turned the key. I almost never listen to the radio when I drive, but I didn't want to be in silence; it was making me feel lonely and teary. Turning on the stereo, there was no music for a few seconds, as the radio station cut to a new track. Out of the speakers came, "Oh, why you look so sad? Tears are in your eyes, come on and come to me now. Don't be ashamed to cry, let me see you through ... " [47]

Yet, every time I asked Jed for guidance, I got the same answer. Everything is fine, stay focused and write. Every time I asked what more I needed to do, I got the same answer ... *"write and speak your truth."*

I had been avoiding writing, because I didn't feel inspired. What I was missing at the time was that writing *was* what made me feel inspired, and sometimes what was to be written was the truth of what that time was like for me. Not for the benefit of others, and not even necessarily to share with others, but rather because writing for myself would comfort me through challenging times and allow me to access wisdom arising from my soul level-self. This insight was far beyond me at the time.

It was over this period where I completely forgot the simple fundamentals of creating your life. Yes, after all that time I was not practising what I preached. Just an ordinary girl, feeling my way forward, sometimes in the dark, and sometimes in the light. Knowing that what you believe, think, feel and do creates your outcomes had somehow sat like a textbook on a shelf too high to reach. My beliefs were rattled by fear. My thoughts wandered, rehearsing for disaster instead of success. My feelings bounced like a high-speed ricocheting tennis ball ... from anxiety to worry, back to confidence and assurance, on to fear and doubt. Up, down, round about, back and forth. Emotional gymnastics. It felt like a small miracle to me that I had days where I felt completely alive, inspired and affirmed in my path. It was no wonder these months played out the way they did, when my predominant energy vibration was that of fear.

This period of my life is what we call an uninvited hiatus. Nothing happening! I'd willingly cut off half my workload and I was either refusing or forgetting to write. Do you think I remembered that I'd had that hiatus message in my future reading all those months ago? That message lay buried in my hand-scribbled notes, in a notebook in the bottom of a drawer. If only I had gone to read my notebooks.

This is also what we call stumbling at the first major hurdle. Well, it's probably a bit more like crash and burn at the first major hurdle. But the point is this, I experienced a prolonged hurdle and I could have given up. The signals were there to guide me to see this was not a red light. I was off on a bad feeling tangent for sure, but I was living on purpose. It was just that I had challenges to face, some very limiting ways of being to let go of, and life was allowing me to see this in all its glory.

Life will *always* give you the experience you need in order to free yourself to evolve.

I would eventually come to see that living my vision with those limiting ways of being and attachments sturdily tucked under my belt was never going to be possible. Never. I could not dwell in the physical manifestation of my vision while dragging baggage around behind me. The dam in the river had to be broken.

It is at times of despair and darkness that faith has to be greatest. There is no other way through. For within ourselves first comes the sight of possibility, second comes taking action with belief and last comes having *absolute faith* that your life will unfold in the best way. All you have to do is be the clearing to allow it to unfold, by unblocking yourself.

Stand in the Empty Space

I reasoned that if by any slim chance I was on the wrong path then something disastrous would have happened. At the very least I hoped I would have woken to hear lyrics in my head akin to "STOP CRAZY WOMAN! YOU ARE HEADING FOR DISASTER, LA LA LA." But instead what I heard was a song that made me literally drop my face into my hands and cry with relief, love and gratitude for the never-ending support I was being given from the universal energy.

These may read like meaningless words to you, but for me it cut to my core. Just as your signal songs will do the same for you at times. These lyrics told my life story ...

"I found no peace, lived like a shy fearful child, I couldn't feel a thing ... an ever nameless dread ... and I could always have stayed there, never to have played my hand, the lament for the numb. The battle memory remains here, only to be fought and won ... and now the journey repays me, lose all the baggage for one ... to burn a trail ahead ... and there is so much to gain here ... " [48]

I was being told quite literally exactly what was going on. Also, Aaron was always there telling me to harden up, chin up, choose your path and walk it with your head up. "Believe in yourself, you're bloody good at what you do, so get on with it." When my soul decided to team up with his soul pre-lifetime, I clearly didn't read the fine print—"Promises to love and support you, and sometimes this means kicking your butt and bluntly shoving you in the right direction."

I could never have envisaged that I would have ended up in such a vulnerable and scared feeling state from stepping out on a limb. I considered the humorous notion that just perhaps what felt like a flimsy limb to me, could well have been (from a higher perspective) a very sturdy trunk better supported than I realised.

Your version of being out on a limb may be different. Consider that the experiences in life that make us feel vulnerable and afraid, are the direct access points to inner greatness. The experiences are uniquely created to push your buttons, buttons that your soul wanted pushed in order to evolve.

Jed would tell me where I was at soul-level, despite where I was in mind and body:

"Dearest, you willingly gave away your old life as you knew it; you stepped away from a career, you broke down the walls you built up, you have opened yourself to life. Let go of labels, let go of having to be settled, let go of position, let go of your attachments, give away the need to know anything ... stand in the empty space for the first time in your life, for the first time since you were a little girl with nothing more than dreams.

"Can you stand in a space with no place to be, no place to call home, no things to surround you in comfort, no knowledge of what will come next, no labels, no clear path ahead, and can you be with it? Can you sit in that space and not be consumed by worry and questions and fear? Can you blaze a trail forward with nothing other than a vision that compels you to follow it? Will you go to Maui on nothing more than faith that you do not need to do anything other than go and be there, to write and to be? Can you let go of the need to plan and plot, and work out how to make it happen, how to make it a success and how to get your passion-felt message to others? Will you trust that the message will reach those who need it in ways you cannot imagine because you have visioned it to be so and that is enough? Your action of going is all the action that you are here to take at this stage. Be with it."

So rather than do what I felt like doing—going to Mum and Dad's house and crawling under a blanket never to come out again (I reasoned they could feed me by passing plates under the edge of the blanket)—I was reminded that you only get what you give ...

"But when the night is falling, you cannot find the light, if you feel your dreams are dying, hold tight ... this world is gonna pull through, don't give up ... you only get what you give." 49

Two Words

Many times I have considered what it is within me that supports me to act in complete faith of my goals and dreams.

What is it that allows me to face my fear, be afraid to the point of nearly being physically debilitated by it but still find the courage to move ahead?

The answer to this question is clear for me. I always come back to this same answer whenever my fear grips me.

The answer is: Why?

Pretty strange answer, I know!

What I mean by this is, more accurately, what is the reason you do what you do? What is your motivating factor? What is your "why"? It goes beyond the push and pull factors in your life, which are surface level and circumstantial. The why is what lies deeper.

If your "why" is big enough, strong enough, motivating enough, then it will exceed your fear. It's just about a tipping point. You are either tipped in favour of fear or tipped in favour of courage.

My why is big for me. It is big enough that it allows me to face fears and to go beyond. What I share with you is not a sad story. On the face of it, it may initially seem like that. I lived it as a sad story until I awoke. But when one looks deeper, there is a magnificent gift.

It was over twenty years ago. A day that started out a seemingly average Tuesday despite the unsettling circumstances that surrounded life at that time. I heard the dogs restless and the tyres churning the gravel long before they turned the car engine off. I leapt up on the bed and peered out of the upstairs window with anticipation and excitement. *They're home, finally. I knew everything would be just fine. Why didn't they call to tell us they were coming?* This was an unexpected turn for the better.

When we last saw them they said they didn't know when they would be back. We were to return to school, for the situation could have carried on for an indefinite time. No good could come from us all staying, waiting and wondering. So we returned home, back to school, back to ordinary life. But life was not ordinary by any stretch. We might have been going about our "normal" routine, but nothing inside felt normal. Not by a long shot.

Peering out the window, I saw the car doors begin to open and so I flew down the stairs and raced to meet them in the kitchen. The rest is a blur. All my memory offers me are the looks of faces showing broken hearts, because Sarah was not with them. In fact Sarah was not coming home, ever. The two words were:

Sarah died.

Two words that felt like a punch in the stomach. Two words that destroyed me. Two words that were destroying everyone around me that I loved. Two words that created the biggest WHY in my life. Two words that made me who I am today. Indeed, two words that actually saved my life, because they marked the beginning of a very long awakening. Two words that contribute, in part, to the source of my courage to push the boundaries to explore, dream and discover, and to be all that I came here to be. Because, quite simply, life is that precious and that much of a gift.

The life that you notice coming and going every day, as the sun rises and falls, as you age each day, as you watch babies born and people pass, your life is that precious, that fragile and that big, bold and wonderful all at the same time.

When Sarah visited with me during my session with Augustus, I had suddenly plummeted backward, regressed from a thirty-two-year-old woman to a thirteen-year-old distressed little sister. Augustus, in all his wisdom, could see that I had not fully dealt with the loss. I had thought back then: *Can anyone ever really deal with it? It just is. It is what it is. And I just have to carry this with me.*

However, Augustus shed new light that day. It was he who explained to me why souls come to choose lives, to be here, and why they leave. His words were so beautiful, he said:

> *Your life is your message to the world.*
> *When you finish your message you go home.*

We might never know what that message (soul intention) truly is for another, or ourselves, in all its complexity, or how, when or why it is determined that the message is complete. But it left me with the knowledge that Sarah's message had been completed, and she had gone home.

Those two words, a large part of my "why," to that date had been a sad story. But a sad story they were not. They were an absolute gift.

I rewrote a story of grief that day I saw Augustus, and the new story said, "Live life like you mean it, like it means that much to you, and do things that matter."

This was Sarah's gift to me, the fine print of a soul agreement that said ... I will help you to awaken.

What stories of tragedy do you carry, like a burden you must bear, that could in fact be a gift you were lovingly given, in order to see behind the veil of life through to the soul you are?

Chapter 16

Dark Before Dawn

What comes next is much like a yo-yo. The lesson, clear in retrospect, is that when you yo-yo life yo-yos with you. It is not the other way around.

Here comes my humanness in all its stark reality. This is what it looks like when the mind takes control of the fortress and starts to attack all other aspects of being. Grenades flying, tear gas unleashed. This is what happens when you accidentally fall prey to identifying with the Sergeant Major Mind like it is who you are. It is a dangerous, but all too common, mistake to make. We either submit to the power of our mind or we empower ourselves to apply the magic of our mind in our creative favour. Thoughts are powerful, they either mould an incredible reality that inspires or they have the power to slowly but surely break down their host, like a virus.

I share the coming final "cave day" episodes with you because they're real, and when you go out on a limb to create something big or small, these are some of the challenges that *can* arise *if* you let your mind run riot. To say that outcomes are primarily down to how you interpret, perceive and react to life is a laughable understatement. That is *all* that it's about.

Holding On

With the prospect of selling our house, what felt like my last remaining security blanket, I asked Jed if there was anything else they wanted to share with me.

They said, *"You are still holding onto your equity like you worry it will be depleted. With the vision you have for your life, there will be no lack; there will be no depletion. You must trust in your vision, in us and have faith. Let it go. Let it go. Let it go."*

After brushing my teeth one morning, I opened the

bathroom window and leaned out, resting my chin in my hands. Watching birds flitting in the tree branches a few feet away, my mind wandered and became lost in calculating how much money we would or would not have after the house sale, depending on the scenarios of how any offer might go. I felt myself sinking into my thoughts and I told myself to resist. I lingered for a few minutes then announced loudly, "Enough already!" I had been playing a reasoning game, working out what level of sale price and equity I would feel comfortable walking away with. The game went like this: *So long as I have the same amount of money I had when I came to Waiheke, then that's okay, at least I haven't gone backwards.* I even tested out the sister game which went like this: *So long as I have the same amount of money I had before I left Wellington, then that's okay, at least I have had a wonderful few years of joy and maintained my level of security in the process.*

Oh dear, I knew all of this was nonsense and that it would likely lead me into danger. For Jed had said to trust and take the offer when it came and not to quibble over dollars. They had said, *"It's irrelevant."*

In the scheme of my dreams, it was most certainly irrelevant. I envisioned no lack and I envisioned no loss. I envisioned expansion and joy. Why would you envision less than that? The question remained—did I truly believe in my vision and was I willing to step out for it? How far out on a limb was I willing to go?

Inside Your Head

When I thought I couldn't sink any further into the gluggy, black mud that I found myself stuck in, I realised I was wrong. It appeared that rock bottom of this cave was a bit further down below the mud than I had suspected. Well, at least the upside of rock bottom is that there is no further to fall.

It felt like a plummet from grace. How did I reach this place? Only months earlier I had been a rock solid, confident woman with a vision so compelling I could taste it every time I breathed in and nothing was going to slow down that train as it careened ahead. I suspect the lesson was this—don't careen ahead but rather allow yourself to unfold and witness how miraculous it is when you don't hold on so tightly!

All the uncertainty had eroded my confidence. I was no longer able to make decisions clearly. I no longer knew how to process advice from others and put far too much weight on advice and not nearly enough on my own inner knowing. I no longer felt so strongly and clearly about my vision as a result. I began questioning everything I knew. I was sure that if I were busy being busy (my habitual ingrained way of being) and if my income stream were secure then I wouldn't have been questioning a single thing. I was so in my head that I thought my head was going to explode.

My logic told me that I had thrown common sense out the window. *How can I just sit here with no certainty, both of us pursuing our dreams at the same time, and then decide to waltz off to Maui because I feel like it, relying on equity I've worked all my life to create. Could I accidentally whittle it all away? Could I have taken things too far this time? Is my vision too big, are my dreams just dreams, and am I about to learn a really big lesson the hard way? Am I being selfish and ridiculous to think that we could both go there, with no clear plan, and hope for the best?*

My language was speaking for itself. Selfish, ridiculous, waltz, whittle, no plan ... the vision had not changed, universal energy had not changed, my perspective of it had. Uncertainty had caused fear to inhabit every cell of my body and the voice in my head was Fearful B. Aaron will tell you what Fearful B looks like—fidgety, unsettled, rarely able to sit still.

When every part of you feels under threat, your body goes into fight or flight mode, running on adrenaline, ready to react in response to threats, to protect all that you are.

There was once a time when I thought that it would all be roses if I took action and tried and acted and kept trying. I now knew from this place of trying and darkness that this was not the answer. There is no doubt that action is key. But not all actions are created equal. When you lose faith and lose track of who you really are, there is no amount of "doing" that can get you anywhere, other than into a pile of old crap. Any action you take from that place is infused with fear, not infused with love, and we know where that leads given that everything is energy and like attracts like.

But Excuse

Whenever Jed told me to be present, to be still and have faith, I always replied "But ... "

They said, *"This 'but' does not serve you well. 'But' only gets you caught in circles like a frenetic kitten with claws out fighting with a ball of wool. You will end up tangled in 'buts' and you will not see the clear path forward, so do not invite 'but' into this journey anymore. You are blocking yourself."*

This was seemingly just an easy case of having faith. I had faith and trust when I started out. But after months it was as weak as a floppy old rag in the middle of a gale force wind.

As time went on, I connected less and less with Jed. My flowing connection to my guides had become a staccato series of pointed questions asking for yes and no responses in order that I could know when the certainty I wanted would arrive in my life. It actually would not have mattered what my circumstances were, I would still have found a way to worry, because that was my weakness. I had put myself into a place where my greatest weakness would be fully exposed and become my greatest undoing. Or perhaps my greatest unfolding.

> *Will you flow like a river into your own unfolding?*
> *Or will you dam that river and*
> *block the life force?*

It was Charlotte, myself and a handset phone on speaker. She was sharing her own goal with me and her realisation that not achieving that goal instantly was not a matter of life or death, it was a journey that one had to be patient with. It came bursting out of my mouth, "Well, it may not be for you. You not achieving that goal isn't going to kill you. But if I don't achieve this, I will die."

She giggled lovingly ... "You will not die B," and I said, "I will, Charlotte, I will actually die inside because of how called I feel to do this. I can't think of anything worse than living with that numb feeling inside knowing I have not lived in alignment with what I feel so compelled to do."

It was clear to me, from my earlier past life vision where I had run out of time, that I had once before died for my beliefs. Perhaps this present do-or-die feeling was just the tenuous remaining link to that past life memory. I might have been sensing my inability to fulfil my soul intention once before.

The Heart of the Issue

There was nowhere to turn from this, I actually blurted out to her, in a defensive way, "I did not build up my entire life just to throw it all away!"

She said, "Is that what you think you are doing, throwing it all away? You do not believe that."

She was right. But the ease and force with which this artillery flew out of my mouth uncovered the severity of my fear. I knew I was not throwing it away; I was giving myself a bridge to cross into a more meaningful life, one that was calling to me. It was just that the journey across the bridge was slightly wobbly. I was in limbo land, not part of life as I previously knew it, and not fully sure how to operate in this new life I was in. I could turn back or change direction at any time, but that was not what I felt compelled to do. Forward facing was the direction my gut kept telling me to go.

Charlotte had ended the conversation with one simple comment. "B, with all we know, perhaps it really is no mistake your being here, experiencing this, writing about this and being willing to honestly say how it is to be in the dark and to rise out of it."

Pod Shaking

And of course I still had Aaron. My rock. Until the rock momentarily turned into sand, in a way that sent me plummeting. Making a toasted sandwich for his lunch, he turned to me and asked, "Do you think we should really be selling our house? Do you think we should really be taking this guidance you keep getting? What if Jed isn't real? What if the signals aren't real and actually we've put blind faith into something that could just turn to complete shit?"

I felt an awful sinking feeling inside. I think I barked out a response like, "I don't know!"

Questioned by Aaron, who had always been my rock, it now

felt like everything solid was gone. I felt devoid of foundation. Every part of me wanted to be swallowed up by the ground. I felt naked. On a thrill ride at the adventure park when you don't know which way is up or down, you become totally disoriented and you wonder why the hell you· ever bought a ticket for the stupid bloody ride in the first place.

I knew it was Aaron's fear talking now. The tone of his voice and the look on his face—it was not his soul speaking to me. The fear in me recognised the fear in him. With both peas shaking, the pod was now rattling. In meeting Aaron's fear face to face, part of me was thankful that I wasn't the only one feeling scared and part of me thought: *Holy shit, my usually fearless husband is worried. There must definitely be something to worry about!*

This was my challenge. I had defined myself, labelled myself and latched myself onto security my whole life, to feel valued, to feel safe and to know who I was.

How do you know your value and your truth when you find yourself in the middle of your worst nightmare? What happens when you realise you put yourself in that very nightmare?

This dark place I had come to on my internal journey was serving a purpose in my life, one that I could not see at that time. If only I could have remembered the truth that:

> ### From the greatest breakdowns come the greatest breakthroughs.

The mother of all breakthroughs had to be just around the corner.

I asked Charlotte to seek guidance for me. I didn't trust my own my connection at this time. Aaron and I were both in a quagmire. My mind was overpowering my soul-level self with its noisy ways. With my blessing, Charlotte called forth Jed in her meditation to hear what they wanted to share, when I wasn't allowing myself to hear it. Within several hours she emailed me the transcript of what she received:

"You can hear the song, can't you? 'The Final Countdown.' Of course it is for her. This is her final countdown. She needs to shift her energy vibration. It is all waiting, but her

vibration is not allowing anything to manifest. B and Aaron are both attracting the circumstances they find themselves in. It spiraled from a seed of doubt, and was fanned by the flames of fear and worry about money. They kept their heads down, got stuck into doing and without staying connected to source they have now put their heads up and thought 'how did we get here?' and 'what are we doing?' The circumstances that exist in the spiritual realm are all still the same—who they each are and what is in store for each of them on their soul journeys. This is a matter of vibration, energy and manifestation. The answer is not in what they are doing, or not doing. They can manifest their vision by doing what they are currently doing. There are many paths to any outcome. It is their energy in the matter that is causing all this pain. If something does not feel right, then it may not be the right path but that is different from feeling scared and different from feeling confronted, both of which are part and parcel of stepping outside familiarity. And right now they are wanting to know 'what to do' to get out of this feeling, to make this all better, and we are saying that what they do right now is not the issue. They can't 'do' their way out of this situation. But they can be differently and it will all transform.

"We understand that is it difficult to comprehend that everything is perfect in the spirit side, just waiting for them to allow it to materialise. It is just a matter of allowing. She forgets that 99.9 percent of it is already complete, ready to show up. Her energy and Aaron's also are attracting circumstances rapidly.

"Let us say that when things turn sour, it is not so much that they are doing anything wrong, but that their state of being is not attracting what they want. It is their being, not their doing that has caused that. And they will know what is right to do next when they can shift their being to one of positivity and love and trusting. And they might say, 'How can we do that when all of this is just sitting here, all wrong?' And we say they cannot fix it from where they are, energetically speaking. They are not accepting what is, they are not allowing what is, they need to make peace with where they are—which is disconnected, and in a low vibration. They first need to accept it. They have landed themselves there. And they can shift it in a moment if they just stop fighting against

where they currently are. As soon as they do, everything shifts. The results of shifting their energy vibration then flow. When they are closely aligned and connected, the shift can be almost instantaneous, as the time space continuum collapses like a concertina file, allowing them to manifest effortlessly. And when they shift their vibration and things return to the state of inner peace, listen to what we have to say to them about this. They got themselves into this state in the first place. They attracted these circumstances by way of their vibration. Do not let it go so long next time.

"When two people get caught up in a vortex of negativity, if they are so energetically matched then they can drag each other down or lift each other up. They can allow others to assist with taking themselves out of it.

"Of course they are both determined and stubborn. B has decided the only way out is to fight and work and try and she has forgotten the truth. The truth is that you are all godly and you are all spirit, and you all have the inherent ability to shift yourselves and shift your outcomes. They both know all of this already. This is B's final countdown. She is free from the bounds of most other things, but when she disconnects so completely by forgetting who she is and why she is there, and who we are for her, this is what happens. And this is the lesson to learn. Everything and all else is possible now that she knows this. She can shift her vibration. She knows how. Accept how things are right now. Do something else that will make her feel good, give herself some time and allow the signals to guide her."

After reading this I took a shower to clear my head. Feeling the weight of everything bearing down on me, I felt tears rising. I sank down to the floor, letting the water envelop me. Trying to assimilate the guidance and conjure the light within myself to guide me out, I wondered what on earth was going to happen. Then I heard, *"Get up off your knees. You are not a victim."*

Battlefield

Fresh from the shower, cocooned in my cosy pyjamas, the house was dark and silent. Quietly admitting that I no longer knew what way was up and what way was down, who I was and what I stood for, and whether in fact I was living in "reality" ... I went and sat on the couch with red eyes and tearstained cheeks. It was now 11:30 p.m. Aaron was asleep at the other end of the house. I cried in a whisper to Jed.

"Please help me, I can't do this on my own. I need you. PLEASE HELP ME." Silence.

"I was so dead inside before, and I won't go back. I can't live with that dead feeling inside of me again. That numbness is something I cannot and will not bear." Silence.

"If I won't turn back, then I can only stay here in this place I find myself in, or move forward. If I stay here in this limbo, unsure of what will happen next, I feel like I will dissolve into nothingness. Everything in me is shaken; I have nowhere else to turn. I don't know how to get myself out of this. My confidence is shot, what have I done wrong to get myself into this space? I am questioning everything about my vision, my abilities and myself. Have I gone too far?" Silence.

"I've heard all you told Charlotte. I hear it and I see it but still I feel lost. Please help me." Silence.

I felt forsaken. I closed my eyes and sat quietly hoping for answers. Were they there, just standing by in silence?

I saw a scene in my minds eye. I was standing on a barren stretch of land. Hills flanked me on the left, right and behind, with a vast expanse of yellow sand stretched before me to the horizon. Then it appeared. I was tiny and looming over me was a large masked figure twice my size. I was shadowed under it. It bent down, bringing its face within an inch of mine. I cowered back, turning my face away, not wanting to see the nasty black mask that gave away nothing, but the hot, wet air that steamed from angry flaring nostrils. In my minds eye, I ripped off the mask. Ugliness—decrepit skin, veins, protruding bone, bulging eyes. The ugliness lay not solely in what I saw but in its way of being, malice seeping from every cell of this thing. Heavy, huffing breathing were not the only signs that this thing wanted to explode and obliterate me in the process. The eyes gave it all away. Menacing eyes that pierced through me. An inch from my face now, I shuddered. Afraid to look and afraid not to look, because I knew what it was. It was the embodiment of human fear, my fear. It was here to fight. I had invited it to battle and allowed it to stay. I could now see that full-blown battle with this beast was not getting me anywhere, it was leaving me tired and small. The ugly truth of what I was looking at started to sink in. It's like it was spitting my fears back at me, taunting me: *"Am I good enough? Am I right to do this? Am I able capable of this? Am I to being too risky? Am I asking too much of myself and of the universe?"*

These are the dark places we go, when nobody knows.

The Work

It seemed in my feeling forsaken that night I was mistaken. Spirit moves in mysterious ways to bring insights to us, to allow us to see things in new light.

Charlotte emailed me what further information she got from Jed when she had said to them, *"Please help her to understand how to be with these feelings, and how to move forward into whatever future is best for her."*

Jed replied, *"We are calm and quiet because we know that everything is alright as it is now and that everything will turn out how she desires. We are operating at the level that she has been vibrating. We have not forgotten what she wants, even if she has. She worries that she doesn't know what she wants now but we know, and the universe is still coordinating things in that respect. She does not need to know how it will work out in order for it to work out. We know that this is an uncomfortable place for her to be in. But we are not troubled by that for her, because we also know what is coming for her in terms of how she comes to understand it and how she copes with these feelings. She will look back on this time with a different understanding of herself, of how the universe works, of energy vibration, of what is possible, of where and how people get stuck and how they move out of it, and people will look at what she has done, and where she is now and what is coming and understand when she shares it that none of it came easily but neither was it hard work in the traditional sense that made it possible. For in the end all of the work is energy. Everything starts first in energy and ends in the manifestation of the physical."*

Then Jed had light to shed on my desire to revert back to my tried and true use of common sense. I had been spouting for weeks that perhaps it was time to use my common sense and that I was concerned my common sense had gone out the window. For all my signal following gone by, I had still *always* used an element of logic, of rationale, of good old common sense to manage risk while following the signals. This time I felt I had gone beyond all of that. I had gone fully into signal following, into spiritual understanding and I was allowing spiritual guidance and my intuition to override logic. This is what they said:

"When she talks about common sense, what she is actually referring to is fear. She had tried common sense in the past, but it was fear. She is talking about common sense now, but that is fear too. There is no such thing as common sense. Common sense refers only to limiting yourself to that which you currently know is possible based on the current physical manifestation. It is like looking at what is, and deciding that is all that there is. And there is some comfort in that, there is no trust required when you base your decisions on what you already know. Trust is basing your decisions on what you know is possible, without knowing how it is possible.

"She has done things such as this plenty of times, following signals and listening to her soul self, but always with the security of money. For some people it is not those same things that would scare them. For some people they would give up money, but not give up being close to family, or whatever it is for them that they think they will die without.

"And here is the truth. It is not even money that triggers her, but what money represents to her. Money is her security and independence. She has defined herself by what she has achieved in terms of security. It means, 'I can look after myself.' It means, 'I am at the mercy of no one.' It is, 'I would rather die than have to rely on someone else because they will not help me.' This is the echo of a past life for her.

"She can look now at what it is that security represents to her. She can name these things for herself. She thought she was at the bottom of this belief already. If she allows herself, she will know what the rest of her beliefs are. She knows what Augustus told her about a past life and why she is like this about security, but she has not felt it before. She has surmised what it would be like, she has felt the threat of it, but she has not had to deal with it and face it and feel it. She has done everything in her power throughout her life to not be in this position. She is in the very position she has worked so hard

not to be in and she therefore feels she has done something wrong to be facing this, like it is some kind of punishment. In fact, that she is finally here is testament that she has done everything right. She has done exactly what she was asked to do—she has trusted and acted and worked harder than she has needed to—all in the name of making a difference. And we want her to know that this could have gone no other way. No person can move forward into their dreams dragging around the one thing that will prevent their dreams from happening. It is impossible. It is the sheer brilliance, vision and compelling possibility of the future that she sees, and is making a reality, that has brought this fear now to the light to be faced, accepted and moved past. There is no other way. There was never going to be any other way. One way or another this would have been faced. This is the work. This is her work. This is her greatest fear. It was not being alone, it was not the diving, it was not facing the orphanage, and it was not being confronted with memories of institutionalisation. It is this.

"It is not real, this fear. It is not true these scenarios she makes out. She makes having security, or not, mean something. And she must go there now—she does not need to build her future on top of this fear, she needs to release it. But there is no power in us telling her the list of negative beliefs she has. She must look this fear in the eye for herself, see it for what it is, understand that it is a falsehood, that there is no power in it when she looks at it square on. This is what she must do. This is why she cannot build on top of it, that is why she pulls herself up and falls down again. That she can even have moments of joy or optimism while facing this fear is testament to what life will be like on the other side of it. And it is good. Life on the other side of this fear is good. It is not going backwards. There is a security she will find that is unlike any other she has ever known. There is more security on the other side of this fear than she has ever found in money on this side."

Charlotte asked, *"So what specifically does she need to do?"*

"There is nothing for her to frenetically connect with us about. Instead, she is to find a way to connect with the wonder and joy of life, and of being. Be with those she loves.

Release negative thoughts and feelings in meditation, through conversation with her soul self. Allow it to come out, transforming it into light. Talk to you about security and what it means to her. Talk about what being in control of her security means. Then do the healing; she can move those negative beliefs. She will start to heal and feel the shift in mood. Then start to trust that all will be well again. Then start to notice the inspiration spark. Then start to notice that signals are flowing. Then start to act on the signals again, and feel the connection, and feel inspired, and receive more signals, and act, and feel and receive and act and so on.

"This is entirely about this fear. She should not entertain doubts or worries about any other thing that is happening at this time. There is nothing amiss. Every feeling she has, every doubt, every difficult thing is all stemming from this fear. This is the work."

If you feel thrown around by the washing machine of life, spat out by a rigorous spin cycle, take some time out. Sit still and quiet, eyes closed, and breathe deeply from your diaphragm. Let your body's natural breathing pattern centre you and bring you peace. Know that no amount of trying to work things out will bring you any result when you're feeling frazzled. In fact it just leaves us more caught up in the problem.

The best gift you can give yourself is the space to let your instincts and intuition be heard, rather than giving your worries and fears the platform.

I could have changed my course on my external journey at any time, to do something else, or to do what I had always done, but this wasn't about an external journey. This was *all* about the internal journey. If not before, then now. If not now, then certainly sometime in the future. For soul-level self was calling for this growth, and nothing could stop it from coming to pass.

Isn't it interesting that the most powerful way to overcome challenges is to release our resistance, to not fight against them? For so many of us, instinctively it feels like the one thing we *should* do is to rally against our challenges (an auto pilot response). As the old saying goes though ... what you resist persists.

Themed signals flowed at this time, telling me what I was

made of, what I was capable of and that this experience would not break me ...

"This time, baby, I'll be bulletproof." [50]

"I'm bulletproof, nothing to lose, fire away." [51]

Gifted a New Foundation

You cannot build something strong upon a shaky foundation. Not a person, not a dream, not a vision, not a life. Eventually something will give. A little push, a shove, and that foundation will shudder.

Coming to this point to be broken down presented me with an extraordinarily inspiring opportunity, the opportunity to be rebuilt on a stable foundation. A foundation based in being, not in doing or having. My mind and body had somewhat willingly come to this point in my life, partially dragged kicking and screaming by my soul-level self that had now taken the reigns. The way life goes is no mistake.

What experiences in life have you had or are you having that leave you feeling lost, distressed or confused?

What purpose could it serve and what learning has it given you? Can you see the gift?

Telling It Like It Is

After righting myself on my path forward, Jed would not sugarcoat the remaining messages that I needed to hear on this learning curve.

"Finally you sit still and listen. You listen with an open heart instead of hearing what you want to hear. You had come to us too many times before with loaded questions and wanting to hear answers that fit with your perspective. It is easy to be flowing in life when you hear and see what works for you, isn't it? When things turn to darkness, that is the time when character is tested. You pushed away your guidance and you disconnected yourself from source. You could not see the wood for the trees. You could not understand what you

were missing. You were missing your connection to source and to the guidance that you have in your life. You do not operate on body alone; you are spirit first, body second. You have learnt this the hard way. And from that place you have now come to know the price that is paid when you stray so far from source.

"What brings you greatest joy are not the moments that you deem to be traditional success but the moments of connection to source. What you traditionally call success is merely a result of that connection and the purposeful creation and flowing of your life stemming from it. Freedom lies in the willingness to open yourself up to face what you fear and to see the limiting beliefs in the negative stories you tell yourself."

At the end of all of this, I sat for two full days and did my work. I wrote. I wrote all of this. Living it had been awful. Feeling it had been awful. Writing it was freeing and at the same time it was quite embarrassing to see in black and white how my mind had caused carnage with a series of destructive stories.

Following those two days it all began to flow freely—the energy that is, the life force. By finally learning what I needed to learn, I had broken down the dam that was blocking the river. Signal bombardment followed. Eleven signals in total, so comical I was left with no doubt that I was 100 percent on my best path forward and 100 percent right where I needed to be. For as a matter of fact, there is no other way it can be. You are always exactly where you are meant to be by the very nature of being there.

Four incoming phone calls, two situations I found myself in, one animal totem, two songs recurring, two emails arriving—I could not deny the perfect synchronicity of the letting go and the simultaneous flowing.

Confirmation

As I picked myself up and moved forward, there were times when I thought about the fact that I had self-selected Maui as a place to be for writing, wondering why I had done that. For I'd never been there. It was just a compelling feeling. Where does that feeling come from? Something in me was drawn to go; to the extent I would go to great lengths to make it possible.

Standing in line at the post shop one day, I stared down at the floor daydreaming about my vision, feeling filled with possibility. I looked to the right to see a postage stamp collection on the very bottom shelf of a glass cabinet next to my feet and emblazoned across the collection was ... "MAUI."

Please Take the Path of Least Resistance

Throughout this entire self-created debacle, I had ignored my writing signals. If only I had taken the path of least resistance.

The signals had been blatant, as blatant as spiders could be to get my attention. One in fact had self-sacrificed.

In a ceramic water font at the front door, one morning I had discovered a mammoth spider upside down, dead. My totem for writing was dead in the water. This is what I call a literal signal.

One of those wintry mornings, I had opened the curtains to see that spiders had been busy all night weaving cobwebs from the roof of the house swinging down to the balustrade of the deck, all the way around the perimeter of the house, a glistening carousel covered in dew drops.

On another occasion, walking out of my bedroom, I found myself nose to nose with a little spider. It was dangling from its thread and swaying from the doorframe above.

These three encounters were just the spidery cherry on top of the pay-attention cake. I had been too off-centre to act upon them. Despite my desire at times to cling to the fact that I know better, I must admit that the signals really do know better. They are divine, they are from "out there," they are from within, they are the better part of you helping you to find your way home to your centred soul-level self.

Let the Light Shine

As I found my way back into the flow of life again, my parents came to visit. Seeing the reinvigorated passion in my eyes as I sat glued to my laptop, Dad lowered his newspaper to peer over at me and say, "You know, some things really are worth working hard for."

He was right. What we desire to create in life doesn't

necessarily come easily, but neither is it about the type of hard work that we may anticipate, just as Jed had said. When I looked back at my laptop, I noticed something odd.

The desktop photo of Maui was now covered in rays of light from the top of the screen shedding out across the image.

I found a forum online where others had also experienced this same fault with their computer, but there was (according to this forum) no explanation. It did not matter either way. The light shining on my dream caught my attention.

Chapter 17

Springing Upwards

Get in the Game

When purposefully creating your life it helps to line yourself up as closely as possible to the attainment of your goal or dream, doing all you can within your means, to the point where you do not know how to go any further, and then allow the universal energy to guide you further with signals. This is about getting in the game, participating in co-creating.

When I told you that I called the agent about selling our house, what I really meant to say was that I called the agent and asked him to keep our house in the back of his mind just in case a willing buyer happened to eventuate and then he was welcome to give me a call. This is called showing your intention a teeny, weeny bit without any commitment. In fact, I could have actually listed the house properly without any solid commitment. Buyer interest wasn't forcing me to commit and sell. I didn't realise I was still sitting on the fence. Fence sitting is wishy-washy, resulting in wishy-washy outcomes.

How often do we sit dormant, knowing there is more we could do to create our lives, but we are either too busy, too scared, too tired, too uncertain, too lazy or any combination of these?

At times we may know exactly what we want, but we may nevertheless sit waiting for divine intervention to confirm it is right before doing what makes us happy or, worse, waiting for it to be delivered to us on a silver platter before taking any action to create it.

What if you took action right now towards creating your goal or dream and it worked? What if it eventuated in joyous outcomes for you?

Still unsure whether to take action? Still wanting confirmation it's the *right* thing to do? In relation to your goal or dream, do you want me to tell you about a signal that you can recognise right now, in this very second, as you read these lines? Are you ready?

When you think about what you want in your life, does it make you happy? Close your eyes and visualise that goal or dream as being your reality. Can you feel the possibility? Do you feel the happiness?

That happy feeling is your heart singing. Your heart singing is your soul-level self guiding you in a direction that serves you well. Your soul-level self is your deepest level of connection to the universal energy, to source, to God, whatever you wish to call it. Therefore that feeling within you *is* a signal!

When we talk about signals, and following signals, they are indicators to guide, confirm, support and intervene on our path. They don't *tell* us what to do, they do not dictate right from wrong. Life isn't about waiting for something to happen to us. There is no right or wrong path. We get in the game and show our intention. We line ourselves up as closely as possible to the goal or dream that we are creating, and signals are part and parcel of flowing in the river of life. They respond beneficially when we get in the river. They are part of the unfolding and they respond to how we show up in our lives.

As co-creators of our reality, we were gifted the wonder of free will and personal accountability. To not exercise your free will and personal accountability is the equivalent of rolling over on your back with all fours up in the air and playing dead.

Is there any area of your life where you have rolled over?
What might happen if you flip back over, stand up and jump in the river?

As time crept on, the "sell your house" signal remained front and centre in my mind. I challenged myself whether I had really taken purposeful action in relation to the signal and then cunningly convinced myself I had.

I attempted to ignore the fact I was inadvertently humming these song lyrics: "What are you waiting for?" [52]

Chatting to Charlotte, she called me out on my fence sitting behaviour. "So your visualising is awesome B, but you seem to be holding back a bit on the action. You know if you really want to follow that signal and sell your house, you could help the universe out a bit and actually list it for sale. On that note, what else are doing to get ready to leave for Maui? Where are you going to put all your furniture when the house does sell? What are you going to do with Cash? Get in the game girl. Prepare for what you are envisioning. If you're serious about this and you believe in the vision and you believe in yourself, then start acting like it!" Two butterflies were dancing around each other outside the window as I listened to Charlotte talk.

I knew a more purposeful action would have been to actually list the house for sale. That's obvious. I was only making it harder for the universe to assist me by putting boundaries around this possible path forward. But listing the house made it all real. Listing the house was to me the most extreme example of my signal following to date.

I was afraid as well; of putting myself out there by listing our house, in case it didn't sell. I was afraid of what people might say if I set a dream and the house didn't sell and somehow we didn't have any answer to how to get to Hawaii and I looked like a failure.

Flies irritated the heck out of me while I continued to write each day, noisily buzzing around the room where I was writing. I noticed there were no flies anywhere else in the house. I looked online for the meaning of the fly totem. It symbolises both perseverance and letting go of ego, "You are giving away passions, dreams, ideas and yourself because you are caring about what others might think or say too much." [53]

It resonated in relation to my situation. My ego didn't want people to know we were selling our house to realise a dream. My ego didn't want people to know if it didn't work out. My ego was afraid of being called "less than." Not a single person in my life would have said those things, they were all beyond supportive, loving and encouraging with complete authenticity. Somehow I have been gifted with extraordinary people in my life.

I had nothing to lose and everything to gain. Tired of being a baby about it, I realised it was *finally* time to start coaching myself. So I stepped up to the batter's plate and called to the pitcher to bring it on.

I contacted every storage unit provider I could find to get quotes and availability confirmed for our move. I placed our passports on the office desk. We submitted our travel visa applications for the United States and made plans to check flights deals from New Zealand to Hawaii every day. We registered with vacation rental companies in Maui to find suitable accommodation and submitted enquiries with every condo and unit for sublet that looked suitable for our needs.

A business contact in New Zealand suggested we make lunch plans for a few weeks out, but I declined and told them I suspected I would be in Hawaii by then.

And so I went on, showing intention and lining myself up in every way possible for what I was creating.

Energy Responds

I did not call the real estate agent to list our house officially. Instead, within twenty-four hours of this renewed level of committed purposeful action, I received an email from the agent asking if we would consider formally listing the property. They were in need of new listings. They later smiled with wide open eyes when I asked if they could please have it sold within three weeks, because I wanted to be in Hawaii approximately two weeks after that. I figured there was no point in holding back on what I really wanted.

The fact that the local market at the time was dictating an average of three months to sell a house, not three weeks, and the fact that there were some additional limiting factors regarding where our house sat in the current market, I decided not to focus on. Focusing on those statistical, factual distractions would not do me any good in creating this dream. I did not want my beliefs, thoughts, feelings and actions hijacked by external stimuli that would limit possibility.

Instead I became grateful for the buyer who would love the house like we had. I imagined how much they would enjoy rows of ripe bananas and baskets full of nectarines and peaches from the garden. I imagined them having fun on the deck in the sun and wandering to the beach down the road for an ice cream and a swim.

Chatting to Marisa again on Skype, who didn't even flinch at the fact I was listing my house for sale based on signals, I said, "I guess if this is the most free flowing, beneficial way for me to move forward, then the house will sell. I know those 'sell your house' incidents were signals. I know it in my heart."

"Well B, it would not happen if it weren't the best outcome for you. You would not be led in a direction that doesn't serve you well in some way for your growth. We don't always know how or why but life always gives us exactly what we need for our soul path at that moment. Get ready, because if the house sells, you know that's your green light."

From being in action, I could feel myself rising. When you get in the game, the universe responds. After another fruitful day of writing, sitting within my self-induced high, I got offered a short contract of coaching/training work for my former employer, timing in perfectly with my goal date to go to Hawaii; a gift of reconnection with friends and a welcome deposit of extra income.

Being back there immediately allowed me to realise that I absolutely adore supporting and coaching people. It lights a fire within me like nothing else. Seeing faces light up and watching people flourish is the greatest gift to receive in response to giving. Walking away at the end of that short contract, I knew that the hiatus was nearly over. The hiatus had served a purpose, taking me to places that forced me to look at myself in daring new ways.

When it rains it pours. Offers of other contract work arrived. Requests to assist. What it told me was this ...

There are opportunities galore in life. You simply have to choose the path you want and follow it. I had been in limbo, no longer the woman I was, and not fully the woman I knew I was here to be. When in limbo the natural reaction is to want to jump all the way forward or all the way back, where there is clarity. I wasn't interested in jumping back, and despite my desire to jump all the way forward I knew I had to first traverse the path to get there. The journey was the point, not the destination.

The incoming opportunities told me that there would always be options, there would always be provision and it was all my choice as to which direction I went in. So I followed my heart, again, and moved forward—closer to clarity in the direction that compelled me.

All of this made me wonder: *If I had just listened to Jed,*

followed my signals and done what was good for me, would
my experience of the preceding months have been different?

There was no point in looking back and I regretted none of it. Everything we experience in life is a gift for evolution. I was a clearer, freer and improved version of myself for experiencing all of that firsthand and for having my weaknesses exposed. It is never a mistake how things turn out. The divine universal energy doesn't make mistakes. It is godliness weaving in perfection.

> ***How can we ever strengthen our weaknesses***
> ***if we never meet them?***

If I ever encountered others stuck in the wasteland I had been in, facing their beast of fear, I would not pity them at all because I would know something they would not be able to see yet. I would know that their being stuck was going to aid them immensely through what they would learn from it. I would simply say to them, "I know, it's rough … " while lovingly reaching out a hand to pull them up and point them towards the way out.

Intersection on a Bridge

One night when I was drifting in Glide Time, I heard: "Sail on silver girl, sail on by. Your time has come to shine, all your dreams are on their way … like a bridge over troubled water, I will ease your mind." [54]

Aside from the obvious bright message these lyrics offered, we had sung this song at Sarah's wake. It was a song that meant a lot to me. *Perhaps Sarah is supporting me?*

It wasn't until a week later that I had a true "pinch me" moment in relation to the synchronicity of energy weaving in unexplainable ways. The unmistakable energetic genius is there if you pay attention.

As I walked across a bridge towards the waterfront on my way to the ferry, I was thinking about my desire to have my writing be a positive contribution to others. The traffic was thick as trucks and buses slowly grunted past me, nose to tail.

Halfway across the bridge, midthought, my phone beeped to announce a new email. As I read the opening, I stopped walking, stood still and with a gaping open mouth I almost cried.

A seventy-nine-year-old woman from the United States named Joanna, a complete stranger to me, had emailed to tell me that *Pinch Me* had flipped a switch inside her. It had come into her path at just the right time, she explained. She was excited to share with me that she recognised her first signal. What followed was the background of what was happening in her life at the time, the challenges and the dreams she had for herself.

She then told me that her first signal was a song that came to her, reaching out to support her: "Sail on silver girl, sail on by, your time has come to shine, all your dreams are on their way." [55]

Intersecting signals. Bringing her to me, me to her, support to her, encouragement to me, perfectly woven on so many levels.

There is no greater gift to give than to reach out to another, for how it touches the heart of another we can never measure or truly know for ourselves.

This is the never-ending cycle of contribution that goes around and around. Be a part of it and benefit from the flow.

Bring Down the Walls

Before these eventful escapades, I would have said: *What walls? I don't have walls.*

Ah ha, but of course I did! That old fierce need for robust security and independence had offered me surface-level benefits, but it had also long been holding at bay all the gifts of life that can flow to you when you open yourself to them.

I had wanted life to look a certain way. I wanted to live in my newly discovered joyful river of life, but my ego was secretly trying to design it so that I could make that river just as independent and secure as my life had always been where nothing could touch me, nothing could break me and nothing would tarnish the fortress I was creating.

Augustus had pointed out my desire to avoid mess, to remain in control. But I had not fully realised that when you build up massive fortress walls to keep out the mess, guess what? You also keep out the gifts.

Whether we build up those walls to keep out mess or to hide what lies within, the walls limit us.

> ***Do you have walls?***
> ***What caused you to put up those walls?***
> ***How high are they?***
> ***What are they hiding?***
> ***What do they keep you from seeing and receiving?***
> ***Are you ready to take them down?***

Having been put under the microscope through this hiatus, I realised that I actually felt quite impotent if I needed other people to help me. That is why I had always strived to be self-contained. Staunch independence had limited my experience of life and the joy that comes from collaboration.

Finally, I was in a situation where I could see this fully and I was invited to allow others to give to me and to support me on my journey. This was a lesson in receiving. One of my unofficial mentors gifted me a ticket to an event, which ended up unlocking insights for me that greatly leveraged me forward on my internal journey. My sister Ella gave me a gift during the cave days at home some months earlier, four bottles of wine and two bottles of champagne. She told me that if one must follow one's dreams and go into caveman isolation while doing so, one must at least have excellent Sauvignon within the cave. I certainly could not disagree.

A Gift of a Different Kind

The official "For Sale" sign had literally just been pegged on the front lawn when the agent called. I'm not sure who was more surprised, the agent or us. Against all the statistics, facts and market conditions, he announced, "We've got an offer. They're serious buyers and it's a clean offer at the asking price."

The message rose up from my memory: *When the offer comes, do not quibble over dollars and cents.*

So rather than do what I usually would have done, negotiate, I had faith that the river in which these wonderful people swam had intersected with mine, aligned in vibration to our goal/dream in order that they could have their goal/dream of this house. We had asked, they had responded and so we received with gratitude.

The contract was signed and the deal was complete one day before my three-week sale goal.

Travelling on the bus in the city, I marvelled at the realisation that the less you focus on *how* to live your goals and dreams, the easier you make it for the universe to deliver a myriad of paths forward and the easier it is for you to recognise them. The key was the *willingness* to follow those signals when they arose, for I could have said no to selling the house. I could have said no to the offer when it came. As passengers off-loaded from the bus, I glanced out the window to see "MAUI" plastered on a building advertisement.

Despite my outrageous desire to fly Cash to Hawaii with us for three months, here is one instance when I did allow logic to lead over heart. I was lying on the floor with my baby as Aaron read out the list of preparatory veterinarian visits, injections, drugs and tests that Cash would be put through in the thirty days prior to reentering New Zealand, and the following days in quarantine after reentry. Despite the exorbitant cost of flying forty-five kilograms of dog around the world (there were moments I wished I had a Chihuahua), looking at Cashy lying there next to me I couldn't quite bring myself to put him through it (maybe my heart was leading?). It was at this time that Cash received an invitation, for a holiday of his own, at my parents. Living rurally, surrounded by native bush on the water's edge, Cash was going to love it there. I hoped he would notice no difference and I vowed to Skype him so he didn't think he'd been abandoned. Having whispered into his ear frequently since our return from Thailand, "I will never leave you again," I lifted one of his big brown floppy ears, lent down and whispered, "Forgive me."

As he prepared to go to a temporary home, I affectionately named him Community Cash—spreading his doggy love and joy amongst many. Just as Kelly and Brent fell in love with him during our Thailand sabbatical, I wondered how I would pry him away from my parents after Hawaii.

Know What You Love & Who You Are

One final arrangement ... we were now officially homeless, so where would we be living in Maui? Aaron had been scouring accommodation sites online. For some reason, humorously, I felt like I should be somewhere remote in the jungle amidst nature and silence in order to write the book. That was potentially going to be very isolating given we would have no car, thus no access to amenities, not to mention contact with other human beings. Then I had remembered something the little old lady Palm Reader in Bangkok had said to me.

It was nearing the end of the hour-long session. It had been compelling and quite entertaining. Part of me had secretly wanted her to mention my reason for being in Thailand, to somehow allude to my newfound passion for writing, my discovery of energy healing and where this signals adventure was leading. She finished the notes she was making and leaned back slightly in her seat. I would have assumed the reading was finished, except for the fact she continued to grip my palm, pulling my arm outstretched. She cocked her head sideways as she stared at my hand, then looked up and locked eyes with me.

"Writing," she announced.

Hoorah! I sparked inside. *I knew it. Writing is my thing.* Leaning forward with eager anticipation of what joys she was about to share ...

"You no natural writer" she stated as a matter of fact.

Bah! I wanted to close my ears; this is not what you want to hear when you're in the middle of writing a book. Then she continued, "You feel bad, you write bad. You feel good, you write good. Remember."

Based on this "feel good, write good" philosophy, I considered where the best place to reside in Maui might be to encourage my ultimate feel good factor.

Despite all that I had experienced and delved into on this adventure in my life spiritually, mentally and physically, I still knew myself well enough to know that of my own choosing:

I don't love being isolated.

I don't love being alone *all* the time.

I don't love meditating 24/7 on a raised platform in the jungle with complete silence like a serene yogi.

I do love the beach.

I do love sunbathing.

I do love cocktails.

So I pictured Aaron and I, with my merry band of spirit guides, lying in the sun, on a beach, cocktail in one hand, laptop on knee, tap tap tapping away, writing up a storm of words flowing from my good feeling space.

It was slim pickings for what we wanted within our budget. When we found a homely little condo a stone's throw from a relatively private stretch of white sand beach, with a swimming pool and Jacuzzi, near a yoga studio and shops, I hoped by some miracle we could afford it. Please ...

Funny enough, the owner was an author, coach and healer. I'm not kidding. If that weren't odd enough, there was another weird coincidence ...

Aaron had been bombarded with references to Bali, Indonesia for several weeks. Everywhere he turned there were references to Bali. From books, movies, conversations, emails and comments online, to TV and radio, and then a dream. He dreamed he had two empty Coke bottles in his hands and he was putting them up to his eyes and looking through them. That was the sum total of the dream.

The following day he was channel surfing and saw a documentary about a tribe of water dwelling people in Southeast Asia and their traditional fishing techniques. The old man explained through a translator, as he placed homemade swimming goggles up to his eyes, that they used the bottom of Coke bottles to make an apparatus that allowed them to see under water when spear fishing. The program was filmed in Indonesia.

The owner of the Maui condo had connections to Balinese healing. Upon request, he then agreed to discount his condo rental to fit our budget. Minds reeling about the possible interconnectedness of all of this, we gratefully took this opportunity and began packing our house for departure.

I joked to my friend Toby that I was now jobless and homeless. I love to bring humour to any situation where possible and I found it comedic that I could say this with truth. I declared, "But this is as far as it goes. I'm not up for letting go of anything else for any spiritual path, no matter how enlightening it may be. God help me if I'm signalled to let go of my possessions. I refuse to be jobless, homeless and possession-less. Don't make me do it!'"

Offload What You Don't Need

A dream that followed was not amusing. I was rushing to catch a train. I didn't know where it was going, but what I did know was that I really had to get on it and I really wanted to be on it. Just as I went to jump on the train, I realised I had left my bag behind. Crisis. *I can't get on the train without my things. I need my things!* I could have gotten on that train without the bag and made it to my destination, but in my dream I chose to turn away and go back to get my things, missing the train.

> *Our dreams can offer us a reflection of what is really going on. In case you're asleep when you're awake, you can rely on being awake when you're asleep.*
>
> *Pay attention to the symbology of your dreams.*

When I awoke, I remembered the story that Debbie, a lady I met at a dinner party years ago, had told me before I went to Thailand. It was a story about a train. You might remember the story from *Pinch Me*. It's a good one, so I relay it here again:

"The train is going to come through. Be ready when it comes. You have two choices. Get ready, grab that train, and jump on it. Or, you can watch it go by. If you watch it go by, you will always wonder what would have happened and you'll have regrets. What's the worst thing that can happen if you jump on the train?"

When you show up in your life with the intention of being your fully expressed self, being present and willing to allow the universal energy to flow through you, you truly are allowing yourself to unfold into your greatness. Clinging to "things" with attachment, be those actual physical things or negative ways of being, blocks the unfolding.

When life calls you to act, please act. If we all had enough faith to jump on the train, knowing it would take us to good places, places where we wouldn't need to worry about the baggage we left behind, life would be so much simpler.

I could not be more grateful for the Divine Timing of our house selling, for the showing of opportunities, influxes of income, and for the experience of the adventure that lay ahead.

Not long before leaving for Maui, as I reached out to grab an apple from the fruit bowl at home, a word came into my head like a lightning bolt cutting through a murky mist of thoughts: "*Providence.*"

My first reaction was to think of the TV program *Providence*. My second thought was the location Providence in the United States.

Then I googled the meaning of providence and it was the tale of the Divine's part to play in the physical: "God's intervention in the world ... A distinction is usually made between 'general providence,' which refers to God's continuous upholding the existence and natural order of the Universe, and 'special providence,' which refers to God's extraordinary intervention in the life of people." [56]

Why don't we always get what we want when we want it? The answer is the truth about manifesting that many of us don't want to hear. It goes like this ...

If you have a great vision for your life, sometimes you just can't go there while dragging a whole lot of useless baggage with you. So life presents you with opportunities, disguised as crappy problems, in order for you to recognise this baggage that you're carrying, in order that you have the opportunity to offload it. Life gives us the chance to see the train doors wide open, to turn around and see the bags behind us, and to chose which direction we want to go in.

Cling on? Or let go? The choice is yours. What looks prettier for the vision of the life you desire—you painted into the picture carrying a sack of crap on your shoulders, or ... wait for it ... you painted into the picture, sans crap.

Remember when you get dealt a hand that looks to be the opposite of what you are manifesting to have in your life, the hand you were dealt is no mistake and it is sometimes the very means by which you will achieve all that you desire, if only you will see the crap for the gift that it is.

Demanding to Instantly Close the Gap

The frustration we experience when we don't get what we want when we want it is partly magnified due to living in an age of instant gratification.

The predominance of promises for instantaneous results in our society has gone beyond a joke. You want entertainment, you press a button. You want food, you dial in. You want a six-pack of abs, you order the two-minute ab machine.

The point is—when we want a new this or that, we want it (and often times get it) instantly. We want our goal or dream as our reality; we want to create it instantly. We discover this phenomenon of signals, and we want them instantly. We get stuck in our journey, and we want guidance instantly.

It just doesn't work that way. Your soul is not seeking instant gratification—there is no room for growth in that. No matter how much instant gratification we get, it will never be enough. Remember the "need vs. want" distinction ... what our soul needs and what our mind/body wants are two very different things. This life you are experiencing is not a sprint race and there are no quick fixes. It's a journey and signals are *one* magical aspect of that journey, if you awaken to them. But never forget that signals are a gift from the universe when the universe knows you need them, from a higher perspective that you cannot see or understand with the thinking mind. As soon as you attempt to control that, or make demands of it, you are setting yourself up for inevitable frustration and disappointment.

When we don't get what we want when we want it, it's all too easy to assume that manifesting in general doesn't work. Then we end up blaming the particular process of manifesting that we have subscribed to, trying another and another and another in the hopes that someone will eventually tell us the secret.

The "not working" and the physical or metaphorical distance between yourself and what you desire is just life calling out to you to learn how to close the gap. Your soul came to evolve and it would defy the very point of your soul intention if you didn't have the opportunity to close the gap.

This will sound simple, but please really allow this to resonate for a moment:

> ### *The gap exists between what you think you are and who really you are.*

The journey of life allows us to discover *how* we create reality, to discover the mechanics of how our world really works, to unblock ourselves, and in doing so bring about (by mirror reflection) all that we desire externally. The distance that you experience between what "is" and what you want, is a gift that calls you home to your soul-level self. Meeting and living in alignment with soul-level self is closing the gap.

Meet Your True Self

Jed helped me to understand a signal song that said, "I've been waiting for a girl like you to come into my life ... only in dreams could it be this way." [57]

They said, *"Your soul self has been waiting for this version of yourself to turn up in your life, waiting for a girl like you to come out. She has come out now and now that she is here she can live the life that was before only a dream. That life stems from within you. The words say, "only in dreams could it be this way" because as you allow yourself to unfold and become the full expression of who you came here to be, in that space your dreams morph into your physical environment. Joy to you, joy for you and share that joy limitlessly."*

What Really Defines Your Life?

Packing up to leave, I did not find it the least bit amusing when it appeared that the storage unit would be too small to fit all our things. "Pack that storage unit like a Lego kit. I'm sure it will all fit!" And it did, just. With inches to spare, I peered into the dark, crammed twenty by ten foot space stacked from floor to ceiling with everything that defined our physical life.

In those last hours preparing to leave the island, I pulled the roller door closed on the unit, clicked the lock, and as I turned to walk away I distinctly remember realising something. For the first time in my entire adult life I now knew firsthand that your life is not what you do or what you have. The career, the house and everything in that storage unit had felt like my life. But of course they were not my life. It was not until I literally stood without any of it that I finally saw where meaning did not lie, and instead saw the space where true meaning existed.

And, so, there no longer stood anything between me and ...

Chapter 18

Valley Isle

Coconut bra—check.
Hula skirt—check.
Frangipani hairclip—check.
50+ SPF sunscreen for very white skin—check.
Laptop—check.
Pile of signal notebooks—check.
Open heart and mind—check.
Okay, not all truth. I actually forgot the hairclip.

Aloha

It was a bright clear morning as the plane descended for landing. At first there seemed little mystery as to what to expect on the ground, for not a single cloud had been in sight to hide the view as we approached the island. Lush sugarcane fields lay like carpet across a plateau between the west mountain and the imposing volcano—Haleakala, House of the Sun.

As tyres touched searing tarmac, a deep breath signified the awe inspiring sense again that turning your dreams into reality is entirely possible.

When I first stepped onto the land that had drawn me over four thousand miles from home, I asked Maui to help me be all that I could be and I asked it to support me in my writing.

Then the good time games began. I immediately nicknamed this blessed place Awesometown.

In Awesometown everyone is happy. Who wouldn't be? Tropical blooms wafting their fragrance, coconut trees lining golden sand stretching over miles of coastline, crystal waters rippled by cool trade winds flowing, and hot days that wrap around you like a warm loving hug from the moment you rise until the moment you drift back to sleep. The Valley Isle that is magical Maui.

Disorientation Week

Our first week in Awesometown involved orientation to the land where everything is back to front. Of course to all of our wonderful American friends, everything is correctly front to back. In New Zealand, however, light switches go from up to down, bus doors are on the left-hand side, car steering wheels are on the right-hand side and we drive on the left-hand side of the road.

After a few times dancing around the car in circles, what do you think happened when two little Kiwis were driving along in their trusty 2004 Nissan rental car, deeply immersed in conversation about the excitement of their adventure?

One Kiwi shrieks, "What the BLEEP!" while the other swerves to avoid a head-on collision with two oncoming pickup trucks. This is called not paying attention to driving on the correct side of the road. This, of course, only happens once, because that's enough to shock you into second by second full attentiveness to remain on the right side of the centre line. It's hard to break an ingrained habit. Little life lesson in there ... when you've been doing something your whole life it takes more than one day to retrain your brain to do it the exact opposite way.

The beauty of Awesometown is that everyone is welcoming and full of aloha. The mere fact that the pickup trucks didn't even toot their horns angrily at us was testament to this. They just smiled and kept driving.

We were booked into Casita Paradiso Condo, so named by me, for one month only, as it was not available beyond that. Therefore, soon after arriving we took purposeful action to identify something suitably wonderful for the rest of our stay. I really wanted to stay in this particular complex; it was peacefully quiet for writing, nestled amongst bougainvilleas, hibiscus and trees which formed an umbrella over expansive green lawn. The only noise came from the zebra doves that also loved Casita Paradiso Condo as much as I did. Nothing not to love really. Alas, the retail price of staying was beyond our budget. We had been gifted this month due to the owner generously dropping his price to fit our budget. What if, though, by some miracle, we could stay? What if another unit in the complex was free and was equally as obliging?

We discovered there was another unit available; it was approximately thirty feet away from the unit we were in but the price was as immovable as the volcano that created the dramatic backdrop for this development.

Aaron could have stood in one door, I could have stood in the other and moving would have involved nothing more than throwing the bags of clothes between us. I looked at that empty unit each morning while eating breakfast, thinking: *It's empty. What a waste. That patio is just begging me to sit on it and write!*

It just so happened that the universe was busy conspiring in our favour. When we went to sign up for our three-month membership to the local yoga classes, there was a limited time special offer of a three-month membership for the price of one month. This budgetary gift of goodness from the universe was the exact amount we needed in order to afford the unit next door. This was an aloha accommodation miracle.

I must give kudos to a random array of other equally spectacular Maui moments that evoked joy during Disorientation Week and all the weeks beyond.

These included hikes into lush rainforest riddled with guava growing wild, being massaged by pounding waterfalls, biking through arid volcanic terrain doing it's best to imitate an alien planet, snorkelling with creatures that are a living testament to the breathtaking capacity of mother nature, unwinding in Jacuzzi bubbles before bedtime, days interspersed with beach walks, sunbathing while sipping lemon iced tea, and savouring mouth watering ensembles of papaya, passionfruit and lime, and last but not least ...

Turtle Alert

TA would become the new call sign, which Aaron would soon find amusing and also a little boring after about the hundredth time. For my love of turtles is only surpassed by my love of dolphins. Standing on the beach, a few feet into the lagoon I saw a little head pop up out of the water and look right at me, like a periscope peering out only to quietly recede.

It took all my might not to jump in and swim after it in my clothes!

So would commence a three-month odyssey that I would forthwith refer to as Turtle Stalking. This pastime embodied my adoration for these green-shelled gems. By stalking, I mean constantly looking for them at any given moment and adoring being in their vicinity in an ecologically friendly, marine protected, nonhazardous, keeping my distance, don't touch the turtle, harmless stalker kind of way.

Aaron would smile, saying nothing, as I would call, "TA!" and stand on the water's edge with my hands clasped under my chin, swaying up on tippee toes, pointing into the water at the turtles that needed no pointing out yet I felt it necessary to do so all the same.

I will never forget how beautiful it was one day to have two gentle giants connect, their flippers touching momentarily, as I floated above them. If it weren't for the fact I had a snorkel in my mouth, unable to talk underwater, I would have been outwardly exclaiming every gratitude for witnessing that moment.

Energetic Pull

Taking up residence in one of the most remote archipelago in the world, led me to wonder what it was that made this place such a special one. *Why do people flock here, besides the obvious reasons?*

A client emailed me to see if we had arrived safely and to tell me that she had read on an email that day that Hawaii was renowned for being a centre of energy for "spiritual opening and special creation." Her email was strangely coincidental, as Aaron and I had been discussing this very matter during our multi-lane, death defying rental car jaunt. It would be much later during our stay that I would really experience this unique energy. It would indeed prove to support spiritual opening and special creation.

In the interim, many nights were spent mesmerised by nature. With the slopes of Haleakala in the background, ocean endlessly searching outward for a horizon, and everything in between swaying sleepily in the breeze, day after day brought evening after evening of heartbreakingly beautiful sunsets commanding the entire sky with hues of orange and pink. Melt into nothingness moments, where from nothingness springs a deep gratitude for life.

After absorbing my new surroundings, the first communication with Jed in Maui had gone like this:

"Do you want to know why you came here? Why you came here at this very time? You came here to be connected to an energy centre that resonates strongly with you. You were born into New Zealand for the same reason. The energy alignment helps to reawaken you to where you came from and why you came. This is what this time is about. Reconnect to the power of your source, to soul self that is free of any of the fears that you have held in mind and body. There is nothing more that you need to know about this other than you are here for a good reason and there is nothing to work out or look for. It will all become clear to you as you settle in. Here is where you will do well for this time and here is where you are belonging at present. Here is where you are cherished in the energy, let your energy radiate, it will be stronger here than anywhere else at this time. You are connected into lines of energy that you have not before experienced; yet at some level you will have moments of familiar recognition. Adjust your polarity."

I had something to say about all of this, *"That is beautiful and amazing and I'm so grateful. Though I can't help but say that I chose to come here. I came here because it appealed to me logically. I picked this place with my mind. Nothing drew me here in particular. It's not like I heard 'Hawaii' in the middle of the night."*

What Jed said next I share with you because it applies to you as it does to me.

"Yes, that is what you think. But why do you think it appealed to you in the first place? Where does the appeal come from? Most people would just come for a holiday; you came here for months to write. You could have gone anywhere in the world, many wonderful places, but you did not go anywhere; you came here. If there is something for you to know, some place to benefit you, the way it works is that you will find your way there if you awaken. You awakened and now you are here. Why do you distrust the system of energy flow, when you have experienced it so often

first hand? There is no better place for you to be at this stage, in belonging and in connection with the land and the energy that will serve you best for your coming alive in this next phase of your journey.

Shed shackles.

Drop pretence.

Let go of worry.

Release concern.

Say hello to yourself.

Welcome and usher in a new age of your life.

Welcome it with open arms.

Give birth to the next self you create, the fullest level of self, let it shine and blossom.

Let it be.

Move on.

Rise up.

Shadow no more.

Release it all.

Allow it all.

Remember where you came from.

Remember why you came.

Allow us to show you.

Forever trust in the source you are from and part of.

Aaron too, he is here for a good reason, for his own alignment and his own guides are with him to show him the way if he will listen.

Nothing to fear.

Nothing to lose.

Nothing to hold back.

Nowhere to go to.

Nothing to ask for.

Only allowing to receive.

Being true to self.

Flow with it.

Go with it.

Allow yourself to be.

"Let the writing come out. Do not underestimate that through the sharing of a message, as dark as it may have been at times, others can benefit in ways that they could not have done without that message. Every soul has a different message to share in new and different ways. It is designed

that way to reach all people, to reach all types, to reach people at different places and stages in their journeys. Energy resonates differently with each. Some will hear you. Others will not. You must be that one for those some. Others will be that one for others. Others have been that one for you. You all have messages to share, each and every one of you, and you all have messages to hear.

"There is no other way, this is the work you must do and from it will come great fulfilment of promise, for that is how it works when you flow in alignment with soul intention and live in the released state—released of all tension and released of all blocks. That releasing has prepared you to be here now at this time, and this will prepare you for the next phase, and on it goes. Life flows as one long journey, each step synchronistically leading to the next, and a wonderful weaving of all things, perceived good or bad, that will aid you in achieving what your soul came here for."

This is the unfolding. This is the way of the life force. You do not need to hear words in the dark of night, or have some epiphany of sorts in order to live in alignment with your soul intention. Simply ask yourself:

What do I feel compelled to be, do or have?
Where do I feel compelled to dwell on
my internal or external journey?

What am I ignoring/hiding from that reinforces the
gap between what I think am and who I really am?

You hold the answers to your own questions. We are sometimes afraid to own our power and vitality as our souls intended us to. We mute ourselves or we fall victim to believing that life has muted us. Yet, within you right now you have every talent, every capability, every knowing that you will ever need to live your soul intention fully. That is the perfection of life; you came with all that you needed. It is simply a case of allowing it to unfold.

You might ask, "How do I allow it?"

You allow it by honouring what you *feel* to be right. You

allow it by being courageous enough to acknowledge your blocks and shedding light on them to dissolve them. You allow it by having conversations with deeper meaning, which give rise to such insights in the first place. You allow it by showing up in your life with the *intention* to live the life your soul chose, without even needing to know what that is. You allow it by letting the universal energy, the life force, flow through you unhindered. You allow it by letting yourself unfold before your own eyes as the miracle that you are. You allow yourself to be surprised.

The Marriage of Free Will & Soul Intention

Sitting on the patio one morning, I asked Jed to help me understand the beautiful message that Augustus had shared with me. Jed's response would in turn shed light on my curiosity about free will to create exactly the life we want, versus soul intention with a leaning toward particular life paths and experiences.

"Jed, Augustus told me that 'your life is your message to the world and when you finish your message you go home.' Can you talk to me about this?"

"Being who you are is a message in and of itself. Being a full expression of who you are is a gift to all, it is a gift to humanity, it is a gift to the whole and that is enough. There comes an intersecting conclusion point, a merging between learning and contribution, divinely conceived and not humanly understood. It is sometimes long coming and sometimes not. We say that when your message is complete you have lived in a way that your learning and your contribution have joined together to complete the soul path in this lifetime, and then you leave. And your leaving in and of itself is part of your message, as it creates openings in which other souls then move forth in understanding, with their learning and their contribution. Your soul intends this.

"What you choose to do to share your message with the world during a lifetime is what you call free will. In exercising your free will, there exists one critical choice—that of listening to your heart singing or not.

"What makes your heart sing is no mistake. Your heart singing is your soul communicating with you in a way you

can understand at a mind and body level. *Honour your heart song and you honour your soul and its intention. In doing so you honour the whole and make a contribution simply by being who you truly are.*

"*A spark of divinity, a soul, is who you are. Soul intention is why you are here. Free will is how you dance the dance. You can use your free will to follow your heart song and the divine guidance that supports your highest soul path through this lifetime. This is free will married hand in hand with soul intention. Or, you can use your free will to ignore the call from within and the guidance. You can choose to live within an illusion of form-based physical reality only.*

"*You make choices and you live your days out in ways that are in alignment with those choices.*"

Chapter 19

Support Everywhere You Turn

Before leaving New Zealand I asked Aaron to promise me something—that he would always remind me of the importance of being my true self and of speaking my truth throughout my lifetime. If I ever looked like my confidence was lagging, I wanted to be reminded.

I believe it is vitally important that we all reach out to those we love and trust to ask for help when we need it. Thriving in life is not a solitary achievement. We are wired for connection at a soul level, and that connection is strengthened through the giving and receiving of love and support.

As it would pan out, my time in Maui would be littered with plenty of reminders about speaking my truth, in whatever form of expression that might take.

Lying on the bed reading one evening, Aaron turned to me and said, "Bingo. You've got to listen to this."

In the condo he had found a book about healing by Dr Zhi Gang Sha. Aaron had been absorbed in the book for days.

He announced, "Negative memories are another type of soul blockage ... They have different sources." [58]

It went on to provide examples, such as people who may have been in service to others in previous lives, including healers, who suffered for those acts.

Aaron continued reading, "You may have been punished or even put to death. Your soul possesses all of the wisdom you have gained in your many lifetimes. It can also retain all of the powerful negative memories. In this lifetime ... [it] may cause you to have great fear and resistance toward accepting your abilities—as a healer ... or as someone who serves others. It may cause you to lack confidence." [59]

Being in Maui, in that condo, reading that book was no mistake. I asked Jed for their input on the matter.

"You've certainly carried some serious beliefs that hinder

you in relation to speaking your truth, a variety of internal dialogue going on that doesn't serve you and you voice it over and over again, and that further embeds the beliefs within yourself. You feed it. Now is the time to release all that nonsense and to guide yourself to a higher place perspective. There is nothing to fear in aligning with your soul intention and you have been creating these negative beliefs your entire life, affirming them, owning them as though you bought them like a toy in a shop. You got them from the collective fear, it's the thing to do to say that you are afraid of public speaking, and it's not true for you. You are not. You are afraid when you have to share and say things that mean nothing to you, but when you talk of your truth and your experiences you flow torrentially like a river ... sharing from your heart with honesty is all you need do and that is all that people will hear. Be clear of these old beliefs now ... You will not be perfect at everything the first time around, that is the point of living; to learn, to practise and to expand over time."

Out walking in the Bamboo Forest the next day, I resolved to never again waver. I would share my truth whenever called to, whenever compelled to. It might be a story that not everyone would "get," but then I guess that's the risk that naughty wee heretics take!

Places and Stages

Each place I had been and lived had served an important purpose in my life journey so far. Each was a stage. My Wellington stage had taught me that the most obvious path is not always the best. My Waiheke stage had taught me how wonderful life can be; how accessible joy and paradise are and it was a haven for me during a transition period that required me to take great leaps of faith into the unknown. My stage in Maui was teaching me how to release all attachments, how to just be like never before, and to write of the fears that broke me down without feeling embarrassment or self-judgment. Maui was my place to stand as my soul intended, to embrace my full self-expression. From that opening to be fully self-expressed, popped a question ...

As I stood on the beach one evening, backed by a sky shot red, with my hair straggly and salty, tangled from the hyperactive breeze rolling down the coastline, I picked up a stick and dragged it across the ground. The sand edged upwards making room for the grooves of each letter, letters that formed words, words that asked the burning question: "What form of light work and healing am I *really* here to do?"

Bee Invasion

It was soon after this that I started to see the significance of a recurring signal.

Visiting family before leaving New Zealand, we had been blessed with the opportunity to go on one of my all time favourite adventures ... a road trip. Driving southwards, a bumblebee had been sucked in the window of the car, buzzing and thudding as it knocked against surfaces and windows trying to find its way out.

Walking Cash at a park during a stopover, a bumblebee had hovered above our heads, trailing after us insistently, swooning left and right.

Riding a water taxi to reach my parents in a remote bush area far from town, I was acutely aware of a bumblebee buzzing around me on the back deck of the boat. A bumblebee, all the way out there in the middle of the sea, far from land, far from flowers, far from wherever bumblebees normally are.

Then again later, sitting with my notebooks on the water's edge, planning out the flow for my book, a bumblebee was humming around me.

Since then, several times in Maui bumblebees had flown a flight path a little too close for my liking, and in one instance a swarm of bees had been hovering in the air as I rounded the corner of a beach walkway.

I had forgotten all about the bee that I saw in my meditation months earlier and was now reminded of the many messages that bee totem offers. Aside from the message of pursuing dreams and achieving what seems impossible through focus and dedication, something else resonated with me. I saw multiple references online to interdependence, cooperation and this idea of pollinating as a service to the eco system.

I wondered: *Pollinating with words, to trigger unfolding?*

It also got me thinking further during the coming months

about cooperation, collaboration and contributing, things that both Augustus and Jed had alluded to.

Interpretation

I wrote every single day in Maui—writing, editing, musing, reading, writing more, editing further, revising and reviewing. On and on it went, every day for three months and I never tired of it, not once.

I reminded myself at all times to stay true to writing what I felt compelled to write. What rose up and came forth to be written was more important than getting caught up with who might read it and what they might want to read. That would become an exercise in second-guessing; overriding the truth that a creation infused with love is able to flow to those who might benefit from it.

As I walked to yoga one morning, I did however ponder whether my writing about the cave days would be a little depressing for readers. I started to draw connections between the flow of my first book and this second book, and I wondered: *Is it going to be joyful enough for readers?*

As the thought moved in and out of my mind on the conveyor belt, a pickup truck drove past carrying four men turning into a building site. One of them leaned out the passenger window and yelled out to me, "Hey, you're doing good work!"

My initial reaction was to frown and think he was a dirty pervert for leering at me out the car window. Not a very Zen reaction. Told you, I'm just an ordinary girl. The B doesn't stand for Buddha.

I could only assume he was making such a statement, as I meandered along in my Lycra yoga pants, to allude to how I physically looked. Even though it sounded like a compliment, I'm not a huge fan of receiving compliments from men who shout at me from passing trucks. A bit lewd, right? Though it was an odd phrase to use if it was lewd in nature.

Then I wondered about the words he said and a different interpretation became apparent when I removed the negative slant I had added.

I'm wondering about the reader's experience of my writing and I just got told, "You're doing good work."

We can drastically shift our experience of what occurs by the meaning we add. This is what Jed meant about the stories we create. You write your story, negatively or positively.

Just as we each have the free will to create and live within a negative or positive story, we also have the ability to interpret signals as meaningless or to recognise signals as divine guidance.

I can tell you everything that I have experienced first-hand and what resonates for me personally, but this is your life and you are being called upon to choose your interpretation of it. Just notice whether or not your interpretation benefits you or limits you.

From this "Lycra meets pickup truck" encounter, I concluded that the universe really does attempt to compliment and support us, and sometimes we refuse to accept it. After all, you must agree, we are not to say *how* the compliments will be delivered to us, just whether we receive them.

Next time the universe compliments you, be acutely aware of how open you are to receiving it. Do you deny it? Do you rebut it to say that it is undeserved or that it's unnecessary? Drop the racket you are using to bat away gifts and then you'll have two free hands to receive them.

Chapter 20

Let Go in Order to Flow

While in Maui, Jed helped me with closure on all I had experienced prior to then, by releasing remaining questions and memories that were nothing but dead weight. Like a game of twenty questions we bantered back and forth, expanding understanding and letting go of it all, in order to flow.

Blocking the Flow

The rally started when I asked Jed to help me to understand more about the flow of life force energy through us. I was primarily interested in what interrupts that flow of energy, thus causing what we deem to be problems or non-manifestation of what we really want to experience in our life. They said:

"When you rally against what you don't like and don't want and you strive to have something look a certain way then you not only rule out all other possibilities but you go directly into the face of the unacceptability of what is. In doing so you give light and energy and vibration to that which you don't want, magnifying it and then you wonder why it isn't the way you want it. You cannot see anything except what you don't want and you feed the situation with more questions about what is not working, thus perpetuating the thing you don't want. You vibrate with the confusion of how you got to that place and while you want to create change, you don't know where to go or what to do and so the cycle continues."

It was exhausting just listening to this explanation of insanity, and I could see from my own previous firsthand experience that it was just as exhausting to live this way, as it was to hear it explained. And yet this insanity comes so naturally to us all, which made this phenomenon all the more intriguing to me. How could it be so?

Jed continued, *"Let go of life having to look a certain way and go a certain way, and decide to be open to all paths, then see what opens up. Pushing up against what already exists, with complete non-acceptance of the 'is-ness' of the present moment, is what blocks the flow; your flow, the flow of life force, the very energy of all that is. Accepting what is doesn't mean you have to embrace it and like it and choose for it to remain that way. Change it by all means, but accept the fact it is as it is now. Don't rally against it, rather acknowledge what is and then rally forward to create something new. There is a difference."*

I then discussed with Jed how the experience had been for me in the dark cave days, when I had done just the opposite of what they were suggesting. I started with:

"Back then things weren't working like I expected them to. I thought it should have gone a certain way. It felt like it shouldn't have been the way it was, that it should have been different."

I was saying should, should, should. I wanted X and so it should have been X, to which Jed gave a very long reply:

"Lots of shoulds and expectations, pervading all the possibilities and blocking out other opportunities and narrowing your life down into a tunnel with a picture at the end where circumstances must match what you envision or if not then all has failed you. In the tunnel you can't find a way back and you don't know which way to turn. Those are the times to take your blinkers off and see the opportunities all around you. Everywhere. Stop forcing things to look a certain way. Choose the opportunities you want, choose to be open to them all and be open to all paths that lead you there, choose what works for you.

"If something doesn't work then the world has not conspired against you, you have not necessarily done anything wrong. Will you consider the possibility that there is something to learn or some better space or place for you to be, some better outcome for you if only you will open up to it. Stop blocking the flow and allow yourself to unfold. You need not meet any expectations, your own or others. You need not live in the 'must have' of a life that looks the only way you thought it could, would or should. You have choices; the

choice to weave your way through life, looking at your options as each day passes and selecting from the menu what looks good that day. There is nothing wrong with multiple choices and options and detours and paths, and following your heart where it leads you. When life does not go as you planned, you are being shown something. Perhaps you are blocking the possibilities by how you are being, or something else exists for you; it may be that you are being shown that other ways and means exist, with higher and greater possibilities.

"The challenge in life is whether you can dance in the midst of that knowledge without the physical proof having shown up yet to support that perspective you have taken. A perspective is nothing more than your choice of how to view a position, a situation, a challenge, a person, life or the world. Your perspective affects your vibration, which in turn has a flow on effect in your life.

"We want you to know that when we told you there was nothing wrong, we really meant there was nothing wrong. Things do not mistakenly turn out the way they do. There was no mistaking the situation you found yourself in with your fear; there was nothing wrong with what happened, it was all perfectly, perfectly created. You created it, at a soul-level, and soul self knew it would be difficult at times and knew it would take time to break down your blocks and rebuild, and knew it would take time for your new path to take flight and you did all of this because of your deep faith in yourself and in your soul intention and the calling to serve others. You were not crazy and you did not take a wrong turn. The turns you took were at times following after things that didn't call to your heart, going in ways that you thought were best because other people said so. Do not move in good thinking ways, instead move in good feeling ways. Now you are moving in ways that your heart truly calls for—contribution, serving, helping, giving and all you ask for is to be guided in this new path. There is nothing wrong with your path.

"The wrongness would have been never opening your mind, never opening your heart, never opening yourself to possibilities and learning all those years ago. The wrongness if anything would have been staying in your life as you had always known it to be, feeling like you were dying inside.

That dying inside is soul self saying, 'I can't take it anymore.' The heart singing about new possibilities is soul self calling out 'yes, yes, yes.'

"When you moved to Waiheke you opened up soul self. When you left your career you listened to soul self. When you took this opportunity to write again, you aligned to soul self and you let yourself have this opportunity. You said it yourself, 'I want to give myself this opportunity to write, to be of service, to help others.' You said, 'I want to know I gave it everything.' You did all of that knowing that you had the ability to be, do and have whatever you want, you knew that because deep down it resonated that this path is for you. This is the path you were born for. You cannot deny it, and that is why you have never turned away from it.

"You might wonder what causes people to be so determined and passionate about their endeavours. We say it is because when soul self rises, soul self always overrides all other aspects of being. When soul self is loud enough to hear, you cannot silence the singing. Lock your soul self into the dark cave at your expense, let it out into the daylight and follow its callings and while it may feel at times that it comes at a cost, the cost is no greater than letting it wither and die in the dark cave.

"When you let it into the light there are challenges; you will have challenges. That is life, that is human life, that is part of being on the life journey in the human being experience. The challenges are manageable when you are going in the direction that serves you best for your soul intention. It is when you are off on a tangent and challenges arise that you feel most lost and alone. But, you have never truly felt alone in this, have you? You have always known that something is with you. You have known this to the extent you felt compelled enough to put your life and your reputation and your existence and your everything on the line to announce it to the world. Why do you think that you did that when you were private, you wanted a simple life, you wanted peace and quiet and you did not like putting your voice out there for fear that it might be disregarded or despised? You do this and have done this and will continue to do this because you know that soul self is singing and in doing so you know you are fulfilling the intention of soul self. Soul

self calling will always see you right. This doesn't mean that you will have a life void of fraught and challenge, you cannot learn without those experiences. You had to have the experience of troubling times, to see what it was like to not have the fundamental things you thought you needed. You had to know what it felt like to push for a dream, to step out bravely to acquire it, to expect results and then to not see it in the way you thought you would in the timeframe you wanted to. For you do not control everything in the world, but you do control your own energy and that is enough. It is your energy that greatly influences the world. Block yourself up, dam the flow and see the consequences."

Desire Without Attachment

This led me onto my next question. *"Why is it that so many people focus intently on what they desire, they diligently practise all that they are taught in order to create their goals and dreams as their reality, and yet sometimes it simply doesn't work for them and this ends in frustration and disarray?"*

Jed said, *"They resist what is and they are attached to particular outcomes. This is denial of the present, living in the future. They block the flow of life force energy because of fierce resistance and attachment and thus they block their own unfolding. The passionate desire without attachment, not having to have, but rather to allow what is to flow freely, from that everything is possible. Nonattachment is being free of the bounds of the 'must have' that so many place on their goals. It is in the 'must-ness' about their goals that they hold it all at bay, and it is in the 'letting go' that their journey more freely unfolds. Letting go is not giving up; it is giving over. Giving over to the flow. Remember, we told you—give over, give over, give over, give over, give over, give over, give over."*

All of a sudden I had clarity on the true meaning of that page long "give over" message from Jed when we first connected.

Face Your Feelings Honestly

My cave days, in time, allowed me to see my own attachment to outcomes and how I had blocked the flow with my decisions (albeit haphazardly and unconsciously) to fly in the face of what I had deemed to be unacceptable. I had emotionally rallied against what was, rather than accepting it and rallying forward to create something else.

Our feelings are *always* an indicator as to whether we are gripping on tightly with attachment or letting go in order to give over to the flow. Never short of a word to say, Jed had something to say about facing feelings honestly.

"If you had stayed in life as you knew it you would never have evolved. You were stuck in Thonburi thinking the walls were closing in on you and wishing to be somewhere else but with no idea where somewhere else would be. And then you were in the cave days, feeling like you were crumbling, and you wanted certainty and you wanted to be somewhere else but you realised there was nowhere else to be at that moment.

"Where you are is always perfect. It is always for your learning, to learn that in running from such feelings you achieve nothing and from facing such feelings you achieve exactly what the situation is offering you. When something feels so disdainful you must ask yourself—why is it that I feel this way? What is there for this situation to teach me? Why has it come to visit me? Why have these events culminated in this way?"

Acceptance, just like nonattachment, is a method by which one can break the dam and allow the flow. Indeed, allow the unfolding of soul-level self.

Look Back, Go Back?

Fear in my life had made me look backwards and forwards too many times, instead of being exactly where I was, in the only place to be—the present. For again, there is no time. It is an illusion that keeps us locked into a mind-made drama.

During my first few weeks in Maui, Jed had challenged me to really look at the face of those previous discomforts and to consider whether I had any remaining questions about my path in life. They were calling out for me to release the dead weight of useless questions and memories that served absolutely no purpose.

They asked, *"Considering all you have learnt and gained from those experiences, if you could turn back the clock and make different decisions would you? Would you not go to Augustus?"*

"No."

"Would you not go to Meredith's course?"

"No. "

"Would you not do the healing course?"

"No. "

"Would you not have taken the leadership role?"

"No."

"Would you not move to Waiheke?"

"No. "

"Would you not go to Thailand?"

"No."

"Would you not have written the book?"

"No."

"Would you not have left your job?"

"No."

"Would you not have offered coaching and healing to people?"

"No."

"Would you not have sold your house?"

"No."

"Would you not have come to Hawaii?"

"No."

"Do you want to go back?"

"No."

"Is there any part of back there that you truly miss?"

"No."

"Not the job?"

"No."

"Not the house?"

"No."

"Not the asleep-ness of your earlier life?"

"No."

"Then precisely what is wrong with where you are?"

"Nothing. "

"Do you want to write?"

"Yes."

"Do you want to be of service to others?"
"Yes."
"Do you want to live a life where you flow and unfold as a full expression of soul self?"
"Yes."
"Do you want to go to places, and be in spaces, where you feel called to be?"
"Yes."
"Do you want to share light and healing with others?"
"Yes."
"Then precisely what is wrong with where you are now?"
"Nothing."

And then, as if it had been too long since their bluntness and humour had come to visit, they said:

"Not everything you need shows up instantly. It is in the delay of the showing up that you learn something about yourself. Like how you feel it is utterly unacceptable to share a message with others unless you are living that message perfectly as a demonstration. You are not the Martha Stewart of self-help B, you are an ordinary girl showing ordinary people that you don't need to be a guru in order to unfold, to follow the signals and to live a life fulfilled."

Press Play

If we were meant to look back and go back, we would each have been born with a rewind button next to our tap. Not sure about you, but I ain't got no rewind button.

Rather than rewind ourselves into the past, into our negative stories, or fast-forward into the future where we deny the present (where life is actually happening and our signals exist), how about we all just press play and dwell in our own unfolding.

Let me ask you—have *you* ever felt alone when you want to create something in your life and you don't know how? Have *you* ever felt alone when you think things are going "wrong" and you don't know what to do? Have *you* ever felt alone when you get lost in the direction your life is taking?

You're not alone in experiencing that alone feeling. This is life for us all at one point or another. We are all ordinary in the sense that we are all equal and not one person is better than the other and we are all extraordinary in the sense that we each have our own unique place to fill in the world that no other soul has or will ever fill. Ever.

It is the ordinariness that people need to know is marvellous. It is your falling into traps and going around in circles that gets you to know yourself better, that allows you to recognise your own blocks and thus gifts you the opportunity to grow from them, in order that you can propel forward in your expansion of self. It is through your ordinariness that you have breakdowns, and then from these come miraculous breakthroughs, which allow your extraordinariness to shine. And this is life, and on it goes.

One of the reasons I felt so compelled to write this journey and help people is that I want "ordinary" people to have a voice, to know that it doesn't take being born with something we perceive to be "special" in order to live your greatness and experience the life your soul intended.

Drop the Facade

Amidst those challenging times, I had become lost in thinking that I had to be someone extraordinary and that all my falling over was showing me to be faulty and broken in some way. I had an image in my mind of what I *should* look like and how my life *should* be going, not just for myself but in order to be of any value for people with my endeavours to share the signals message I'm so passionate about. Here is the rest of what Jed said about the illusionary façade I thought I had to fulfil:

"Do not be what you are not. Don't dress yourself as someone who must pretend to be faultless and perfect. Don't be someone who says, 'Hey I did this and it was wonderful and it worked perfectly and I left my old life behind and look how wondrous it is. Come on, fly like I am!' No, there is no power in that. If that is what you want to be, then join the queue of all the people who tell their fellow man and woman all about the ways to be and the glory that then results without any truth for the journey that takes you there. It is the journey that people must hear. It is the journey wherein lies the gold."

Not one person is better than you, more capable than you

or more knowing than you. We each have the one thing that levels the playing field when we journeyed into life. That one thing is our soul self and our infinite connection to and place within the universal energy. That energy holds divine wisdom. It is our choice to allow it to flow through us, to listen to it and to see life from a paradigm beyond this current time, space and circumstance illusion. Beyond that illusion, all things are possible. Beyond the illusion, soul intention is possible.

So here I am, writing to share what I know to be true, without being perfect, without having all the results or all the answers. No one does. Sometimes I do things and they work out great. Other times I do things and they do not work great (like the time I tried to make an Italian, Asian and Greek infused salad which Aaron can attest did not come out great at all!). Some things I do work the first time around, other things I do take quite some time before they work, and I'm sure there are plenty of things I have done and will do which might not work at all. I'm not perfect. Being perfect is not the point. So if you're in that boat, the one whose mast is flying the flag "Gotta look like everything's working perfectly" then feel free to jump overboard, because guess what ... I heard a story once about a lifeboat standing by.

All you have to do is accept the support that is there for you. The universe is giving you that support every day.

Is there an illusory façade you are fulfilling? Are you playing a part in life that you feel you need to fill in order to be valued, accepted, liked or indeed to "fit in"?

Are you ready to drop the façade and embrace your authentic self without any dead weight weighing you down?

Chapter 21

Shedding, Shifting & Anchoring

Planetary Reflection

A few weeks before leaving New Zealand, I met with Meredith for coffee. She was in town visiting at the time, so we snuck an hour together as she transited through.

Devouring pecan fudge brownie and coffee, through conversation we ended up chatting briefly about astrology. Meredith told me about a close friend of hers, Daniella, who did astrological chart interpretations. My thirst to know more about my soul had not been quenched, so I asked for Daniella's contact details.

I considered, again, that maybe I had done enough seeking already, and it was time to let myself live with what I knew and to dam the torrent of questions. But, again, that consideration didn't last long. On the basis that the greatest tool we have for creating our life is in fact ourselves, I wanted to continue to understand that tool.

So I contacted Daniella, asking if she would be willing to do my astrological chart reading. Unfortunately, she was busy but said she would start it whenever she was free.

A month or so passed, and while sitting on the patio of our condo in Maui I received the first email from Daniella, letting me know she was about to commence interpreting my chart. Before that had even taken place, we hit it off with our words flying back and forth through the ether across the world.

I didn't know anything about astrology, other than my star sign was Aries. Daniella shared a few early insights about Arian nature with me in those initial emails.

"The positive Arian spirit is fearless ... Arians are here to act and survive by being independent, pioneering warriors."

Independent at all costs had certainly been true of me. This was the opposite of the cooperation, collaboration and interdependence messages I had been pondering lately. I considered that perhaps there was a way to be independent without costs.

Pioneer also rang in my ears from the early morning message months before, and while I had not been fearless by any stretch of the imagination, I had acted and continued to act despite my fear, so I wondered if that was perhaps in part due to the Arian nature. I considered it was no mistake then that I had come into life as an Arian. After all, to come for my soul intention after experiences in past lives that did not go well for me, I clearly needed the energy of courage deep within. After all, we are born with everything we need in order to unfold into our soul intention. That is the perfection of life. As it is for me, it is for you. It's no mistake that you were born with the sign you have, with your chart exactly as it is. Within that chart lies truth.

Several weeks would pass before I would hear further from Daniella. In that time I mused how influential the planets could really be in relation to someone's life journey. Was it the planets *influencing* the journey, or was it that the soul had incarnated at a particular point in time and the planetary alignment at that moment in time was merely a *reflection* of the choices the soul made and its intention for the journey?

I was already converted to the fact that your date of birth has much soul wisdom to offer, having found life path numbers within numerology to be incredibly accurate indicators as to the nature of the life path that one is here to experience. Astrology, as I understood it, was derived from that birth date as well, going further to look at birth time and the placement of planets at that moment as well as their placement throughout your lifetime.

On the basis of all I had learnt, finding guidance hidden in mysterious places, I strongly sensed that the planets were simply another *reflection*, from a different angle, of the soul's intention.

Shedding What We Do Not Need

Had it not been for Charlotte I would have missed an upcoming signal to consolidate my understanding of what the Maui phase of my journey was all about.

I knew being in Maui was for my writing and for connecting with the energy there, but I had also started to sense there was something else. There was something I couldn't quite put my finger on. Something available to me that would help me crystallise my learnings of the last six months and prepare me for whatever lay ahead in my life. Jed had said it would become clearer to me and that there was no need to search it out.

It was partway through our time in Maui when I shared this with Charlotte during a phone call. She suggested going for a big walk to help clear my mind and allow inspired insights to rise up. Aaron then randomly announced he was going walking along the coastline, so I donned my sneakers and 50+ SPF to join him.

We walked and walked and walked. Four miles later, after climbing over rocky points, along beaches, crossing nature reserves, lava outcrops and resorts, we came to the edge of a rugged little cove. There was no one around; the access was limited. To reach the black sand beach in the cove ahead we balanced arms out left and right, tiptoeing over rocks piled high. There was a sharp drop to the water a few feet below. Waves were pounding to within inches of our feet.

Leaping from the rocks up to a grassy bank above the beach, I was slightly taken aback when from out behind a bush appeared a bright-eyed, bushy-tailed, very enthusiastic lady.

She clasped her hands together and with a genuine look of glee she asked, "Do you know anything about Monk Seals?"

I wanted to ask who she was and why on earth she was jumping out from behind a bush in this remote cove, but her enthusiasm was contagious, like that of a Children's School Holiday Programme Coordinator after ten cups of coffee. I was enraptured by her question.

"No, I don't." I replied with intrigue.

"Well, just pop around here with me." She had already turned and was waving us on as she snuck back behind the bush from whence she came.

Shrouded by shrubbery, pointing toward the other end of the beach, she showed me a magnificent, imposing and silent Monk Seal. She explained the habits of Monk Seals and that this particular female Monk Seal had decided to come ashore at this very place for a special purpose and it was important that we not disturb her by going any closer. I watched as the Monk Seal momentarily lifted her head in our direction and then returned to her immobile beached position.

After hearing a long explanation, feeling like I had just been on a visit to a nature and wildlife exhibition, we discovered this lady was in fact from the organisation responsible for wildlife preservation. Her job was to protect the Monk Seal and to ensure that no one drew attention to its presence there, so we headed back the way we had come with sealed lips.

I was so busy telling Charlotte about how magnificent it was to see a Monk Seal like that, and all about what the lady had explained to me, that I completely missed any potential significance. However, Charlotte didn't miss a beat, as I regaled her with my seal tale ...

"Apparently this Monk Seal had come ashore somewhere remote like this beach on Maui where she felt safe, and the lady told us it was a special and important time for her. She was actually malting, shedding all her fur. The lady said that it's a very fragile time for the Monk Seal when they malt, because it's like losing an entire layer of skin in order to grow new fur. So they were keeping people away from her so that she could have solitude to malt without any intrusion."

"So B, a very special and important time for shedding what she no longer needs, in seclusion. Do you see how relevant that is?"

I did, but I almost had not. When we think we're not getting signals, sometimes we're just so caught up in the joy or the drama that we don't recognise the significance. I could not have been any more secluded there in Maui, having insights while writing my own unfolding.

Seal totem also stands for trusting your inner voice. I was later told that sightings of Monk Seals up close like that are considered a rare gift.

I then saw the connection of this seal totem back to the cicada totem incidents, which had referred to "shed one's skin" and "share your own voice."

Maui, to shed what I no longer needed. Maui, to allow me to do this without questions I didn't have answers to. Maui, the place where I could write my way through important realisations, without reminders of what I had been caught up worrying about in the past. Seclusion to bring forth honesty and to let go of any façade.

A season for change, but not the explosive nature of change which propelled me in the past, but a quiet going within and grounding type of change.

When I awoke one morning to the word "transmigration" rolling around in my head, I attempted to work out its meaning before heading online for verification. It sounded a lot like shifting of some description.

At the top of the search results online I saw "transmigration of the soul". One particular reference touched my heart. There was a musical composition called *On the Transmigration of Souls*, and the composer, John Adams, suggested that the music would allow the listener to be in a memory space, where you could go and be alone with your thoughts and emotions. Adams referred to transmigration as, "The movement from one place to another or the transition from one state of being to another." [60]

A life is made up of seasons. We move from season to season with something new to learn each time. Moving in cycles like nature. Expanding and contracting, expanding and contracting, expanding and contracting. Life cannot be continued expansion. That is exhausting and it would be imbalanced. Everything has an opposite, a counter balance, an opposing axis.

Summer for creative flourishing, winter for restorative hibernation. Day for being in creative action, night for being in restorative sleep. Birth for coming forth into creation, death for returning home on the soul journey with lessons learnt and a message delivered. We expand in our creative process, and we contract for restoration and learning. I had been within restoration and learning, and it felt like it would feed my creative processes.

Sparks of Recognition

Silently making our way along another coastal track one afternoon, we stopped to take a breather under a tree and I noticed a man walk past behind us. I noticed him because there was no one else around and he seemed so peaceful out for a walk on his own. As we ventured out again into the scorching sun, this time to walk along the sand, cooling our feet in water, Aaron pointed ahead to the same man I had seen, "That guy is really present, he's really loving the moment. You can tell by the way he is being."

As the man turned to walk back past us, Aaron smiled at him and said hello. The man smiled and both of them hesitated for a moment looking at each other, then struck up a conversation about the beauty of the day and sharing stories of what had brought them to Maui. As it would eventuate, this man called Paul invited us to his condo later that week.

It turned out that Paul was also a light worker, as many of us are, whether we realise it or not. Paul also knew of his soul intention. Over several hours we chatted, and I noticed several glimpses of information come together in my mind.

Paul mentioned Lemuria, a supposed lost land and civilisation that is often spoken about as being closely linked to Hawaii. From what I discovered through research, it is believed by many that the land of the Hawaiian Islands is in fact what remains of the original land of Lemuria.

Back in New Zealand when I had followed signals to an evening at Laurie's house to talk about Maui, she had also mentioned Lemuria.

It was while in Maui that Aaron, through seeking out his own Akashic Reading from Rosanna, had learnt of his soul connection to Lemuria from a past lifetime. In meditation, I asked source whether my soul had been in Lemuria as well. The answer was yes.

I sensed there was something important about Lemuria in relation to my path now, and Aaron's, but I couldn't put my finger on it. It had come up multiple times, signalling something perhaps. But what?

When we returned home from Paul's condo, it was something else that he said which sent us into action. He mentioned a particular channeling that he followed online, much like Augustus in some ways, except this was a set of publicly available general channelings, versus private channeling specific for individuals.

We researched online and found the material Paul had referred to. The particular sessions we listened to had been channeled in Hawaii and were full of references to Lemuria. It referred over and over again to the shifts in energy in our world in 2012, to the ending of a cycle and the beginning of a new cycle. I had long been aware of this, as it had been widely spoken and written about as the moving into a new era, a new earth. Ultimately, it was about the shifting of consciousness.

The channeling went on to talk about particular people being drawn to the Hawaiian Islands as part of this energy shift, people whose souls had come for light work whether they were aware of it or not. Souls that had links to Lemuria; drawn to Hawaii now for holidays, for business, for whatever reason they *thought* they were coming. And yet, the channeling said, it was a soul-level choice to be there in energy familiar to the soul at this time of change, for realignment.

As I listened to the message, it mirrored what Jed had said to me when we first arrived, that I thought I had logically decided to go to Hawaii, but in fact it was my soul intention to be there. That was where the compelling desire had stemmed from. It was the energy of Hawaii that I needed to be in at that time, and the same for Aaron. It was not a place, but a space (energetically speaking) to transition, to align and to anchor.

Despite how out there this all seemed to me, going way beyond anything I could logically process, somehow it resonated strongly as truth. I could not deny the feelings that arose upon hearing all of it. There were sparks of recognition, but not from my mind.

Learning to Hold the Light

After meeting this stranger on a beach and ending up in his home, finding our way to this channeling material and recognising the connection to what Jed had told me, I started to see more clearly that my being in Maui, in fact both of us being there, was about learning to hold the light.

When you live unconsciously with no awareness and in the illusion of separation, blind to the truth of oneness and how our world works, then this is the metaphorical dark.

When you awaken and you begin to live consciously, with awareness and resonating with the truth of oneness and how the world works, then this is the metaphorical light.

Transitioning between the two had not been difficult, per se. Yet, holding oneself consistently in the light was a little more challenging. Here is why.

Emerging on your journey through life as something new and different to what you have been before can be challenging. You live in particular places, you work in particular places and the people around you perceive you in particular ways, according not to the present moment alone (which is all there is) but according to an interpretation of the past, of what you have been in their minds (which is nothing more than a collection of memories and stories).

So, we are perceived through this paradigm held by others, the lens through which they see the world. We may shift, but if their lens does not shift then it can seem difficult in some ways to emerge comfortably as the evolving soul-level self. This may sound familiar from *Pinch Me*; an apple transforming into a pear but people still thinking you're an apple.

This doesn't at all mean that their lens is wrong or that there is anything about their paradigm that needs fixing. In fact it is *nothing* at all about others. It is completely, utterly and *only* about oneself and one's own ability to be fully self-expressed without inhibition and without playing into an old role that fits the paradigm of others. It is about being soul-level self, not surface self. It is about not looking to validate self through the perception of others, which is what we are conditioned to do our entire lives—seek validation. Nothing can validate the truth that you are. It just is.

It became very blatantly clear to me that my time in Maui was to align to the energy of that place to teach myself how to hold the light, the light of my true self and the light of truth about the invisible realm of life that creates the reality that we see around us.

I was surrounded by light workers everywhere in Maui. Everywhere I turned there were people speaking truth, writing truth, accepting and loving people for their own paths, each one knowing where they came from and why they came into this life. It was a liberating experience to be within that light and to learn how to hold it in order that no matter where I would go, what I would do or whom I might be with, I could hold the light of my truth.

Looking to have the world around you reflect back to you *who* you are in order to validate yourself is crippling, as you are relying upon externality for that validation, indeed externality for your joy. Allowing the truth of *who* you are to shine brightly negates the need for validation. The truth is that you are divine light, which requires no externality to exist and to shine. Can you see how freeing that is?

> ***Only you know who you truly are.***
> ***The question is—will you own it and show it?***

Chapter 22

All Pointing One Way

When the astrology report arrived from Daniella, I was even clearer on one thing—the truths of our world most definitely, categorically, unmistakably do *not* sit solely in what we can see, hear and touch in our three-dimensional world. The world we know is merely a reflection of the mysterious hidden mechanics that I was now so enamoured with.

These truths of our world lie in places that while seemingly hidden, are actually available to all of us right now, if we seek to know those truths. The compulsion to share this invisible realm with others was pulling at me more and more each day.

Signals had guided me to this space in my life after a long journey of discovery. Their guidance was now reinforced by what I read in the astrology report. It all pointed in one direction. We are all pointed to what we need to know, when we need to know it, and I would not stop at taking this message to those who could benefit from it.

I share these following findings with you not because I believe that the details of my own personal path and astrological chart will somehow be of interest to you. I sincerely believe that we do not read to learn of the paths of others; rather we read to learn of our own path as reflected in their words. I simply want you to see that just as signals led me to this space in my life and this greater understanding, so it is for me, it is for you. In the invisible realm are all the answers *you* have been seeking. They will be unique to you and they can guide you into soul intention and inner joy, just like they have for me.

From a woman I had never met, came a report covering the good, the bad and the ugly in relation to my life path—all points proving to be nuggets of gold, access points for growth. I shivered as particular words in the report mirrored exact words I had already written into my draft manuscript for this book, which no one had read. The parallels with Augustus' messages, my Akashic Reading and my life number were blatant and undeniable.

Most interestingly, it went further and pointed directly to my compulsion to follow this path I found myself on. It pointed to the very truth of why I had followed signals in the first place, where they had led me and why my soul chose this life. None of it was by chance.

"Your mission here, in this life, is to direct passionate Arian energy and action into a conscious investigation of life's hidden dimensions ... An explorer of the invisible realms ... Where we are wounded, is exactly where we have the capacity to heal ourselves and become a healer of others ... To live a life where truth is explored and difficult feelings and discoveries are not avoided."

As if in direct response to the question I had carved into the sand at dusk, came the answer to my form of light work and healing ...

"Communicative channels are important ... the purpose of this aspect is to use words ... in service of a worthy cause ... the cause, or causes, are related to healing, empowerment and transformation; of self and others ... making connections (through communication) with others."

The natural inclination I had to experience and delve into the invisible was apparently akin to "shaking up the status quo" and my work in this lifetime was to channel this into and through communication.

What made me stop and stare at the report in astonishment was the next section. In relation to this delving into the invisible aspects of life, the placement of the planets in particular houses in my chart alluded to this path directly involving an element of risk, more specifically risking personal resources and security. It said, " ... challenges temper the steel in human character ... the results are to be treasured, for they steer you in the direction of your mission." The high path that my soul intended in this life, in relation to my journey into the invisible and doing the soul work I was here to do, was "to risk going to emotional limits." I was at a loss for words when I read that the planetary placement also suggested I had been through a "life-changing crisis or a rite of passage."

I thought: *Yes and yes. Been to the limit, walked the*

passage. In other words, an initiation/rebirth as earlier dream symbology had suggested.

"Your work in healing, transformation, regeneration, bringing what is hidden up to the light—*is* your healing path ... Your mission is to forge ahead, like a pioneer, explore these hidden realms and come back to tell others about them ... A greater part of your helping heal others, lies in communicating insights and awareness to others on the nature of reality."

From palm readers to spirit channelers, from spirituality courses to numerology, from energy healing to meditation, from spirit guidance to intuition, from Akashic Records to astrology, and back to signals. For all our questions, the answers lie at our fingertips.

Is it the path for each of us to go venturing out, seeking all of this information and piecing it together to discover our soul intention? Not necessarily, certainly not unless it compels you to do so. It was my path because I felt compelled to do so and all that I discovered along the way in these hidden depths of information and through my signals brought me to this point of understanding. This understanding and connection to source was the catalyst for experiencing the light within.

Your path and what lies within it is unique to you. All I know for sure is that my work is to go out there and explore life, to heal myself of blocks in the process of doing so, and to come back and tell you what I know to be truth, and to say it like it is. That is what I have done. There is *nothing* at all in this book that you do not already know. Indeed, there is *nothing* in our entire universe that you do not already know. Your soul-level self knows it, it is merely a case of bringing that knowledge up to the light, the light of consciousness and letting it shine through you.

Maui marked the culmination of three years of investigation. What before were many fragments of insights were now all coming together through the process of my writing. As I sat on the patio and wrote each day, the glimpses melded together.

Before leaving for Hawaii, I knew I could not see the full picture. I could not at that time have articulated what causes the unfolding, nor could I have articulated what blocks the unfolding. I still had questions because I was still unfolding.

Indeed life, end to end, is an unfolding. You unfold from the moment your soul breathes into life through your body, until the moment it goes home.

Many of my lifelong questions dissipated. The torment of the void created by "Why am I here? Who am I? What is life about? What's the point?" was gone and I was left with a sense of peace with the light that remained. A song then lulled me one morning, poignant in lyrics, title and artist name. "World I Know" by Collective Soul was telling me about the present moment I found myself in:

" ... love is gathering. All the words that I've been reading have now started the act of bleeding into one ... so I walk upon high and I step to the edge, to see my world below." [61]

The Pact

Each afternoon when I sat writing on the patio, Aaron would walk the beach heading north along the coastline to a spot he liked to visit. He called the spot his "grassy knoll." He enjoyed going there to sit atop that little rise above the sand dunes, looking out over the expanse of water before him, as he worked through, reflected upon and embraced his own unfolding.

On one particular day near the end of our time in Maui, Aaron invited me to walk with him. I welcomed a break from staring at my laptop screen and we headed out.

I considered myself a lucky woman as he invited me to sit with him upon the grassy knoll, while we both reflected on the magnificent unfolding of life. To witness someone you love unfold into their true self, transforming their inner landscape by letting go of all that limits them, is a gift and an honour. We both cherished the continuing awakening we were having, and gave thanks that we were able to take the journey together.

My mother once gifted me a lovely piece of wall art that had this quote written on it: "Love makes your heart swell larger and larger, until you float away." [62]

This quote reflects how I felt while sitting atop that grassy knoll with my soul mate, so light and filled with love that I felt like I might float away on the breeze.

As Aaron and I wandered back toward the condo along the beach, we were deep in conversation about change, growth and our dreams. Our conversation sparked a thought. I turned to Aaron and said, "I think we should make a pact. A pact to never live in fear. To not let fear rule our lives. To never let fear play a part in our decisions. And, to always support each other in this way."

Aaron is quite used to my flair for the dramatic after nine years together, so it was no surprise to him that I wanted to stand facing each other right there on the beach, joining our hands together to make this pact by promising each other aloud (like wedding vows) that fear would never again rule our lives. So the pact was made, a moment we will always remember and lovingly hold each other to.

Into the Heart

I met Marisa in person for the first time two weeks before leaving Maui. We hugged like family and immediately commenced a conversation that lasted several hours, much like meeting an old friend after years apart. We agreed we had met before, not in this lifetime, but somewhere, sometime. The connection was unmistakable.

Together we went to a labyrinth in Maui, set amongst the jungle at the base of a cliff face. It was Laurie who had first mentioned labyrinths to me back in New Zealand when I went to her home. She had explained that labyrinths are sacred spaces, mystical circular shapes laid on the ground that form a maze-like path for one to follow as a walking meditation. The walk into the centre of the labyrinth is considered symbolic of a walk into the centre of oneself.

Before entering the labyrinth, I closed my eyes and asked to be shown whatever was in my best interests to know at that time. I held my vision for my life in my mind's eye, and with the knowledge I would soon be leaving Maui to return to New Zealand, I entered the labyrinth.

As I silently and slowly wove my way along the path, the message coming to me was this:

"No questions remain. Feel the spaciousness. Do not let the mind make up questions or look for problems to fill the space of peace. Answers to needless questions will always elude you."

When I reached the centre of the labyrinth, marked out on

the ground before me with stones in the shape of a heart, I paused. I held my vision for my life again in my mind's eye, stepped into the centre and closed my eyes. I heard:
"Here in your heart no problems exist."

Chapter 23

Allowing & Blocking

The only block to the life force of universal energy that naturally flows through us is our unwillingness to allow the mysterious unfolding. The unwillingness equates to attachments—our ways of being, the desire to control everything to fit our expected outcomes or rallying against anything that does not fit.

Why is the unfolding mysterious? Because your highest path, your soul intention, may not be at all what you anticipate in mind and body. Your thinking mind cannot conceive of all the possibilities. It likes to interrupt the great unfolding by hatching plans that it thinks are best.

The unwillingness that blocks the flow shows up under many guises. We create these blocks. It is our expectation and attachment to things that we want to happen that sees us willing those things to happen through foreseeable ways and means. We place these demands upon life, through judgment of what is, judgment of others and judgment of self. We create blocks through our negative stories, backed by limiting belief systems we have built up like layers of bedrock over a life or lifetimes. This all creates a dam in our river that blocks the energy flow and holds at bay all that we desire at a soul-level. This creation of a dam is often unconscious. As a result, life's intervention mechanisms kick in to help us. We then see the interventions as further evidence that we need to rally against what is, thus building the dam higher and stronger.

Accept that you yourself, at some level, created the dam in the river and blocked the flow, even if unconsciously. By acknowledging that life interventions are actually gifts to allow the breaking down of that dam and the free flow of the river, then you can truly allow the unfolding of your life in the highest and best way forward for your soul-level self.

You still apply your free will, you choose to create and

design your life, visioning with intent and taking purposeful action, but it's all about how you show up with that vision that ultimately makes the difference to your experience of life. When you allow and accept and unblock, then magical moments occur—"pinch me" moments.

There is a subtle, almost unnoticeable difference on the exterior of the person who shows up flowing with their vision, intentional and passionate, allowing their own unfolding, versus that of the person who shows up demanding their vision, forcing their action and feeling aggrieved at not having what they want.

Imagine yourself walking down the street and you feel the heat of the sun on your skin. You feel the breeze and are grateful as it cools you off. In fact, you are grateful for life itself. Your body feels energised and you are acutely aware of what blessings you have. Your head is up and your gaze is up. You are present. This is flow. From flow comes unfolding. From flow, signals are recognisable and universal energy corresponds beautifully with you.

Now, imagine yourself walking down the street talking to yourself, playing out what happened yesterday and wondering how everything is going to work out based on the challenges of your current situation. Your head is down, there is tension in your jaw and you gaze at the ground as you walk. You don't consciously notice the ache in your back, other than the generic feeling of irritation that pervades you. This is not flow, this is blocking.

Characteristics of Allowing & Blocking

It is from my own experiences as chronicled in both books in this series, *Pinch Me* and *Going Out On A Limb*, that I documented twenty-two characteristics of allowing and blocking. I used my own unfolding initially from darkness into light (then into darkness and then into light again!) to construct what I sense is a model that many of us can relate to when we observe ourselves objectively and observe others.

These characteristics come in pairs, each pair is designed to illustrate the polar ends of a spectrum denoting allowing your life or blocking your life, allowing the energy to flow or blocking the energy, allowing your unfolding or blocking your unfolding.

When "allowing your life" characteristics tip the balance over "blocking your life" characteristics, you are flowing more freely and the experience you have of life is considerably different to when "blocking your life" characteristics dominate. We have a choice to dwell more frequently and consistently at the "allowing your life" end of the scale, in doing so we feed oxygen to the light within us, thus we nourish our inner peace and joy.

Picture each pair of characteristics outlined in the forthcoming table as a scale from 10—0, where fully allowing your life sits at 10 on the scale and completely blocking your life sits at 0 on the scale.

10 ←——————————→ 0
Allowing Your Life   Blocking Your Life

10/10?

Do you want to aim to be ten on the scale for each allowing your life characteristic? Do you want a perfect score so that allowing your life characteristics whitewash over blocking your life characteristics?

No, you don't, not in all the pairs we are about to cover. In many of them yes, but overall the point is not perfection, the point is *balance* in most respects. It's about balancing the aspects in favour of allowing your life. Heart leading over head, not heart only without a head! "Being" as the platform for doing, not being without any doing!

We can willingly and consciously choose of our own accord to shift ourselves along the scale. Alternatively, blocking your life at times will give rise to interventions that look like life crises, bumping you into learning life lessons that are designed to awaken you and shift you on the scale, sometimes in small steps and sometimes in quantum leaps. There is no disdain for the blocking your life characteristics; they serve a purpose at one point or another. It is not right or wrong, it just is. Once you see it for what it is, you can choose to tip the balance.

ALLOWING Your Life (10)	BLOCKING Your Life (0)
Conscious living	Unconscious living
Connected	Disconnected
Sense of oneness	Illusion of separation
Heart led	Head led
Passion driven	Necessity driven
Enthusiasm to create	Creating from must-ness
Open to all paths	Fixed on one path
Sees life as a journey	Solely focused on destination
Moving forward	Running away from
Facing causes	Burying causes
Experiencing feelings	Muting feelings
Inward sensing	Outward sensing
Creating and manifesting	Demanding
Free will and personal accountability	Blame
Awe and wonder	Blinkers on
Being	Doing
Internal journey	External journey
Accepting what is	Resisting what is
Dwelling in the present	Dwelling in past and future
Benefiting all	Benefiting no one
Signals co-creating	Signals intervening
Life affirming choices	Destructive choices

We will go through each of these pairs. But first, you might have noticed that many models similar to this give you the *current* state of being on the left and the *desired* state of being on the right, indicating a left to right movement away from what we don't want and towards what we desire. This aligns to that inherent sense that we have to move towards what we desire, to create it. It engenders a feeling that on the left is where we are and on the right is the future, where we want to be. Books are read from left to right, graphs are read from left to right, we naturally look from left to right to denote here and over there. This further embeds a sense of *not* being where we want to be right *now*. Now is all there is. So, I shun that structure and I have instead listed our desired state of being, allowing your life, on the left-hand side of the model so that you will subconsciously pick up that where you want to be is actually where you are right *now*. You have everything, and I mean everything, that you need right now to be allowing your life, to embody the allowing your life characteristics. Right now. Not in the future, but right now. This is who you were born to be, and as Jed said ... this is your greatness. You simply need to claim it, by choosing it moment by moment.

Can you swing back and forth on the scale? Yes, you can. Tap on or tap off? Your awareness, that is your level of consciousness, has everything to do with where you sit on the scale in every pair of characteristics.

The blocking your life characteristics on the right-hand side embody all the things that can dominate, that we can accidentally fall into, as we grow up and forget who we are. Blocking your life doesn't come naturally; it grows instead from the illusion that society has conditioned us to believe to be true. This illusion comes to an end when you go beyond the visible, into the invisible and discover your soul-level self and your truth.

There is a reason that I use zero to denote the far end of the scale for blocking your life characteristics. Zero degrees Celsius is the temperature at which water freezes. Freezing is a pretty inhospitable place to be. In fact, it's polarising to the warmth and love of your greatness, to your soul-level self. Therefore, zero is the perfect point on the scale to denote the ultimate embodiment of blocking your life.

The Way It Looks

What does it look like when someone dwells at either end of the spectrum? All of these characteristics you have already witnessed played out in my journey as I swung back and forth on the continuum.

Take time to reflect upon each pair of characteristics if you wish, to sense where *you* stand and whether you choose to, in this very moment, reposition yourself. The repositioning does not take time and it does not take much effort. It simply takes choice, to let go and let be. In the choice, the shift is immediate.

Note that we do not make the choice once, we make the choice *every moment of our life*. That is what conscious living is all about.

Conscious living or unconscious living—the extent to which you are self-aware and present in each moment to consciously create and enjoy your life versus living by default, blind to how you influence your life and outcomes.

10 ◀━━━━━━━━━━━━━▶ 0

Connected or disconnected—the extent to which you choose to embrace your inherent connection with source, purposefully drawing upon guidance and living out life-affirming practises (living in the light) versus ignoring any signs of connection, living in the illusion of disconnectedness and experiencing a strange pervading sense of "alone" (living in the dark).

10 ◀━━━━━━━━━━━━━▶ 0

Sense of oneness or illusion of separation—the extent to which you can sense for yourself the oneness that exists between all things, versus living in the illusion that all things are completely separate, physically and energetically, including yourself.

10 ◀━━━━━━━━━━━━━▶ 0

Heart led or head led—the extent to which you move through life led by and acting upon the guidance of your intuition and singing heart, which is soul-level self, versus moving through life led by and acting upon the instructions of your thinking mind alone, telling you what you *should* feel and *should* do.

10 ◀━━━━━━━━━━━━━▶ 0

Passion driven or necessity driven—the extent to which you bring passion into what you do (whatever you want to or have to do right now), which generates the necessities for your life, versus driving forward out of necessity hoping to generate passion in what you do as a result. It's a mindset.

10 ◀━━━━━━━━━━━━━▶ 0

Enthusiasm to create or creating from must-ness—the extent to which you feel possibility and purposefully create your life from a base of genuine enthusiasm versus a strong sense of "must," driven solely by intention to get out of whatever situation you are in.

10 ◀━━━━━━━━━━━━━▶ 0

Open to all paths or fixed on one path—the extent to which you are open to the many paths that can take you to any one outcome, versus being fixated on the only way you can see as possible or the only way you want to get there.

10 ←——————————————→ 0

Journey or destination—the extent to which you do whatever you do with passion and for the joy of the journey, with the outcome/destination being secondary, versus being totally attached to the outcome/destination as the only reason, making you completely reliant on reaching that outcome/destination in order to experience any joy.

10 ←——————————————→ 0

Moving forward or running away from—the extent to which you perceive yourself as moving ahead on your journey, exploring and adventuring in life to create versus spending your life trying to get away from the past, out of a need (conscious or subconscious) to be as far as possible away from what has hurt you and/or defined you in the past (emotionally or physically).

10 ←——————————————→ 0

Facing the cause or burying the cause—the extent to which you face the cause of any unrest or dis-ease as being something within yourself that you can powerfully unblock, versus burying the cause and/or assuming the cause to have been only the external circumstance that triggered you.

10 ←——————————————→ 0

Experiencing feelings or muting feelings—the extent to which you allow yourself to feel your emotions fully, be those positive or negative, in order to understand the message your feeling guidance system is giving you, versus muting those feelings with stimulus to avoid them.

10 ←——————————————→ 0

Inward sensing or outward sensing—the extent to which you perceive and make sense of the world around you by utilising your innate inner sense of intuition to process what you experience, versus processing the world only by your outward senses of sight, sound, touch, taste and smell as filtered by your thinking mind.

10 ←——————————————→ 0

Creating and manifesting or demanding—the extent to which you design your life from the truth that you create and manifest based on belief, thought, feeling and action versus demanding that life show up to meet your expectations, and frustration with it when it does not play your game.

10 ◄————————————————► 0

Free will and personal accountability or blame— the extent to which you take ownership for your beliefs, thoughts, feelings, actions and outcomes created through free will, versus blaming (others, life, the world, the universe, circumstances, timing) for the outcomes of your life.

10 ◄————————————————► 0

Awe and wonder or blinkers on—the extent to which you see and enjoy the magic of the universe and life, experiencing awe and wonder at the beauty that is in front of you every day in the simplest of things versus having blinkers on (being stuck in your head) where you can no longer see the magnificence that lies all around you.

10 ◄————————————————► 0

Being or doing—the extent to which you recognise and practise that your state of being is the primary influencer of outcomes, versus believing that it is only what you do and how much you do that defines your outcomes.

10 ◄————————————————► 0

Internal journey or external journey—the extent to which you understand and live from the paradigm that your internal journey leads and reflects into the creation of your external journey versus the illusion that there is only an external journey which seems to create positive or negative internal experiences as a result.

10 ◄————————————————► 0

Accepting "what is" or resisting "what is"—the extent to which you can accept what is in your life at present, knowing you do not control everything in life but rather you control your own energy and your experience of life, which has immense influence as you rally forward versus resisting what is and rallying against it in the hope you will give rise to change as a result of that opposition.

10 ◄————————————————► 0

Dwelling in the present or dwelling in the past/future—the extent to which you are living your life in the only place you can be, namely the present moment, versus letting your mind drift to replay past moments over and over or living the moment as a means to an end to get you to a future point, which inevitably ends up being the present moment anyway, which perpetuates the cycle of never getting to the future because it doesn't exist, leaving you endlessly dissatisfied.

10 ←—————————————————→ 0

Benefiting all or benefiting no one—the extent to which your choices automatically benefit all in a win-win scenario be it emotionally, physically, psychologically, materially or karmically, versus your choices benefiting no one.

10 ←—————————————————→ 0

Signals co-creating or signals intervening—the extent to which you are receiving guiding, confirming and supporting signals helping you to co-create versus signals predominantly coming to intervene and encourage you out of the dark towards the light of truth.

10 ←—————————————————→ 0

Life affirming choices or destructive choices—the extent to which your choices are life affirming versus destructive; choices that then play out in your health, your well-being, your relationships, your career/vocation, your finances, your outcomes and your joy (or your unhappiness as the case may be).

10 ←—————————————————→ 0

Chapter 24

The 6 Cs

What follows is what I call the 6 Cs for thriving on our internal and external journey through life. They are part of the *overarching* intention of every soul. They are the foundation of life, which we can play out in a myriad of ways as we live our individual *unique* soul intention, rounding out our learning and soul experience.

There is nothing to work out and nothing to be concerned about, because when you dwell in the characteristics of allowing your life, you are automatically (a) feeding the 6 Cs and thus flowing with your *overarching soul intention* and (b) unfolding in your life magically and beautifully which carries you into playing out your *unique* soul intention.

The system is designed perfectly to allow all of this to happen when you discover and live from the truths that lie beyond the three-dimensional world that you know, indeed that lie at the foundation of creation for the world that you know.

These 6 Cs are consciousness, connection, compassion, collaboration, creation and contribution.

Consciousness—living in conscious awareness in the present, knowing our consciousness creates our experience of reality.

Connection—living in connection to source, soul-level self and all others.

Compassion—living with compassion for ourselves and for others, basing all we do upon compassion.

Collaboration—living in collaboration with others, with nature, for the benefit of all.

Creation—living as active, purposeful creators of our lives with life-affirming choices.

Contribution—living as a contribution to our world in whatever unique, special ways we do by being our fully expressed true selves.

What would it look like if we all lived within these 6 Cs? On the flip side, what would it look like if we all lived *outside* of these 6 Cs? Perhaps we think it is too idealistic to live by these 6 Cs, to embody them in who we are.

It isn't hard to live the 6 Cs, because we were born conscious, we are connected, we have inbuilt compassion, we benefit from collaboration, we are creators and we have a deep need to contribute. The system is designed in every way for you to want to, need to and have to live within these 6 Cs. This is who you are.

It was our developing perception of the world, and our experiences of life that we interpreted and added negative stories to, that led us to believe we had to *try* to be these ideologies, rather than knowing we *are* these ideologies at the core of our soul-level selves.

Consciousness

No one would ever choose to be unconscious. It is not a choice, but rather an accident. If you chose to be unconscious, you would have to be consciously aware enough to make the choice in the first place. Unconsciousness is never preferable, but if you want a sense of what it looks like then simply think of a robot operating on autopilot banging up against a brick wall over and over again until it short circuits.

Connection

With regards to living in connection to source, to yourself and to others, truthfully you cannot help but live in connection. The choice lies in whether you *embrace* that connection or pretend it isn't real. In pretending it isn't real, you feed the illusion of your separateness and the pervading sense of aloneness that lurks quietly.

If you attempted to live your life disconnected from source, from yourself and from others (all being one in the same— universal energy), just ponder a few examples of what it looks like when things become disconnected. A stereo that is unplugged from its power source doesn't function. A tree that is ripped from the ground where it draws its life force from doesn't live; it dies. Embracing connection to source, on the other hand, is affirming, rejuvenating and flowing.

Compassion

I don't think anyone would volunteer to admit they live outside of compassion, but the truth is a significant number of people do live partially, if not fully, outside of compassion. Living outside of compassion is a direct result of living disconnected. When you know that you are inherently connected to everything and everyone, your compassion for everything and everyone is equivalent to having compassion for yourself, because you are one and the same.

Compassion is not about loving those you love. Loving those you love is easy. Compassion is loving all. It is allowing your soul-level self to recognise and acknowledge the soul-level self in every other person, animal, tree, flower, anything that you encounter. Compassion doesn't mean you have to love what they *do*, it is loving the soul that they *are* for the journey they are on, being compassionate for the lessons they are learning and the evolution that is occurring.

Most of all, compassion is loving self and embracing self without judgment and with full acceptance.

Collaboration

Collaboration is perhaps the most obviously under-demonstrated C of all. We live in a world of competition (another side effect of disconnection), with the illusion of scarcity. Competition for love, competition for jobs, competition for products and services, competition for housing, competition for resources and on it goes.

I don't use this word competition in the way you might assume. We can all be in the world and create what we desire and some of us will be creating the same things and desiring the same things and selling the same things. We can compete in the same market and be collaborative in spirit. Instead, many of us live with the perception that we must fight for what we need, metaphorically or literally, and that when we win someone else loses, or if we have lost then someone else has clearly won and stolen our opportunity.

Collaboration is a core fundamental of human life that allows *the whole* to thrive. When one helps another, both thrive. The system is designed this way. When one steps on another, there are no winners. Collaboration is a vibration of love. It is founded upon the truth that we are connected, so competing with another is competing with oneself and so is pure insanity.

Creation

We are a creation in and of ourselves, a creation from source. Additionally, we came into life for the purpose of creation, as creators of our own reality. Given tools to create our life but without a manual as to how to use those tools, we can be left with the assumption that we are not creators but puppets in a play. When you know the truth of your ability to create and you own that truth, that ownership is life affirming for yourself and for everyone else who witnesses you within their reality.

Contribution

Finally, saving the best for last ... contribution. As souls we intend to contribute—to our learning, to the learning of other souls we encounter, and to the world. We are not here to take and take and take and wonder how much more we can get from others and from the world around us. When you give openly of *who* you are, infusing passion and joy into whatever you do, you will never need to think about taking, because in giving you will receive in equal and greater amounts. That is the flow of energy, the vibrational flow of life.

Most importantly, it is not our job to judge ourselves for how valuable or worthy our contribution is, or what type of contribution we *should* be making, or to worry about how many might benefit from our contribution. Our job is simply to *be* the expression of who we truly are and trust that it is always enough.

Be the free flow. Ask less about what you can get from life and more about what you can give as your unique expression, that is, wherever your heart sings loudest.

Don't want for life to give you more in order to be in a position to give. You have plenty to give right now ... your unique expression. There is nothing to wait for. Source gave you what you need, unfold into it.

> **What if we all lived by these 6 Cs?**
> **What sort of world would we be living in?**
> **What would it take to have this be the case?**

The answer to this last question is a seventh C ... choice. The choice is ours. The choice is yours. The choice is available every moment. The choice *needs* to be made in this moment, and the next moment, and the next, and the next. There is no one on this planet, not even the most holy of holy, who can say they are the embodiment of the 6 Cs always just because they declare themselves to be so. This is because the next moment has not happened yet and it is in the face of that coming moment, in the face of triggers and experiences that we *choose* to be the 6 Cs in that very moment. We make that choice every moment of every day of our entire life.

Conclusion

Trekking through a Maui rainforest one morning, it felt good to be tucked away in nature. The thick tree canopy let in speckles of sunlight dispersing like a kaleidoscope design dancing on the dirt trail. There was not a sound. Nothing.

As we emerged out of the covering, after climbing hundreds and hundreds of feet, I was confronted by a scene so soul striking that I could not help my reaction. Resonance causes us to respond in ways our thinking mind does not always understand. Some part of me knew this place and had come here because of that knowing. That knowing was now vibrating in reaction to being there.

On the edge of a cliff, with a deep creviced valley below, the expanse before me displayed a family of jagged peaks and sheer cliff faces dropping away, painted green with life. Mist hung in the air and far below a sliver of silver marked the path of a stream snaking the base of the valley.

This was not just a place, a location or a piece of land. It was a space, and a space is much different to merely a place. This was a sacred space, for spiritual opening and special creation.

Letting Go

To come to this sacred space, I had been asked to let go. That process of letting go had not been what I would have thought by definition before this journey began. For letting go used to sound to me like giving up. I don't do giving up. Instead I came to realise that letting go in this context meant something entirely different. It meant giving over, not resisting, but rather accepting and allowing. And, it most definitely meant not feeding fear with all the input that gave it legs to run riot. When you stop feeding fear, the malnutrition kills its power. It cannot live in the light of consciousness, in the light of being completely present in the moment.

Letting go seemingly goes against the grain of how we are instinctively conditioned to behave. We are taught to fight for "it," to compete for "it," to go after "it," to drive forward for "it." When in fact the truth is that we can let go and create at the very same time, and get more powerful results. To fight, to compete, to drive—all comes at a cost. The question is whether that cost is worth it. The answer will always, eventually, be no.

You either live without fear from a choice to let the light dissolve it as you move powerfully through it, or you live without fear from avoiding going near your fear at all costs. If you live a half-happy life, because true happiness for you would mean doing things that you are too afraid to try, or risking things you are too afraid to lose, then you are not living without fear. You are living in a safety zone where you know it is fearless to operate.

When this life comes to an end, and you realise that you are about to become more soul than body once again, returning to the divine space from where soul-level self originally sprang forth, you could be standing in one of two places.

One place will evoke a statement of inner freedom that goes like this, "I felt fear, I shed light upon it and I moved through it. The outcomes are just what they are. I lived this gift of life as a full expression of *who* I am and that is what I came here to do. I unfolded."

The other place will force out a statement of inner suffocation that goes like this, "I kept away from fear. I still do not know what lay beyond it. I guess I will never know. I lived this gift of life with caution. I'm not sure who I am. Better luck next time."

It is *never* too late to choose which place you want to stand in.

Availability of the Blank Page

The signal song that had lured me to write again all those months ago, " ... staring at a blank page before you ... " turned out not to be just a blank page on which to write words, but a blank page on which to recreate myself from a foundation of pure truth, of who I am. A foundation of nothing but energy and soul, yet more stable and secure than any form-based foundation I had previously clung to.

It can seem, at first glance, to be a rare gift during life to be able to stand on a blank page this way. One might go an entire lifetime without realising that nothing stops any one of us from placing ourselves on that proverbial blank page, ready to paint the picture of who we truly are. It's just a choice.

From the blank page springs forth inspiration of a divine nature, inspiration that cannot break through until the dark cloud of self-created negative stories dissipates. That inspiration is soul-level self calling you into action, action which is in complete alignment with source.

Dissolution and Re-creation

There may be times when we purposefully create that blank page or it may feel like we got dumped there by life circumstances. The beauty of the world we live in is that the universal energy recognises a vacuum of nothingness and sends forth possibilities to fill that space. For those facing a blank page, a vacuum calling possibilities, there is a window of time that feels both fleeting like a nanosecond painted upon eternity yet at the same time it can feel like a forever game of limbo.

If you've ever played the game of limbo, where you have to walk under a stick as it goes lower and lower, and you walk ahead bending yourself to go lower and lower to get under, you'll know how flexible you need to be to succeed at the game of limbo.

Life had taught me what it was to play in the great unfolding. To create a vacuum and call forth possibilities in alignment with my vision, I was called upon to play a good game of limbo. Flexibility teamed with tremendous faith are assets that see you triumph in limbo.

Life can be incredibly exciting and incredibly uncomfortable at the very same time. It is in realising that the uncomfortable space serves an extremely important and *divine purpose* that one has access to one of the great mysteries of life ...

A butterfly emerges after much time enclosed in a cramped space where its former caterpillar self dissolves in order to call forth greater form, with greater capabilities and more profound beauty. We think nothing of this and we do not grieve for the caterpillar that is asked to step aside, because we know it has given birth to its highest level of self.

For new order to arise in your life, there might first be a

collapsing of previous states of being and dysfunctions in order for there to be opportunities for your soul-level self to emerge.

> *In order to move forth in your journey, what parts of your former state will now dissolve, to call forth new possibilities?*
>
> *Will you purposefully choose to dissolve these or would you rather wait for life to bring that dissolution upon you?*

Your Journey

I surmised that you did not want to hear that living a Pinch Me life, following the signals, is all roses and glory. No one's life is like that. There would have been nothing available to you in such a story. So instead of telling you a story, I told you the truth. From my truth, I hope you see your own light, for your own journey.

Sometimes creating the life you want and the life your soul-level self is calling for, involves going out on a limb. Sometimes it takes faith to believe that the limb is strong enough to hold you and that what you are reaching for is worth the risk.

All the work is energy. It starts first in energy and ends in the physical manifestation. What happens in the gap in between is all up to you, carrying you from *what* you think you are, to *who* you really are. You are here to shed the baggage, to drop the negative stories and to learn how to close the gap. Live the 6 Cs and tip the balance to *allow* your life to unfold.

Paint Yourself into the Picture

Let me finish by telling you a brief tale of a girl. She might sound familiar, almost like you know her, but something changed. Once a well-protected fortress, her walls slowly but surely collapsed outwards, unfolding to expose a truth that lay within.

Now she stands on the beach, framed by the mountain in the distance. A scene that once held true only as a picture she looked at each day and a glimpse of a vision in a meditation.

Somehow she painted herself into this picture. Glancing back at the other end of the vast cove, she wonders what the vision looks like now that she is standing in the middle of it. Is someone else looking over this vista now and seeing the very picture she had seen herself almost a year ago?

Sounds of waves dumping ashore, skin tingling, breathing salty air, she realises fully that she is no longer the girl that she used to be, but rather the girl that she truly is, the one that was waiting to come out her whole life.

Not fearless, just fear conquering.

No labels to define who she is.

No address to define where she lives.

No place she has to be.

Nowhere she has to go.

No reason to fence herself in.

When you strip it all away there is nothing.

When there is nothing, what is left?

The answer, categorically, is everything.

For the first time ever, she knows and deeply appreciates that everything.

She thanks her soul-level self for setting her free and marvels at the mysterious unfolding that had been the key.

Standing on the beach, the girl turns to face *you* and asks you a question.

"Will you allow yourself to unfold?"

Your response right now is defining.
It's time to decide.
If not now, then when?

Feel the warmth of the sun on your cheeks. Feel love for yourself. Hear the gentle whispers of *your* soul-level self. Answer the call.

What Next?

Who knows what lies ahead for B ... her vision and path expands and weaves day by day, week by week, month by month as the unfolding continues, as new possibilities spark into life on the blank page. She has her arms wide open for life learning and for the inner peace and joy that arise from the unfolding.

She loves you for who you are, and says to you:

"You are never alone, you are infinitely connected and loved beyond measure. Love yourself. Own your unique expression and place in this world. Dream big and follow your signals."

PS. She still doesn't hug trees, burn incense, or wear tie-dyed clothing. But her new motto is NEVER SAY NEVER ...

About the Author

Bernadette is an ordinary girl—a daughter, a wife, a puppy mother, a sister, an aunty, a signal follower, a life lover, and just one of many, many souls who are passionately here to share light and healing with others.

To connect with Bernadette, and for more information on private coaching, retreats, live events, as well as free resources, please visit **www.pinchmeliving.com**.

Also by the Author:

Pinch Me

Unleash Your Life

References

1. Lyrics from "Price Tag" by Jessie J, featuring B.o.B. Written by Jessica Cornish, Lukasz Gottwald, Claude Kelly and Bobby Ray Simmons, Jr. (source: http://www.wikipedia.org).
2. Lyrics from "Creep" by Radiohead. Written by Radiohead, Albert Hammond and Mike Hazlewood (source: http://www.wikipedia.org).
3. Lyrics from "You and I" by Lady Gaga. Written by Lady Gaga (source: http://www.wikipedia.org).
4. Lyrics from "Price Tag" by Jessie J featuring B.o.B. Written by Jessica Cornish, Lukasz Gottwald, Claude Kelly and Bobby Ray Simmons, Jr. (source: http://www.wikipedia.org).
5. Lyrics from "Crazy" by Gnarls Barkley. Written by Brian Burton, Thomas Callaway, Gian Franco Reverberi and Gian Piero Reverberi (source: http://www.wikipedia.org).
6. Lyrics from "Crush" by Jennifer Paige. Written by Andy Goldmark, Mark Mueller, Berny Cosgrove and Kevin Clark (source: http://www.wikipedia.org).
7. Lyrics from "Will You Be There" by Michael Jackson. Written by Michael Jackson (source: http://www.wikipedia.org).
8. Lyrics from "The Edge of Glory" by Lady Gaga. Written by Lady Gaga, Fernando Garibay and Paul Blair (source: http://www.wikipedia.org).
9. Lyrics from "What About Now" by Daughtry. Written by Ben Moody, David Hodges and Josh Hartzler (source: http://www.wikipedia.org).
10. Lyrics from "Don't Let Me Get Me" by Pink. Written by Pink and Dallas Austin (source: http://www.wikipedia.org).
11. Lyrics from "King of Anything" by Sara Bareilles. Written by Sara Bareilles (source: http://www.wikipedia.org).
12. Lyrics from "King of Anything" by Sara Bareilles. Written by Sara Bareilles (source: http://www.wikipedia.org).

13. Quote from *Animal-Speak: The Spiritual & Magical Powers of Creatures Great & Small* by Ted Andrews, 2002 (p. 338).
14. Lyrics from "Someone Like You" by Adele. Written by Adele and Dan Wilson (source: http://www.wikipedia.org).
15. Definition of "enlightenment" sourced from http://www.merriam-webster.com
16. Definition of "hiatus" sourced from http://www.webstersonline-dictionary.org
17. Lyrics from "I Knew You Were Waiting (For Me)" by Aretha Franklin and George Michael. Written by Simon Climie and Dennis Morgan (source: http://www.wikipedia.org).
18. Lyrics from "Fix You" by Coldplay. Written by Chris Martin, Jonny Buckland, Guy Berryman and Will Champion (source: http://www.wikipedia.org).
19. Lyrics from "Count On Me" by Bruno Mars. Written by Bruno Mars, Philip Lawrence and Ari Levine (source: http://www.wikipedia.org).
20. Lyrics from "The Flame" by Cheap Trick. Written by Bob Mitchell and Nick Graham (source: http://www.wikipedia.org).
21. Lyrics from "Come Back" by Depeche Mode. Written by Dave Gahan, Christian Eigner and Andrew Phillpott (source: http://www.wikipedia.org).
22. Lyrics from "Blinded By The Light" by Manfred Mann's Earth Band. Written by Bruce Springsteen (source: http://www.wikipedia.org).
23. Quote from *Animal-Speak: The Spiritual & Magical Powers of Creatures Great & Small* by Ted Andrews, 2002 (p. 341-342).
24. Lyrics from "Someone Like You" by Adele. Written by Adele and Dan Wilson (source: http://www.wikipedia.org).
25. Lyrics from "Broken Arrow" by Rod Stewart. Written by Robbie Robertson (source: http://www.wikipedia.org).
26. Lyrics from "Somebody That I Used To Know" by Gotye, featuring Kimbra. Written by Wally de Backer (source: http://www.wikipedia.org).

27. Lyrics from "Talking To The Moon" by Bruno Mars. Written by Bruno Mars, Philip Lawrence, Ari Levine, Albert Winkler and Jeff Bhasker (source: http://www.wikipedia.org).
28. Lyrics from "Count On Me" by Bruno Mars. Written by Bruno Mars, Philip Lawrence and Ari Levine (source: http://www.wikipedia.org).
29. Definition of "should" sourced from http://www.thefreedictionary.com
30. Lyrics from "Out Of Touch" by Hall & Oates. Written by Daryl Hall and John Oates (source: http://www.wikipedia.org).
31. Definition of "resonate with" sourced from http://www.macmillandictionary.com
32. Lyrics from "You're The Voice" by John Farnham. Written by Andy Qunta, Keith Reid, Maggie Ryder and Chris Thompson (source: http://www.wikipedia.org).
33. Quote sourced from http://www.paganspace.net
34. Quote sourced from http://www.totemwisdom.com
35. Quote from Maggie Kuhn. Activist and Founder of the Gray Panthers (source: http://www.wikipedia.org).
36. Quote from *Animal-Speak: The Spiritual & Magical Powers of Creatures Great & Small* by Ted Andrews, 2002 (p. 346-347).
37. Lyrics from "Unwritten" by Natasha Bedingfield. Written by Natasha Bedingfield, Danielle Brisebois and Wayne Rodriguez (source: http://www.wikipedia.org).
38. Lyrics from "We Are Young" by Fun. Written by Nate Ruess, Andrew Dost, Jack Antonoff and Jeffrey Bhasker (source: http://www.wikipedia.org).
39. Definition of "paradise" sourced from http://www.wikipedia.org
40. Lyrics from "Everybody's Changing" by Keane. Written by Tim Rice-Oxley, Tom Chaplin and Richard Hughes (source: http://www.wikipedia.org).
41. Lyrics from "You and I" by Lady Gaga. Written by Lady Gaga (source: http://www.wikipedia.org).
42. Lyrics from "Baker Street" by Gerry Rafferty. Written by Gerry Rafferty (source: http://www.wikipedia.org).

43. Lyrics from "Price Tag" by Jessie J, featuring B.o.B. Written by Jessica Cornish, Lukasz Gottwald, Claude Kelly and Bobby Ray Simmons, Jr. (source: http://www.wikipedia.org).
44. Lyrics from "Love Song" by Sara Bareilles. Written by Sara Bareilles (source: http://www.wikipedia.org).
45. Lyrics from "Don't Stop Me Now" by Queen. Written by Freddie Mercury (source: http://www.wikipedia.org).
46. Lyrics from "You'll Never Take That Away" by Jamie McDell. Written by Jamie McDell (source: http://www.wikipedia.org).
47. Lyrics from "I'll Stand By You" by The Pretenders. Written by Chrissie Hynde, Tom Kelly and Billy Steinberg (source: http://www.wikipedia.org).
48. Lyrics from "Lament For The Numb" by Dave Dobbyn. Written by Dave Dobbyn (source: http://www.wikipedia.org).
49. Lyrics from "You Get What You Give" by New Radicals. Written by Gregg Alexander and Rick Nowels (source: http://www.wikipedia.org).
50. Lyrics from "Bulletproof" by La Roux. Written by Elly Jackson and Ben Langmaid (source: http://www.wikipedia.org).
51. Lyrics from "Titanium" by David Guetta, featuring Sia. Written by David Guetta, Sia Furler, Giorgio Tuinfort and Nick Van De Wall (source: http://www.wikipedia.org).
52. Lyrics from "Animal" by Neon Trees. Written by Tyler Glenn, Tim Pagnotta, Branden Campbell, Elaine Doty and Christopher Allen (source: http://www.about.com).
53. Quote from http://www.wildspeak.com
54. Lyrics from "Bridge Over Troubled Water" by Simon & Garfunkel. Written by Paul Simon (source: http://www.wikipedia.org).
55. Lyrics from "Bridge Over Troubled Water" by Simon & Garfunkel. Written by Paul Simon (source: http://www.wikipedia.org).
56. Definition of "providence" sourced from http://www.wikipedia.org
57. Lyrics from "Waiting For A Girl Like You" by Foreigner. Written by Mick Jones and Lou Gramm (source: http://www.wikipedia.org).

58. Quote from *Divine Soul Mind Body Healing and Transmission System: The Divine Way to Heal You, Humanity, Mother Earth, and All Universes* by Dr Zhi Gang Sha, 2009 (p. 40).
59. Quote from *Divine Soul Mind Body Healing and Transmission System: The Divine Way to Heal You, Humanity, Mother Earth, and All Universes* by Dr Zhi Gang Sha, 2009 (p. 40).
60. Quote from John Adams, Composer of *On the Transmigration of Souls* (source: http://www.wikipedia.org).
61. Lyrics from "The World I Know" by Collective Soul. Written by Ed Roland and Ross Childress (source: http://www.wikipedia.org).
62. Quote from wall art designed by Crispin Korschen, sourced from Barkingmad (http://www.barkingmad.net.nz).

Reflections